C000134209

STATING THE GOSPEL

STATING THE GOSPEL

Formulations and Declarations of Faith
from the Heritage of the United Reformed
Church

Edited by
David M. Thompson

T&T CLARK LTD
EDINBURGH

T&T CLARK
59 GEORGE STREET
EDINBURGH EH2 2LQ
SCOTLAND

First Published 1990

ISBN 0 567 09508 8

British Cataloguing in Publication Data

Stating the Gospel
1. The United Reformed Church. History
I. Thompson, David M
274.1

Typeset by Bookworm Typesetting Ltd, Edinburgh
Printed and bound in Great Britain by Billing & Sons Ltd, Worcester

Contents

Introduction

The United Reformed Church was formed in 1972 by a union of the Presbyterian Church of England and a majority of the churches of the Congregational Church in England and Wales. In 1981 the Re-formed Association of Churches of Christ in Great Britain and Ireland united with the Church. A confession of the Church's faith at the date of formation was included in paragraph 17 of the Basis of Union. In the following paragraph the Church acknowledged its duty 'to be open at all times to the leading of the Holy Spirit', and therefore affirmed its right 'to make such new declarations of its faith and for such purposes as may from time to time be required by obedience to the same Spirit'. Furthermore the Church accepted with thanksgiving 'the witness borne to the Catholic faith by the Apostles' and Nicene Creeds'; and recognised as 'its own particular heritage the formulations and declarations of faith which have been valued by Congregationalists, Presbyterians and members of Churches of Christ as stating the gospel and seeking to make its implications clear'.

A footnote to paragraph 18 listed five statements as examples of such formulations and declarations of faith:

The Westminster Confession, 1647 (Presbyterian)
The Savoy Declaration, 1658 (Congregationalist)
Thomas Campbell's *Declaration and Address*, 1809
  (Churches of Christ)
A Statement of the Christian Faith, 1956 (Presbyterian)
A Declaration of Faith, 1967 (Congregationalist).

This list was not intended to be exhaustive; nor were the examples listed to be regarded as 'subordinate standards' in the sense in which that term was used in the former Presbyterian Church of England. They are intended as reminders of the roots from which the constituent parts of the United Reformed Church have come.

Until now, however, these statements have not been readily available to any member or minister of the United Reformed Church wishing to study them, except in very good libraries. Even those that are in print are not to be found in óne volume. For this reason,

1

the Doctrine and Worship Committee of the General Assembly, following a suggestion from the Council of the United Reformed Church History Society, has authorised the publication of this collection. It does not provide a critical study of the documents concerned: but each statement is given a brief historical introduction, with suggestions for further reading. The Committee hopes that the book will be a useful work of reference for all who wish to explore the heritage of the United Reformed Church, whether they are members or not. May it prompt us all to be ready to give an account of the hope that is in us.

David M. Thompson
March 1989

English translation of the Apostles' Creed and the Nicene Creed prepared by the English Language Liturgical Consultation, 1988.

1. The Apostles' Creed

The Apostles' Creed is probably the best-known of all the creeds of the Church, because of its place in Morning and Evening Prayer in the Book of Common Prayer of the Church of England. Traditionally in the Western Church it has been the creed associated with baptism, and it has often been used in ecumenical services.

The Latin text of the Apostles' Creed which is now accepted as authoritative is first found in documents of the eighth century from the Frankish dominions. Its origins probably lie two centuries earlier in Burgundy; and it is in many respects similar to the ancient Roman baptismal creed described in a treatise by Rufinus (c 404), which also contains the legend that it was composed by the twelve apostles. Even though the legend is discredited, it is clear that fragments of the text go back to the second and third centuries. The widespread adoption of the present text in the West is due to the influence of Charlemagne's reform of the Church in the eighth century, and it probably became part of the Roman liturgy in the tenth century.

The English text given here is that produced by the English Language Liturgical Consultation in 1988.

For further reading, see page 264.

The Apostles' Creed

Credo in Deum
  Patrem omnipotentem,
  creatorem caeli et terrae,

et in Iesum Christum,
  Filium eius unicum, Dominum nostrum,
  qui conceptus est de Spiritu Sancto,
  natus ex Maria virgine,
  passus sub Pontio Pilato,
  crucifixus, mortuus et sepultus,
  descendit ad inferna,
  tertia die resurrexit a mortuis,
  ascendit ad caelos,
  sedet ad dexteram Dei Patris omnipotentis,
  inde venturus est
  iudicare vivos et mortuos.

Credo in Spiritum Sanctum,
  sanctam Ecclesiam catholicam,
  sanctorum communionem,
  remissionem peccatorum,
  carnis resurrectionem,
  et vitam aeternam. Amen.

The Apostles' Creed

I believe in God,
   the Father almighty,
   creator of heaven and earth.

I believe in Jesus Christ,
   God's only Son, our Lord,
   who was conceived by the Holy Spirit,
   born of the Virgin Mary,
   suffered under Pontius Pilate,
   was crucified, died, and was buried;
   he descended to the dead.
   On the third day he rose again,
   he ascended into heaven,
   He is seated at the right hand of the Father,
   and he will come again
   to judge the living and the dead.

I believe in the Holy Spirit,
   the holy catholic Church,
   the communion of saints,
   the forgiveness of sins,
   the resurrection of the body,
   and the life everlasting. Amen.

2. The Nicene Creed

Although many people think of the Apostles' Creed as being the most ancient of Christian creeds, the complete text in its present form is later in date than the complete text of the Nicene Creed.

The Greek text of what we have come to call the Nicene Creed was included in its present form in the decrees of the Council of Chalcedon in 451. Its origins are extremely complex, and have been the subject of long discussions among scholars. The Council of Nicaea met in 325 under the presidency of the Emperor Constantine in order to bring peace to the Church, which had been divided by the views of a presbyter from Alexandria, named Arius. Arianism, as it came to be called, was the belief that Jesus, whilst divine, was not the Son from all eternity. The Council agreed upon a creed which declared the Son to be 'of one substance with the Father' (*homoousios*), and the opinions held by Arius were condemned. However, the Arian controversy was not ended by the Council, and the creed agreed at Nicaea was later amended to take account of subsequent arguments.

According to the decrees of the Council of Chalcedon, the present text was the work of the Council of Constantinople in 381, and this is why the creed is sometimes called the Nicaeno-Constantinopolitan Creed. In the later nineteenth and early twentieth centuries many scholars became sceptical of this claim, but more recently fresh evidence has made it more plausible.

Since Chalcedon the authority of the creed has not been questioned. It is the only creed which is accepted as authoritative by the Western and Eastern Churches, although there is a continuing disagreement over the status of the *filioque* clause (i.e., the statement that the Holy Spirit proceeds from the Father *and the Son*). This clause was added by the Western Church from the eighth century under Charlemagne, though it was probably not added to the Roman liturgy until the eleventh century. The creed has been the baptismal creed of the Eastern Church, and the eucharistic creed of East and West. From the time of the Reformation it has been translated into the vernacular. The English text given here is that produced by the English Language Liturgical Consultation. The

Faith and Order Commission of the World Council of Churches has published a valuable study paper on the Nicene Creed which is listed in the further reading.

For further reading, see page 264.

The Nicene Creed

Πιστευομεν εις ενα Θεον.
   πατερα παντοκρατορα,
   ποιητην ουρανου και γης
   ορατων τε παντων και αορατων

και εις ενα κυριον Ιησουν Κριστον,
   τον υιον του θεου τον μονογενη,
   τον εκ του πατρος γεννηθενια προ παντων των αλωνων,
   ψως εκ ψωτος,
   Θεον αγηθινον εκ Θεου αληθινου,
   γεννηθεντα ου ποιηθεντα,
   ομοουβιον τω παιρι,
   δι ου τα παντα εγενετο
   τον δι ημας τους ανθρωπους και δια την ημετεραν σωτηριαν
     κατελθοντα εκ των ουρανων
   και σαρκωθεντα εκ πνευματος αγιου
     και Μαριας της παρθενου,
     και ενανθρωπησαντα,
   σταυρωθεντα τε υπερ ημων επι Ποντιου Πιλατου
     και παθοντα και ταψεντα
και ανασταντα τη τριτη ημερα
κατα τας γραφας,
και ανελθοντα εις τους ουρανους,
     και καθεςουμενον εν δεξια του πατρος,
   και παλιν ερχομενον μετα δοξης κριναι ζωνιας και νεκρους
     ου της [β]ασιλειας ουκ εσται τελος

και εις το πνευμα το ανιον,
   το κυριον και ζωοποιον,
   το εκ του πατρος εκπορευομενον,
   το συν πατρι και υιω συμπροσκυνουμενον και συνδοξαςομενον,
   το λαλησαν δια των προφητων.
   Εις μιαν αγιαν καθολικην και αποστολικην εκκληοιαν.
   Ομολογουμεν εν [β]απτισμα εις αφεσιν αμαρτιων.
   Προσδοκωμεν αναστασιν νεκρων
     και ζωην του μελλοντος αιωνος. Αμην.

The Nicene Creed

We believe in one God,
   the Father, the Almighty,
   maker of heaven and earth,
   of all that is, seen and unseen.

We believe in one Lord, Jesus Christ,
   the only son of God,
   eternally begotten of the Father,
   God from God, Light from Light,
   true God from true God,
   begotten, not made,
   of one being with the Father;
   through him all things were made.
   For us and for our salvation
   he came down from heaven,
   was incarnate of the Holy Spirit and the Virgin Mary
   and became truly human.
   For our sake he was crucified under Pontius Pilate;
   he suffered death and was buried.
   On the third day he rose again
   in accordance with the Scriptures;
   he ascended into heaven
   and is seated at the right hand of the Father.
   He will come again in glory to judge the living and the dead,
   and his kingdom will have no end.

We believe in the Holy Spirit, the Lord, the giver of life,
   who proceeds from the Father,
   who with the Father and the Son is worshipped and glorified,
   who has spoken through the Prophets.
   We believe in one holy catholic and apostolic Church.
   We acknowledge one baptism for the forgiveness of sins.
   We look for the resurrection of the dead,
   and the life of the world to come. Amen.

3. The Westminster Confession, 1647

The Westminster Confession has been regarded as the classic statement of faith among Presbyterian Churches, since its formulation
by the Westminster Assembly of Divines during the English Civil
War. The history of that assembly, which met from 1643 to 1649
in Henry VII's Chapel in Westminster Abbey, is inextricably entangled with the religious and political background of the Civil War.

In 1641 the House of Commons in its Grand Remonstrance to
Charles I had asked for 'a general synod of the most grave, pious,
learned, and judicious divines of this island . . . who may consider
of all things necessary for the peace and good government of the
Church' (para 185). Nothing was done until June 1643, when
Parliament passed an Ordinance convening an assembly to effect
a more perfect reformation in the liturgy, discipline and government of the Church. One hundred and twenty-one ministers were
named, together with ten members of the House of Lords and
twenty members of the House of Commons, though most of
those with episcopalian sympathies never took their seats. Since
part of the political purpose of the assembly was to cement the
alliance between Parliament and the Scots, the General Assembly
of the Church of Scotland was invited to appoint commissioners:
four ministers and two elders were appointed. The Ordinance made
it clear that the Assembly was not to have any ecclesiastical jurisdiction or authority, although after the abolition of episcopacy it was
asked to examine candidates for ordination.

Several members of the Assembly had taken part in the Synod
of Dort (1619), which was probably the most representative
international gathering of Reformed church leaders in the seventeenth century. That Synod had rejected the views of the Dutch
theologian, Jacob Arminius, and had agreed that election was the
result of the pure grace of God, without regard to good works,
that grace once given cannot be altogether lost, and that Christ
had died only for the elect. The views of Arminius, however, had
won support in the Church of England in the 1630s, and those who
had demanded a synod of learned divines wanted to reverse this
trend. The Westminster Assembly therefore tended to be not only
anti-episcopalian on matters of church polity, but also anti-Arminian
in its theology.

10

The first tasks of the Assembly were to prepare the *Directory of Public Worship* and the *Form of Church Government*. A long campaign against the adoption of presbyterianism was carried out by a small group of Independents in the Assembly, which is one reason why the Confession, as distinct from the *Form of Church Government* contains nothing which is unequivocally presbyterian. The Assembly sent the *Form of Church Government* to Parliament on 3 July 1645, and Parliament passed an Ordinance regulating the election of elders on 19 August. In February 1645/6[1] the General Assembly of the Church of Scotland approved both the *Directory of Public Worship* and the *Form of Church Government*.

The Westminster Assembly then turned its attention to the Confession of Faith. This was in large part based on the Articles of Religion for the Irish Church, drafted by Archbishop Ussher in 1615. It has been described as 'the product of numerous theological traditions: native British Augustinianism, Puritan Covenant theology, the Reformed theology of the Rhineland, and Calvinism'. The first nineteen articles of the Confession were approved by the Assembly on 25 September 1646 and sent to Parliament, where they were approved by the House of Lords on 6 November: the remaining articles were approved by the Assembly on 4 December 1646 and submitted to Parliament. The House of Lords approved the complete Confession on 16 February 1646/7[1], but the House of Commons made a number of amendments, especially in relation to chapters 30 and 31, and final agreement with the Lords was not reached until 20 June 1648. The text printed here, and adopted as authoritative by Presbyterians in Scotland and elsewhere, is the unamended text approved by the General Assembly of the Church of Scotland on 27 August 1647. The scripture proofs, provided by the Assembly after they had approved the text, are not reprinted here.

For further reading, see page 264.

---

[1]   At this time the last day of the year was 31 March rather than 31 December, so dates in the first three months of the year are usually cited with both years given. The later of the two years would be the year according to modern usage.

The Westminster Confession of Faith

Chapter 1
Of the Holy Scripture

1 Although the light of nature, and the works of creation and providence, do so far manifest the goodness, wisdom, and power of God, as to leave men inexcusable; yet are they not sufficient to give that knowledge of God, and of his will, which is necessary unto salvation; therefore it pleased the Lord, at sundry times, and in divers manners, to reveal himself, and to declare that his will unto his Church; and afterwards, for the better preserving and propagating of the truth, and for the more sure establishment and comfort of the Church against the corruption of the flesh, and the malice of Satan and of the world, to commit the same wholly unto writing; which maketh the holy Scripture to be most necessary, those former ways of God's revealing his will unto his people being now ceased.

2 Under the name of holy Scripture, or the Word of God written, are now contained all the Books of the Old and New Testament, which are these:

Of the Old Testament

Genesis	Ecclesiastes
Exodus	The Song of Songs
Leviticus	Isaiah
Numbers	Jeremiah
Deuteronomy	Lamentations
Joshua	Ezekiel
Judges	Daniel
Ruth	Hosea
I. Samuel	Joel
II. Samuel	Amos
I. Kings	Obadiah
II. Kings	Jonah
I. Chronicles	Micah
II. Chronicles	Nahum
Ezra	Habakkuk
Nehemiah	Zephaniah
Esther	Haggai
Job	Zechariah
Psalms	Malachi
Proverbs	

Of the New Testament

The Gospels according to
- Matthew
- Mark
- Luke
- John

The Acts of the Apostles

Paul's Epistles to the Romans

Corinthians I

Corinthians II

Galatians

Ephesians

Philippians

Colossians

Thessalonians I

Thessalonians II

To Timothy I

To Timothy II

To Titus

To Philemon

The Epistle to the Hebrews

The Epistle of James

The First and Second
    Epistles of Peter

The First, Second and
    Third Epistles of John

The Epistle of Jude

The Revelation

All which are given by inspiration of God, to be the rule of faith and life.

3 The books commonly called Apocrypha, not being of divine inspiration, are no part of the canon of the Scripture; and therefore are of no authority in the Church of God, nor to be any otherwise approved, or made use of, than other human writings.

4 The authority of the holy Scripture, for which it ought to be believed and obeyed, dependeth not upon the testimony of any man or church, but wholly upon God (who is truth itself), the Author thereof; and therefore it is to be received, because it is the Word of God.

5 We may be moved and induced by the testimony of the Church to an high and reverent esteem of the holy Scripture; and the heavenliness of the matter, the efficacy of the doctrine, the majesty of the style, the consent of all the parts, the scope of the whole (which is to give all glory to God), the full discovery it makes of the only way of man's salvation, the many other incomparable excellencies, and the entire perfection thereof, are arguments whereby it doth abundantly evidence itself to be the Word of God; yet, notwithstanding, our full persuasion and assurance of the infallible truth, and divine authority thereof is from the inward work of the Holy Spirit, bearing witness by and with the Word in our hearts.

6 The whole counsel of God, concerning all things necessary for his own glory, man's salvation, faith, and life, is either expressly

set down in Scripture, or by good and necessary consequence may be deduced from Scripture: unto which nothing at any time is to be added, whether by new revelations of the Spirit, or traditions of men. Nevertheless we acknowledge the inward illumination of the Spirit of God to be necessary for the saving understanding of such things as are revealed in the Word; and that there are some circumstances concerning the worship of God, and government of the Church, common to human actions and societies, which are to be ordered by the light of nature and Christian prudence, according to the general rules of the Word, which are always to be observed.

7 All things in Scripture are not alike plain in themselves, nor alike clear unto all; yet those things which are necessary to be known, believed, and observed, for salvation, are so clearly propounded and opened in some place of Scripture or other, that not only the learned, but the unlearned, in a due use of the ordinary means, may attain unto a sufficient understanding of them.

8 The Old Testament in Hebrew (which was the native language of the people of God of old), and the New Testament in Greek (which at the time of writing of it was most generally known to the nations), being immediately inspired by God, and by his singular care and providence kept pure in all ages, are therefore authentical; so as in all controversies of religion the Church is finally to appeal unto them. But because these original tongues are not known to all the people of God who have right unto, and interest in the Scriptures, and are commanded, in the fear of God, to read and search them, therefore they are to be translated into the vulgar language of every nation unto which they come, that the Word of God dwelling plentifully in all, they may worship him in an acceptable manner, and, through patience and comfort of the Scriptures, may have hope.

9 The infallible rule of interpretation of Scripture is the Scripture itself; and therefore, when there is a question about the true and full sense of any Scripture (which is not manifold, but one), it must be searched and known by other places that speak more clearly.

10 The supreme judge, by which all controversies of religion are to be determined, and all decrees of councils, opinions of ancient writers, doctrines of men, and private spirits, are to be examined, and in whose sentence we are to rest, can be no other but the Holy Spirit speaking in the Scripture.

Chapter 2
Of God, and of the Holy Trinity

1 There is but one only living and true God, who is infinite in being and perfection, a most pure Spirit, invisible, without body, parts, or passions, immutable, immense, eternal, incomprehensible, almighty, most wise, most holy, most free, most absolute, working all things according to the counsel of his own immutable and most righteous will, for his own glory, most loving, gracious, merciful, long-suffering, abundant in goodness and truth, forgiving iniquity, transgression, and sin; the rewarder of them that diligently seek him; and withal most just and terrible in his judgments; hating all sin, and who will by no means clear the guilty.

2 God hath all life, glory, goodness, blessedness, in and of himself; and is alone in and unto himself all-sufficient, not standing in need of any creatures which he hath made, nor deriving any glory from them, but only manifesting his own glory in, by, unto, and upon them: he is the alone foundation of all being, of whom, through whom, and to whom are all things; and hath most sovereign dominion over them, to do by them, or upon them whatsoever himself pleaseth. In his sight all things are open and manifest; his knowledge is infinite, infallible, and independent upon the creature; so as nothing is to him contingent or uncertain. He is most holy in all his counsels, in all his works, and in all his commands. To him is due from angels and men, and every other creature, whatsover worship, service or obedience, he is pleased to require of them.

3 In the unity of the Godhead there be three Persons, of one substance, power, and eternity; God the Father, God the Son, and God the Holy Ghost. The Father is of none, neither begotten nor proceeding, the Son is eternally begotten of the Father; the Holy Ghost eternally proceeding from the Father and the Son.

Chapter 3
Of God's Eternal Decree

1 God from all eternity did, by the most wise and holy counsel of his own will, freely and unchangeably ordain whatsoever comes

to pass; yet so as thereby neither is God the author of sin, nor is violence offered to the will of the creatures, nor is the liberty or contingency of second causes taken away, but rather established.

2 Although God knows whatsoever may or can come to pass upon all supposed conditions, yet hath he not decreed any thing because he foresaw it as future, or as that which would come to pass upon such conditions.

3 By the decree of God, for the manifestation of his glory, some men and angels are predestinated unto everlasting life, and other foreordained to everlasting death.

4 These angels and men, thus predestinated and foreordained, are particularly and unchangeably designed; and their number is so certain and definite that it cannot be either increased or diminished.

5 Those of mankind that are predestinated unto life, God, before the foundation of the world was laid, according to his eternal and immutable purpose, and the secret counsel and good pleasure of his will, hath chosen in Christ, unto everlasting glory, out of his mere free grace and love, without any foresight of faith or good works, or perseverance in either of them, or any other thing in the creature, as conditions, or causes moving him thereunto; and all to the praise of his glorious grace.

6 As God hath appointed the elect unto glory, so hath he, by the eternal and most free purpose of his will, foreordained all the means thereunto. Wherefore they who are elected, being fallen in Adam, are redeemed by Christ, are effectually called unto faith in Christ by his Spirit working in due season; are justified, adopted, sanctified, and kept by his power through faith unto salvation. Neither are any other redeemed by Christ, effectually called, justified, adopted, sanctified, and saved, but the elect only.

7 The rest of mankind God was pleased, according to the unsearchable counsel of his own will, whereby he extendeth or withholdeth mercy as he pleaseth, for the glory of his sovereign power over his creatures, to pass by, and to ordain them to dishonour and wrath for their sin, to the praise of his glorious justice.

8 The doctrine of this high mystery of predestination is to be handled with special prudence and care, that men attending the will of God revealed in his Word, and yielding obedience thereunto, may, from the certainty of their effectual vocation, be assured for their eternal election. So shall this doctrine afford matter of praise,

reverence, and admiration of God; and of humility, diligence, and abundant consolation to all that sincerely obey the Gospel.

Chapter 4
Of Creation

1 It pleased God the Father, Son, and Holy Ghost, for the manifestation of the glory of his eternal power, wisdom, and goodness, in the beginning, to create or make of nothing the world, and all things therein, whether visible or invisible, in the space of six days, and all very good.

2 After God had made all other creatures, he created man, male and female, with reasonable and immortal souls, endued with knowledge, righteousness and true holiness, after his own image, having the law of God written in their hearts, and power to fulfil it; and yet under a possibility of transgressing, being left to the liberty of their own will, which was subject unto change. Beside this law written in their hearts, they received a command not to eat of the tree of the knowledge of good and evil; which while they kept they were happy in their communion with God, and had dominion over the creatures.

Chapter 5
Of Providence

1 God, the great Creator of all things, doth uphold, direct, dispose, and govern all creatures, actions and things, from the greatest even to the least, by his most wise and holy providence, according to his infallible foreknowledge and the free and immutable counsel of his own will, to the praise of the glory of his wisdom, power, justice, goodness, and mercy.

2 Although in relation to the foreknowledge and decree of God, the first cause, all things come to pass immutably and infallibly, yet by the same providence he ordereth them to fall out, according to the nature of second causes, either necessarily, freely, or contingently.

3 God, in his ordinary providence, maketh use of means, yet is free to work without, above, and against them, at his pleasure.

4 The almighty power, unsearchable wisdom, and infinite goodness of God so far manifest themselves in his providence that it extendeth itself even to the first fall, and all other sins of angels and men, and that not by a bare permission, but such as hath joined with it a most wise and powerful bounding, and otherwise ordering and governing of them, in a manifold dispensation, to his own holy ends; yet so as the sinfulness thereof proceedeth only from the creature, and not from God; who, being most holy and righteous, neither is nor can be the author or approver of sin.

5 The most wise, righteous, and gracious God doth oftentimes leave for a season his own children to manifold temptations and the corruption of their own hearts, to chastise them for their former sins, or to discover unto them the hidden strength of corruption and deceitfulness of their hearts, that they may be humbled; and to raise them to a more close and constant dependence for their support unto himself, and to make them more watchful against all future occasions of sin, and for sundry other just and holy ends.

6 As for those wicked and ungodly men whom God, as a righteous judge, for former sins, doth blind and harden, from them he not only withholdeth his grace, whereby they might have been enlightened in their understandings and wrought upon in their hearts, but sometimes also withdraweth the gifts which they had, and exposeth them to such objects as their corruption makes occasion of sin; and withal, gives them over to their own lusts, the temptations of the world, and the power of Satan; whereby it comes to pass that they harden themselves, even under those means which God useth for the softening of others.

7 As the providence of God doth, in general, reach to all creatures, so, after a most special manner, it taketh care of his Church, and disposeth all things to the good thereof.

Chapter 6
Of the Fall of Man, of Sin, and of the Punishment thereof

1 Our first parents, being seduced by the subtlety and temptation of Satan, sinned in eating the forbidden fruit. This their sin God was

pleased, according to his wise and holy counsel, to permit, having purposed to order it to his own glory.

2 By this sin they fell from their original righteousness and communion with God, and so became dead in sin, and wholly defiled in all the faculties and parts of soul and body.

3 They being the root of all mankind, the guilt of this sin was imputed, and the same death in sin and corrupted nature conveyed to all their posterity descending from them by ordinary generation.

4 From this original corruption, whereby we are utterly indisposed, disabled, and made opposite to all good, and wholly inclined to all evil, do proceed all actual transgressions.

5 This corruption of nature, during this life, doth remain in those that are regenerated; and although it be through Christ pardoned and mortified, yet both itself and all the motions thereof are truly and properly sin.

6 Every sin, both original and actual, being a transgression of the righteous law of God, and contrary thereunto, doth, in its own nature, bring guilt upon the sinner, whereby he is bound over to the wrath of God and curse of the law, and so made subject to death, with all miseries spiritual, temporal, and eternal.

Chapter 7
Of God's Covenant with Man

1 The distance between God and the creature is so great that although reasonable creatures do owe obedience unto him as their Creator, yet they could never have any fruition of him as their blessedness and reward but by some voluntary condescension on God's part, which he hath been pleased to express by way of covenant.

2 The first covenant made with man was a covenant of works, wherein life was promised to Adam, and in him to his posterity, upon condition of perfect and personal obedience.

3 Man by his fall having made himself incapable of life by that covenant, the Lord was pleased to make a second, commonly called the covenant of grace: wherein he freely offered unto sinners life and salvation by Jesus Christ, requiring of them faith in him that they

may be saved, and promising to give unto all those that are ordained unto life his Holy Spirit, to make them willing and able to believe.

4 This covenant of grace is frequently set forth in the Scripture by name of a testament, in reference to the death of Jesus Christ the testator, and to the everlasting inheritance, with all things belonging to it, therein bequeathed.

5 This covenant was differently administered in the time of the law and in the time of the gospel: under the law it was administered by promises, prophecies, sacrifices, circumcision, the paschal lamb, and other types and ordinances delivered to the people of the Jews, all foresignifying Christ to come, which were for that time sufficient and efficacious, through the operation of the Spirit, to instruct and build up the elect in faith in the promised Messiah, by whom they had full remission of sins and eternal salvation; and is called the Old Testament.

6 Under the gospel, when Christ the substance was exhibited, the ordinances in which this covenant is dispensed are the preaching of the word and the administration of the sacraments of Baptism and the Lord's Supper; which, though fewer in number, and administered with more simplicity and less outward glory, yet in them it is held forth in more fullness, evidence, and spiritual efficacy, to all nations, both Jews and Gentiles; and is called the New Testament. There are not, therefore, two covenants of grace differing in substance, but one and the same under various dispensations.

Chapter 8
Of Christ the Mediator

1 It pleased God, in his eternal purpose, to choose and ordain the Lord Jesus, his only-begotten Son, to be the Mediator between God and man, the Prophet, Priest, and King; the Head and Saviour of his Church, the Heir of all things, and Judge of the world; unto whom he did, from all eternity, give a people to be his seed, and to be by him in time redeemed, called, justified, sanctified, and glorified.

2 The Son of God, the second person in the Trinity, being very and eternal God, of one substance, and equal with the Father, did,

when the fullness of time was come, take upon him man's nature, with all the essential properties and common infirmities thereof, yet without sin: being conceived by the power of the Holy Ghost in the womb of the Virgin Mary, of her substance. So that two whole, perfect, and distinct natures, the Godhead and the manhood, were inseparably joined together in one person, without conversion, composition, or confusion. Which person is very God and very man, yet one Christ, the only Mediator between God and man.

3 The Lord Jesus, in his human nature thus united to the divine, was sanctified and anointed with the Holy Spirit above measure; having in him all the treasures of wisdom and knowledge, in whom it pleased the Father that all fulness should dwell; to the end that, being holy, harmless, undefiled, and full of grace and truth, he might be thoroughly furnished to execute the office of a Mediator and Surety. Which office he took not unto himself, but was thereunto called by his Father, who put all power and judgment into his hand, and gave him commandment to execute the same.

4 This office the Lord Jesus did most willingly undertake, which, that he might discharge, he was made under the law, and did perfectly fulfil it; endured most grievous torments immediately in his soul, and most painful sufferings in his body; was crucified, and died; was buried, and remained under the power of death, yet saw no corruption. On the third day he arose from the dead, with the same body in which he suffered; with which also he ascended into heaven, and there sitteth at the right hand of his Father, making intercession; and shall return to judge men and angels at the end of the world.

5 The Lord Jesus, by his perfect obedience and sacrifice of himself, which he through the eternal Spirit once offered up unto God, hath fully satisfied the justice of his Father, and purchased not only reconciliation, but an everlasting inheritance in the kingdom of heaven, for all those whom the Father hath given unto him.

6 Although the work of redemption was not actually wrought by Christ till after his incarnation, yet the virtue, efficacy, and benefits thereof were communicated unto the elect, in all ages successively, from the beginning of the world, in and by those promises, types, and sacrifices, wherein he was revealed, and signified to be the seed of the woman which should bruise the serpent's head, and the lamb

slain from the beginning of the world, being yesterday and to-day the same and forever.

7 Christ, in the work of mediation, acteth according to both natures; by each nature doing that which is proper to itself; yet, by reason of the unity of the person, that which is proper to one nature is sometimes, in Scripture, attributed to the person denominated by the other nature.

8 To all those for whom Christ hath purchased redemption he doth certainly and effectually apply and communicate the same; making intercession for them, and revealing unto them, in and by the Word, the mysteries of salvation; effectually persuading them by his Spirit to believe and obey; and governing their hearts by his Word and Spirit; overcoming all their enemies by his almighty power and wisdom, in such manner and ways as are most consonant to his wonderful and unsearchable dispensation.

Chapter 9
Of Free-Will

1 God hath endued the will of man with that natural liberty, that is neither forced nor by any absolute necessity of nature determined to good or evil.

2 Man, in his state of innocency, had freedom and power to will and to do that which is good and well-pleasing to God, but yet mutably, so that he might fall from it.

3 Man, by his fall into a state of sin, hath wholly lost all ability of will to any spiritual good accompanying salvation; so as a natural man, being altogether averse from that good, and dead in sin, is not able, by his own strength, to convert himself, or to prepare himself thereunto.

4 When God converts a sinner, and translates him into the state of grace, he freeth him from his natural bondage under sin, and by his grace alone enables him freely to will and to do that which is spiritually good; yet so as that, by reason of his remaining corruption, he doth not perfectly, nor only, will that which is good, but doth also will that which is evil.

5 The will of man is made perfectly and immutably free to good alone, in the state of glory only.

Chapter 10
Of Effectual Calling

1 All those whom God hath predestinated unto life, and those only, he is pleased, in his appointed and accepted time, effectually to call, by his Word and Spirit, out of that state of sin and death, in which they are by nature, to grace and salvation by Jesus Christ; enlightening their minds, spiritually and savingly, to understand the things of God; taking away their heart of stone, and giving unto them an heart of flesh; renewing their wills, and by his almighty power determining them to that which is good, and effectually drawing them to Jesus Christ; yet so as they come most freely, being made willing by his grace.

2 This effectual call is of God's free and special grace alone, not from any thing at all foreseen in man; who is altogether passive therein, until, being quickened and renewed by the Holy Spirit, he is thereby enabled to answer this call, and to embrace the grace offered and conveyed in it.

3 Elect infants, dying in infancy, are regenerated and saved by Christ through the Spirit, who worketh when, and where, and how he pleaseth. So also are all other elect persons, who are incapable of being outwardly called by the ministry of the Word.

4 Others, not elected, although they may be called by the ministry of the Word, and may have some common operations of the Spirit, yet they never truly come unto Christ, and therefore cannot be saved: much less can men, not professing the Christian religion, be saved in any other way whatsoever, be they never so diligent to frame their lives according to the light of nature and the law of that religion they do profess; and to assert and maintain that they may is very pernicious, and to be detested.

Chapter 11
Of Justification

1 Those whom God effectually calleth he also freely justifieth; not by infusing righteousness into them, but by pardoning their sins, and by accounting and accepting their persons as righteous: not for any thing wrought in them, or done by them, but for Christ's

sake alone; nor by imputing faith itself, the act of believing, or any other evangelical obedience to them, as their righteousness; but by imputing the obedience and satisfaction of Christ unto them, they receiving and resting on him and his righteousness by faith; which faith they have not of themselves, it is the gift of God.

2 Faith, thus receiving and resting on Christ and his righteousness, is the alone instrument of justification; yet is it not alone in the person justified, but is ever accompanied with all other saving graces, and is no dead faith, but worketh by love.

3 Christ, by his obedience and death, did fully discharge the debt of all those that are thus justified, and did make a proper, real, and full satisfaction to his Father's justice in their behalf. Yet inasmuch as he was given by the Father for them, and his obedience and satisfaction accepted in their stead, and both freely, not for anything in them, their justification is only of free grace; that both the exact justice and rich grace of God might be glorified in the justification of sinners.

4 God did, from all eternity, decree to justify all the elect, and Christ did, in the fulness of time, die for their sins, and rise again for their justification: nevertheless, they are not justified until the Holy Spirit doth, in due time, actually apply Christ unto them.

5 God doth continue to forgive the sins of those that are justified; and although they can never fall from the state of justification, yet they may by their sins fall under God's fatherly displeasure, and not have the light of his countenance restored unto them, until they humble themselves, confess their sins, beg pardon, and renew their faith and repentance.

6 The justification of believers under the Old Testament was, in all these respects, one and the same with the justification of believers under the New Testament.

Chapter 12
Of Adoption

All those that are justified God vouchsafeth, in and for his only Son Jesus Christ, to make partakers of the grace of adoption; by which they are taken into the number, and enjoy the liberties and privileges of the children of God; have his name put upon them; receive the Spirit of adoption; have access to the throne of grace with boldness; are enabled to cry, Abba, Father; are pitied, protected, provided for, and chastened by him as by a father; yet never cast off, but sealed to the day of redemption, and inherit the promises, as heirs of everlasting salvation.

Chapter 13
Of Sanctification

1 They who are effectually called and regenerated, having a new heart and a new spirit created in them, are further sanctified, really and personally, through the virtue of Christ's death and resurrection, by his Word and Spirit dwelling in them; the dominion of the whole body of sin is destroyed, and the several lusts thereof are more and more weakened and mortified, and they more and more quickened and strengthened, in all saving graces, to the practice of true holiness, without which no man shall see the Lord.

2 This sanctification is throughout in the whole man, yet imperfect in this life; there abideth still some remnants of corruption in every part, whence ariseth a continual and irreconcilable war, the flesh lusting against the spirit, and the spirit against the flesh.

3 In which war, although the remaining corruption for a time may much prevail, yet, through the continual supply of strength from the sanctifying Spirit of Christ, the regenerate part doth overcome; and so the saints grow in grace, perfecting holiness in the fear of God.

Chapter 14
Of Saving Faith

1 The grace of faith, whereby the elect are enabled to believe to the saving of their souls, is the work of the Spirit of Christ in their hearts, and is ordinarily wrought by the ministry of the Word; by which also, and by the administration of the sacraments and prayer, it is increased and strengthened.

2 By this faith a Christian believeth to be true whatsoever is revealed in the Word, for the authority of God himself speaking

therein; and acteth differently upon that which each particular passage thereof containeth; yielding obedience to the commands, trembling at the threatenings, and embracing the promises of God for this life and that which is to come. But the principal acts of saving faith are accepting, receiving, and resting upon Christ alone for justification, sanctification, and eternal life, by virtue of the covenant of grace.

3 This faith is different in degrees, weak or strong; may be often and many ways assailed and weakened, but gets the victory; growing up in many to the attainment of a full assurance through Christ, who is both the author and finisher of our faith.

Chapter 15
Of Repentance unto Life

1 Repentance unto life is an evangelical grace, the doctrine whereof is to be preached by every minister of the gospel, as well as that of faith in Christ.

2 By it a sinner, out of the sight and sense, not only of the danger, but also of the filthiness and odiousness of his sins, as contrary to the holy nature and righteous law of God, and upon the apprehension of his mercy in Christ to such as are penitent, so grieves for and hates his sins as to turn from them all unto God, purposing and endeavouring to walk with him in all the ways of his commandments.

3 Although repentance be not to be rested in as any satisfaction for sin, or any cause of the pardon thereof, which is the act of God's free grace in Christ; yet is it of such necessity to all sinners that none may expect pardon without it.

4 As there is no sin so small but it deserves damnation, so there is no sin so great that it can bring damnation upon those who truly repent.

5 Men ought not to content themselves with a general repentance, but it is every man's duty to endeavour to repent of his particular sins particularly.

6 As every man is bound to make private confession of his sins to God, praying for the pardon thereof, upon which, and the forsaking of them, he shall find mercy; so he that scandalizeth his brother, or

the Church of Christ, ought to be willing, by a private or public confession and sorrow for his sin, to declare his repentance to those that are offended, who are thereupon to be reconciled to him, and in love to receive him.

Chapter 16
Of Good Works

1 Good works are only such as God hath commanded in his holy Word, and not such as, without the warrant thereof, are devised by men out of blind zeal, or upon any pretence of good intention.

2 These good works, done in obedience to God's commandments, are the fruits and evidences of a true and lively faith; and by them believers manifest their thankfulness, strengthen their assurance, edify their brethren, adorn the profession of the gospel, stop the mouths of the adversaries, and glorify God, whose workmanship they are, created in Christ Jesus thereunto, that, having their fruit unto holiness, they may have the end, eternal life.

3 Their ability to do good works is not at all of themselves, but wholly from the Spirit of Christ. And that they may be enabled thereunto, besides the graces they have already received, there is required an actual influence of the same Holy Spirit to work in them to will and to do of his good pleasure; yet are they not hereupon to grow negligent, as if they were not bound to perform any duty unless upon a special motion of the Spirit; but they ought to be diligent in stirring up the grace of God that is in them.

4 They who in their obedience attain to the greatest height which is possible in this life, are so far from being able to supererogate and to do more than God requires, as that they fall short of much which in duty they are bound to do.

5 We cannot, by our best works, merit pardon of sin, or eternal life at the hand of God, by reason of the great disproportion that is between them and the glory to come, and the infinite distance that is between us and God, whom by them we can neither profit nor satisfy for the debt of our former sins; but when we have done all we can, we have done but our duty, and are unprofitable servants; and because, as they are good, they proceed from his Spirit; and as they are wrought by us, they are defiled and mixed with so much

weakness and imperfection that they can not endure the severity of God's judgment.

6 Yet notwithstanding, the persons of believers being accepted through Christ, their good works also are accepted in him, not as though they were in this life wholly unblameable and unreproveable in God's sight; but that he, looking upon them in his Son, is pleased to accept and reward that which is sincere, although accompanied with many weaknesses and imperfections.

7 Works done by unregenerate men, although for the matter of them they may be things which God commands, and of good use both to themselves and others; yet because they proceed not from a heart purified by faith, nor are done in a right manner, according to the Word, nor to a right end, the glory of God; they are therefore sinful, and cannot please God, or make a man meet to receive grace from God. And yet their neglect of them is more sinful and displeasing unto God.

Chapter 17
Of the Perseverance of the Saints

1 They whom God hath accepted in his Beloved, effectually called and sanctified by his Spirit, can neither totally nor finally fall away from the state of grace, but shall certainly persevere therein to the end, and be eternally saved.

2 This perseverance of the saints depends, not upon their own free-will, but upon the immutability of the decree of election, flowing from the free and unchangeable love of God the Father; upon the efficacy of the merit and intercession of Jesus Christ; the abiding of the Spirit and of the seed of God within them; and the nature of the covenant of grace: from all which ariseth also the certainty and infallibility thereof.

3 Nevertheless they may, through the temptations of Satan and of the world, the prevalency of corruption remaining in them, and the neglect of the means of their preservation, fall into grievous sins; and for a time continue therein: whereby they incur God's displeasure, and grieve his Holy Spirit; come to be deprived of some measure of their graces and comforts; have their hearts hardened, and their consciences wounded; hurt and scandalize others, and bring temporal judgments upon themselves.

Chapter 18
Of the Assurance of Grace and Salvation

1 Although hypocrites and other unregenerate men may vainly deceive themselves with false hopes and carnal presumptions of being in the favour of God and estate of salvation, which hope of theirs shall perish: yet such as truly believe in the Lord Jesus, and love him in sincerity, endeavouring to walk in all good conscience before him, may in this life be certainly assured that they are in a state of grace, and may rejoice in the hope of the glory of God, which hope shall never make them ashamed.

2 This certainty is not a bare conjectural and probable persuasion, grounded upon a fallible hope; but an infallible assurance of faith, founded upon the divine truth of the promises of salvation, the inward evidence of those graces unto which these promises are made, the testimony of the Spirit of adoption witnessing with our spirits that we are the children of God: which Spirit is the earnest of our inheritance, whereby we are sealed to the day of redemption.

3 This infallible assurance doth not so belong to the essence of faith, but that a true believer may wait long, and conflict with many difficulties before he be partaker of it: yet, being enabled by the Spirit to know the things which are freely given him of God, he may, without extraordinary revelation, in the right use of ordinary means, attain thereunto. And therefore it is the duty of every one to give all diligence to make his calling and election sure; that thereby his heart may be enlarged in peace and joy in the Holy Ghost, in love and thankfulness to God, and in strength and cheerfulness in the duties of obedience, the proper fruits of this assurance: so far is it from inclining men to looseness.

4 True believers may have the assurance of their salvation divers ways shaken, diminished, and intermitted; as, by negligence in preserving of it; by falling into some special sin, which woundeth the conscience, and grieveth the Spirit; by some sudden or vehement temptation; by God's withdrawing the light of his countenance, and suffering even such as fear him to walk in darkness and to have no light: yet are they never utterly destitute of that seed of God, and life of faith, that love of Christ and the brethren, that sincerity of heart and conscience of duty, out of which, by the operation of the Spirit, this assurance may in due time be revived, and by the which, in the mean time, they are supported from utter despair.

Chapter 19
Of the Law of God

1 God gave to Adam a law, as a covenant of works, by which he bound him and all his posterity to personal, entire, exact and perpetual obedience; promised life upon the fulfilling, and threatened death upon the breach of it; and endued him with power and ability to keep it.

2 This law, after his fall, continued to be a perfect rule of righteousness; and, as such, was delivered by God upon mount Sinai in ten commandments, and written in two tables; the first four commandments containing our duty towards God, and the other six our duty to man.

3 Beside this law, commonly called moral, God was pleased to give to the people of Israel, as a Church under age, ceremonial laws, containing several typical ordinances, partly of worship, prefiguring Christ, his graces, actions, sufferings, and benefits; and partly holding forth divers instructions of moral duties. All which ceremonial laws are now abrogated under the New Testament.

· 4 To them also, as a body politic, he gave sundry judicial laws, which expired together with the state of that people, not obliging any other, now, further than the general equity thereof may require.

5 The moral law doth forever bind all, as well justified persons as others, to the obedience thereof; and that not only in regard of the matter contained in it, but also in respect of the authority of God the Creator who gave it. Neither doth Christ in the gospel any way dissolve, but much strengthen, this obligation.

6 Although true believers be not under the law as a covenant of works, to be thereby justified or condemned; yet is it of great use to them, as well as to others; in that, as a rule of life, informing them of the will of God and their duty, it directs and binds them to walk accordingly; discovering also the sinful pollutions of their nature, hearts and lives; so as, examining themselves thereby, they may come to further conviction of, humiliation for, and hatred against sin; together with a clearer sight of the need they have of Christ, and the perfection of his obedience. It is likewise of use to the regenerate, to restrain their corruptions, in that it forbids sin; and the threatenings of it serve to show what even their sins deserve, and what afflictions in this life they may expect for them, although freed

from the curse thereof threatened in the law. The promises of it, in like manner, show them God's approbation of obedience, and what blessings they may expect upon the performance thereof; although not as due to them by the law as a covenant of words; so as a man's doing good, and refraining from evil, because the law encourageth to the one, and deterreth from the other, is no evidence of his being under the law, and not under grace.

7 Neither are the forementioned uses of the law contrary to the grace of the gospel, but do sweetly comply with it: the Spirit of Christ subduing and enabling the will of man to do that freely and cheerfully which the will of God, revealed in the law, requireth to be done.

Chapter 20
Of Christian Liberty, and Liberty of Conscience

1 The liberty which Christ hath purchased for believers under the gospel consists in their freedom from the guilt of sin, the condemning wrath of God, the curse of the moral law; and in their being delivered from this present evil world, bondage to Satan, and dominion of sin, from the evil of afflictions, the sting of death, the victory of the grave, and everlasting damnation; as also in their free access to God, and their yielding obedience unto him, not out of slavish fear, but a child-like love and willing mind. All which were common also to believers under the law; but under the New Testament the liberty of Christians is further enlarged in their freedom from the yoke of the ceremonial law, to which the Jewish Church was subjected; and in greater boldness of access to the throne of grace, and in fuller communications of the free Spirit of God, than believers under the law did ordinarily partake of.

2 God alone is Lord of the conscience, and hath left it free from the doctrines and commandments of men which are in any thing contrary to his Word, or beside it in matters of faith or worship. So that to believe such doctrines, or to obey such commands out of conscience, is to betray true liberty of conscience; and the requiring of an implicit faith, and an absolute and blind obedience, is to destroy liberty of conscience, and reason also.

3 They who, upon pretence of Christian liberty, do practise any sin, or cherish any lust, do thereby destroy the end of Christian

liberty; which is, that, being delivered out of the hands of our enemies, we might serve the Lord without fear, in holiness and righteousness before him, all the days of our life.

4 And because the power which God hath ordained, and the liberty which Christ hath purchased, are not intended by God to destroy, but mutually to uphold and preserve one another; they who, upon pretence of Christian liberty, shall oppose any lawful power, or the lawful exercise of it, whether it be civil or ecclesiastical, resist the ordinance of God. And for their publishing of such opinions, or maintaining of such practices, as are contrary to the light of nature, or to the known principles of Christianity, whether concerning faith, worship, or conversation; or to the power of godliness; or such erroneous opinions or practices, as, either in their own nature, or in the manner of publishing or maintaining them, are destructive to the external peace and order which Christ hath established in the Church; they may lawfully be called to account, and proceeded against by the censures of the Church, and by the power of the Civil Magistrate.

Chapter 21
Of Religious Worship and the Sabbath Day

1 The light of nature showeth that there is a God, who hath lordship and sovereignty over all; is good, and doeth good unto all; and is therefore to be feared, loved, praised, called upon, trusted in, and served with all the heart, and with all the soul, and with all the might. But the acceptable way of worshipping the true God is instituted by himself, and so limited to his own revealed will, that he may not be worshipped according to the imaginations and devices of man, or the suggestions of Satan, under any visible representations or any other way not prescribed in the Holy Scripture.

2 Religious worship is to be given to God, the Father, Son, and Holy Ghost; and to him alone: not to angels, saints, or any other creature: and since the fall, not without a Mediator; nor in the mediation of any other but of Christ alone.

3 Prayer with thanksgiving, being one special part of religious worship, is by God required of all men; and that it may be accepted, it is to be made in the name of the Son, by the help of his Spirit,

according to his will, with understanding, reverence, humility, fervency, faith, love, and perseverance; and, if vocal, in a known tongue.

4 Prayer is to be made for things lawful, and for all sorts of men living, or that shall live hereafter; but not for the dead, nor for those of whom it may be known that they have sinned the sin unto death.

5 The reading of the Scriptures with godly fear; the sound preaching; and conscionable hearing of the Word, in obedience unto God with understanding, faith, and reverence; singing of psalms with grace in the heart; as, also, the due administration and worthy receiving of the sacraments instituted by Christ; are all parts of the ordinary religious worship of God: besides religious oaths, vows, solemn fastings, and thanksgivings upon several occasions; which are, in their several times and seasons, to be used in an holy and religious manner.

6 Neither prayer, nor any other part of religious worship, is now under the gospel, either tied unto or made more acceptable by any place in which it is performed, or towards which it is directed: but God is to be worshipped every where in spirit and truth; as in private families daily, and in secret each one by himself, so more solemnly in the public assemblies, which are not carelessly or wilfully to be neglected or forsaken, when God, by his Word or providence, calleth thereunto.

7 As it is of the law of nature, that, in general, a due proportion of time be set apart for the worship of God; so, in his Word, by a positive, moral, and perpetual commandment, binding all men in all ages, he hath particularly appointed one day in seven for a Sabbath, to be kept holy unto him; which, from the beginning of the world to the resurrection of Christ, was the last day of the week; and, from the resurrection of Christ, was changed into the first day of the week, which in Scripture is called the Lord's day, and is to be continued to the end of the world, as the Christian Sabbath.

8 This Sabbath is then kept holy unto the Lord, when men, after a due preparing of their hearts, and ordering of their common affairs beforehand, do not only observe an holy rest all the day from their own works, words, and thoughts, about their worldly employments and recreations; but also are taken up the whole time in the public and private exercise of his worship, and in the duties of necessity and mercy.

Chapter 22
Of Lawful Oaths and Vows

1 A lawful oath is a part of religious worship, wherein, upon just occasion, the person swearing solemnly calleth God to witness what he asserteth or promiseth; and to judge him according to the truth or falsehood of what he sweareth.

2 The name of God only is that by which men ought to swear, and therein it is to be used with all holy fear and reverence; therefore to swear vainly or rashly by that glorious and dreadful name, or to swear at all by any other thing, is sinful, and to be abhorred. Yet as, in matters of weight and moment, an oath is warranted by the Word of God, under the New Testament, as well as under the Old, so a lawful oath, being imposed by lawful authority, in such matters ought to be taken.

3 Whosoever taketh an oath ought duly to consider the weightiness of so solemn an act, and therein to avouch nothing but what he is fully persuaded is the truth. Neither may any man bind himself by oath to any thing but what is good and just, and what he believeth so to be, and what he is able and resolved to perform. Yet it is a sin to refuse an oath touching any thing that is good and just, being imposed by lawful authority.

4 An oath is to be taken in the plain and common sense of the words, without equivocation or mental reservation. It can not oblige to sin; but in any thing not sinful, being taken, it binds to performance, although to a man's own hurt: nor is it to be violated, although made to heretics or infidels.

5 A vow is of the like nature with a promissory oath, and ought to be made with the like religious care, and to be performed with the like faithfulness.

6 It is not to be made to any creature, but to God alone: and that it may be accepted, it is to be made voluntarily, out of faith and conscience of duty, in way of thankfulness for mercy received, or for the obtaining of what we want; whereby we more strictly bind ourselves to necessary duties, or to other things, so far and so long as they may fitly conduct thereunto.

7 No man may vow to do any thing forbidden in the Word of God, or what would hinder any duty therein commanded, or which is not in his own power, and for the performance whereof he hath no

promise or ability from God. In which respect, popish monastical vows of perpetual single life, professed poverty, and regular obedience, are so far from being degrees of higher perfection, that they are superstitious and sinful snares, in which no Christian may entangle himself.

Chapter 23
Of the Civil Magistrate

1 God, the Supreme Lord and King of all the world, hath ordained civil magistrates to be under him, over the people, for his own glory and the public good, and to this end hath armed them with the power of the sword, for the defence and encouragement of them that are good, and for the punishment of evil-doers.

2 It is lawful for Christians to accept and execute the office of a magistrate when called thereunto; in the managing whereof, as they ought especially to maintain piety, justice, and peace, according to the wholesome laws of each commonwealth, so, for that end, they may lawfully, now under the New Testament, wage war upon just and necessary occasion.

3 The civil magistrate may not assume to himself the administration of the Word and Sacraments, or the power of the keys of the kingdom of heaven: yet he hath authority, and it is his duty to take order, that unity and peace be preserved in the Church, that the truth of God be kept pure and entire, that all blasphemies and heresies be suppressed, all corruptions and abuses in worship and discipline prevented or reformed, and all the ordinances of God duly settled, whereof he hath power to call synods, to be present at them, and to provide that whatsoever is transacted in them be according to the mind of God.

4 It is the duty of people to pray for magistrates, to honour their persons, to pay them tribute and other dues, to obey their lawful commands, and to be subject to their authority, for conscience' sake. Infidelity or difference in religion doth not make void the magistrate's just and legal authority, nor free the people from their due obedience to him: from which ecclesiastical persons are not exempted; much less hath the Pope any power or jurisdiction over them in their dominions, or over any of their people; and least

of all to deprive them of their dominions or lives, if he shall judge them to be heretics, or upon any other pretence whatsoever.

Chapter 24
Of Marriage and Divorce

1 Marriage is to be between one man and one woman: neither is it lawful for any man to have more than one wife, nor for any woman to have more than one husband at the same time.

2 Marriage was ordained for the mutual help of husband and wife; for the increase of mankind with a legitimate issue, and of the Church with an holy seed; and for preventing of uncleanness.

3 It is lawful for all sorts of people to marry who are able with judgment to give their consent. Yet it is the duty of Christians to marry only in the Lord. And, therefore, such as profess the true reformed religion should not marry with infidels, Papists, or other idolaters; neither should such as are godly be unequally yoked, by marrying with such as are notoriously wicked in their life, or maintain damnable heresies.

4 Marriage ought not to be within the degrees of consanguinity or affinity forbidden in the Word; nor can such incestuous marriages ever be made lawful by any law of man, or consent of parties, so as those persons may live together, as man and wife. The man may not marry any of his wife's kindred nearer in blood than he may of his own, nor the woman of her husband's kindred nearer in blood than of her own.

5 Adultery or fornication, committed after a contract, being detected before marriage, giveth just occasion to the innocent party to dissolve that contract. In the case of adultery after marriage, it is lawful for the innocent party to sue out a divorce, and after the divorce to marry another, as if the offending party were dead.

6 Although the corruption of man be such as is apt to study arguments, unduly to put asunder those whom God hath joined together in marriage; yet nothing but adultery, or such wilful desertion as can no way be remedied by the Church or civil magistrate, is cause sufficient of dissolving the bond of marriage; wherein a public and orderly course of proceeding is to be observed; and the persons concerned in it, not left to their own wills and discretion in their own case.

Chapter 25
Of the Church

1 The catholic or universal Church, which is invisible, consists of the whole number of the elect, that have been, are, or shall be gathered into one, under Christ the head thereof; and is the spouse, the body, the fulness of him that filleth all in all.

2 The visible Church, which is also catholic or universal under the gospel (not confined to one nation as before under the law) consists of all those, throughout the world, that profess the true religion, and of their children; and is the kingdom of the Lord Jesus Christ, the house and family of God, out of which there is no ordinary possibility of salvation.

3 Unto this catholic visible Church Christ hath given the ministry, oracles, and ordinances of God, for the gathering and perfecting of the saints, in this life, to the end of the world: and doth by his own presence and Spirit, according to his promise, make them effectual thereunto.

4 This catholic Church hath been sometimes more, sometimes less visible. And particular churches, which are members thereof, are more or less pure, according as the doctrine of the gospel is taught and embraced, ordinances administered, and public worship performed more or less purely in them.

5 The purest churches under heaven are subject both to mixture and error; and some have so degenerated as to become no churches of Christ, but synagogues of Satan. Nevertheless, there shall be always a Church on earth to worship God according to his will.

6 There is no other head of the Church but the Lord Jesus Christ: nor can the Pope of Rome, in any sense be head thereof; but is that Antichrist, that man of sin and son of perdition, that exalteth himself in the Church against Christ, and all that is called God.

Chapter 26
Of the Communion of Saints

1 All saints that are united to Jesus Christ their head, by his Spirit and by faith, have fellowship with him in his graces, sufferings, death, resurrection, and glory: and being united to one another in

love, they have communion in each other's gifts and graces, and are obliged to the performance of such duties, public and private, as do conduce to their mutual good, both in the inward and outward man.

2 Saints, by profession, are bound to maintain an holy fellowship and communion in the worship of God, and in performing such other spiritual services as tend to their mutual edification; as also in relieving each other in outward things, according to their several abilities and necessities. Which communion, as God offereth opportunity, is to be extended unto all those who, in every place, call upon the name of the Lord Jesus.

3 This communion which the saints have with Christ, doth not make them in anywise partakers of the substance of his Godhead, or to be equal with Christ in any respect: either of which to affirm is impious and blasphemous. Nor doth their communion one with another, as saints, take away or infringe the title or propriety which each man hath in his goods and possessions.

Chapter 27
Of the Sacraments

1 Sacraments are holy signs and seals of the covenant of grace, immediately instituted by God, to represent Christ and his benefits, and to confirm our interest in him: as also to put a visible difference between those that belong unto the Church and the rest of the world; and solemnly to engage them to the service of God in Christ, according to his Word.

2 There is in every sacrament a spiritual relation or sacramental union, between the sign and the thing signified; whence it comes to pass that the names and the effects of the one are attributed to the other.

3 The grace which is exhibited in or by the sacraments, rightly used, is not conferred by any power in them; neither doth the efficacy of a sacrament depend upon the piety or intention of him that doth administer it, but upon the work of the Spirit, and the word of institution, which contains, together with a precept authorizing the use thereof, a promise of benefit to worthy receivers.

4 There be only two sacraments ordained by Christ our Lord in the gospel, that is to say, Baptism and the Supper of the Lord: neither of which may be dispensed by any but by a minister of the Word lawfully ordained.

5 The sacraments of the Old Testament, in regard of the spiritual things thereby signified and exhibited, were, for substance, the same with those of the New.

Chapter 28
Of Baptism

1 Baptism is a sacrament of the New Testament, ordained by Jesus Christ, not only for the solemn admission of the party baptized into the visible Church, but also to be unto him a sign and seal of the covenant of grace, of his ingrafting into Christ, of regeneration, of remission of sins, and of his giving up unto God, through Jesus Christ, to walk in newness of life: which sacrament is, by Christ's own appointment, to be continued in his Church until the end of the world.

2 The outward element to be used in this sacrament is water, wherewith the party is to be baptized in the name of the Father, and of the Son, and of the Holy Ghost, by a minister of the gospel lawfully called thereunto.

3 Dipping of the person into the water is not necessary; but baptism is rightly administered by pouring or sprinkling water upon the person.

4 Not only those that do actually profess faith in and obedience unto Christ, but also the infants of one or both believing parents are to be baptized.

5 Although it be a great sin to contemn or neglect this ordinance, yet grace and salvation are not so inseparably annexed unto it, as that no person can be regenerated or saved without it, or that all that are baptized are undoubtedly regenerated.

6 The efficacy of baptism is not tied to that moment of time when it is administered; yet, notwithstanding, by the right use of this ordinance the grace promised is not only offered, but really exhibited and conferred by the Holy Ghost, to such (whether of age

or infants) as that grace belongeth unto, according to the counsel of God's own will, in his appointed time.

7 The sacrament of baptism is but once to be administered to any person.

Chapter 29
Of the Lord's Supper

1 Our Lord Jesus, in the night wherein he was betrayed, instituted the sacrament of his body and blood, called the Lord's Supper, to be observed in his Church, unto the end of the world; for the perpetual remembrance of the sacrifice of himself in his death, the sealing all benefits thereof unto true believers, their spiritual nourishment and growth in him, their further engagement in, and to all duties which they owe unto him; and to be a bond and pledge of their communion with him, and with each other, as members of his mystical body.

2 In this sacrament Christ is not offered up to his Father, nor any real sacrifice made at all for remission of sins of the quick or dead, but only a commemoration of that one offering up of himself, by himself, upon the cross, once for all, and a spiritual oblation of all possible praise unto God for the same; so that the Popish sacrifice of the mass, as they call it, is most abominably injurious to Christ's one only sacrifice, the alone propitiation for all the sins of the elect.

3 The Lord Jesus hath, in this ordinance, appointed his ministers to declare his word of institution to the people, to pray, and bless the elements of bread and wine, and thereby to set them apart from a common to an holy use; and to take and break the bread, to take the cup, and (they communicating also themselves) to give both to the communicants; but to none who are not then present in the congregation.

4 Private masses, or receiving this sacrament by a priest, or any other, alone; as likewise the denial of the cup to the people; worshipping the elements, the lifting them up, or carrying them about for adoration, and the reserving them for any pretended religious use, are all contrary to the nature of this sacrament, and to the institution of Christ.

5 The outward elements in this sacrament, duly set apart to the uses ordained by Christ, have such relation to him crucified, as that

truly, yet sacramentally only, they are sometimes called by the name of the things they represent, to wit, the body and blood of Christ; albeit, in substance and nature, they still remain truly, and only, bread and wine, as they were before.

6 That doctrine which maintains a change of the substance of bread and wine, into the substance of Christ's body and blood (commonly called transubstantiation) by consecration of a priest, or by any other way, is repugnant, not to Scripture alone, but even to common-sense and reason; overthroweth the nature of the sacrament; and hath been, and is the cause of manifold superstitions, yea, of gross idolatries.

7 Worthy receivers, outwardly partaking of the visible elements in this sacrament, do then also inwardly by faith, really and indeed, yet not carnally corporally, but spiritually, receive and feed upon Christ crucified, and all benefits of his death: the body and blood of Christ being then not corporally or carnally in, with, or under the bread and wine; yet as really, but spiritually, present to the faith of believers in that ordinance, as the elements themselves are, to their outward senses.

8 Although ignorant and wicked men receive the outward elements in this sacrament, yet they receive not the thing signified thereby; but by their unworthy coming thereunto are guilty of the body and blood of the Lord, to their own damnation. Wherefore all ignorant and ungodly persons, as they are unfit to enjoy communion with him, so are they unworthy of the Lord's table, and cannot, without great sin against Christ, while they remain such, partake of these holy mysteries, or be admitted thereunto.

Chapter 30
Of Church Censures

1 The Lord Jesus, as king and head of his Church, hath therein appointed a government in the hand of Church officers, distinct from the civil magistrate.

2 To these officers the keys of the kingdom of heaven are committed, by virtue whereof they have power respectively to retain and remit sins, to shut that kingdom against the impenitent, both by the Word and censures; and to open it unto penitent sinners, by the

ministry of the gospel, and by absolution from censures, as occasion shall require.

3 Church censures are necessary for the reclaiming and gaining of offending brethren; for deterring of others from the like offences for purging out of that leaven which might infect the whole lump; for vindicating the honour of Christ, and the holy profession of the gospel; and for preventing the wrath of God, which might justly fall upon the Church, if they should suffer his covenant, and the seals thereof, to be profaned by notorious and obstinate offenders.

4 For the better attaining of these ends, the officers of the Church are to proceed by admonition, suspension from the Sacrament of the Lord's Supper for a season, and by excommunication from the Church, according to the nature of the crime and demerit of the person.

Chapter 31
Of Synods and Councils

1 For the better government and further edification of the Church, there ought to be such assemblies as are commonly called synods or councils.

2 As magistrates may lawfully call a synod of ministers and other fit persons to consult and advise with about matters of religion; so, if magistrates be open enemies of the Church, the ministers of Christ, of themselves, by virtue of their office, or they, with other fit persons, upon delegation from their churches, may meet together in such assemblies.

3 It belongeth to synods and councils, ministerially, to determine controversies of faith, and cases of conscience; to set down rules and directions for the better ordering of the public worship of God, and government of his Church: to receive complaints in cases of maladministration, and authoritatively to determine the same: which decrees and determinations, if consonant to the Word of God, are to be received with reverence and submission, not only for their agreement with the Word, but also for the power whereby they are made, as being an ordinance of God, appointed thereunto in his Word.

4 All synods or councils since the apostles' times, whether general or particular, may err, and many have erred; therefore

they are not to be made the rule of faith or practice, but to be used as a help in both.

5 Synods and councils are to handle or conclude nothing but that which is ecclesiastical: and are not to intermeddle with civil affairs which concern the commonwealth, unless by way of humble petition in cases extraordinary; or by way of advice for satisfaction of conscience, if they be thereunto required by the civil magistrate.

Chapter 32
Of the State of Men after Death, and of the Resurrection of the Dead

1 The bodies of men, after death, return to dust, and see corruption; but their souls (which neither die nor sleep), having an immortal subsistence, immediately return to God who gave them. The souls of the righteous, being then made perfect in holiness, are received into the highest heavens, where they behold the face of God in light and glory, waiting for the full redemption of their bodies: and the souls of the wicked are cast into hell, where they remain in torments and utter darkness, reserved to the judgment of the great day. Besides these two places for souls separated from their bodies, the Scripture acknowledgeth none.

2 At the last day, such as are found alive shall not die, but be changed; and all the dead shall be raised up with the self-same bodies, and none other, although with different qualities, which shall be united again to their souls forever.

3 The bodies of the unjust shall, by the power of Christ, be raised to dishonour; the bodies of the just, by his Spirit, unto honour, and be made conformable to his own glorious body.

Chapter 33
Of the Last Judgment

1 God hath appointed a day wherein he will judge the world in righteousness by Jesus Christ, to whom all power and judgment is given of the Father. In which day, not only the apostate angels shall be judged, but likewise all persons, that have lived upon earth,

shall appear before the tribunal of Christ, to give an account of their thoughts, words and deeds; and to receive according to what they have done in the body, whether good or evil.

2 The end of God's appointing this day, is for the manifestation of the glory of his mercy in the eternal salvation of the elect; and of his justice in the damnation of the reprobate, who are wicked and disobedient. For then shall the righteous go into everlasting life, and receive that fulness of joy and refreshing which shall come from the presence of the Lord: but the wicked, who know not God, and obey not the gospel of Jesus Christ, shall be cast into eternal torments, and be punished with everlasting destruction from the presence of the Lord, and from the glory of his power.

3 As Christ would have us to be certainly persuaded that there shall be a day of judgment, both to deter all men from sin, and for the greater consolation of the godly in their adversity: so will he have that day unknown to men, that they may shake off all carnal security, and be always watchful, because they know not at what hour the Lord will come; and may be ever prepared to say, Come, Lord Jesus, come quickly. Amen.

Charles Herle, Prolocutor
Cornelius Burges, Assessor
Herbert Palmer, Assessor
Henry Robroughe, Scriba
Adoniram Byfield, Scriba

The Form of Presbyterial Church-Government

The Preface

Jesus Christ, upon whose shoulders the government is, whose name is called Wonderful, Counsellor, the mighty God, the everlasting Father, the Prince of Peace; of the increase of whose government and peace there shall be no end; who sits upon the throne of David, and upon his kingdom, to order it, and to establish it with judgment and justice, from henceforth, even for ever; having all power given unto him in heaven and in earth by the Father, who raised him from the dead, and set him at his own right hand, far above all principalities and power, and might, and dominion, and every name that is named, not only in this world, but also in that which is to come, and put all things under his feet, and gave him to be the head over all things to the Church, which is his body, the fulness of him that filleth all in all: he being ascended up far above all heavens, that he might fill all things, received gifts for his Church, and gave officers necessary for the edification of his Church, and perfecting of his saints.

Of the Church

There is one general Church visible, held forth in the New Testament.

The ministry, oracles, and ordinances of the New Testament, are given by Jesus Christ to the general Church visible, for the gathering and perfecting of it in this life, until his second coming.

Particular visible churches, members of the general Church, are also held forth in the New Testament. Particular churches in the primitive times were made up of visible saints, *viz.* of such as, being of age, professed faith in Christ, and obedience unto Christ, according to the rules of faith and life taught by Christ and his apostles; and of their children.

Of the Officers of the Church

The officers which Christ hath appointed for the edification of his Church, and the perfecting of the saints, are, some extraordinary, as apostles, evangelists, and prophets, which are ceased.

Others ordinary and perpetual, as pastors, teachers, and other church-governors, and deacons.

Pastors

The pastor is an ordinary and perpetual officer in the Church, prophesying of the time of the gospel.

First, it belongs to his office,

To pray for and with his flock, as the mouth of the people unto God, Acts 6:2, 3, 4 and 20:36, where preaching and prayer are joined as several parts of the same office. The office of the elder (that is, the pastor) is to pray for the sick, even in private, to which a blessing is especially promised; much more therefore ought he to perform this in the public execution of his office, as a part thereof.

To read the scriptures publicly; for the proof of which,

1 That the priests and Levites in the Jewish church were trusted with the public reading of the word is proved.

2 That the ministers of the gospel have as ample a charge and commission to dispense the word, as well as other ordinances, as the priests and Levites had under the law, proved, Isa. 66:21. Mat. 23:34 where our Saviour entitleth the officers of the New Testament, whom he will send forth, by the same names of the teachers of the Old.

Which propositions prove, that therefore (the duty being of a moral nature) it followeth by just consequence, that the public reading of the scriptures belongeth to the pastor's office.

To feed the flock, by preaching of the word, according to which he is to teach, convince, reprove, exhort, and comfort.

To catechise, which is a plain laying down the first principles of the oracles of God, or of the doctrine of Christ, and is a part of preaching.

To dispense other divine mysteries.

To administer the sacraments.

To bless the people from God, Num. 6:23, 24, 25, 26. *Compared with* Rev. 14:5 (where the same blessings, and persons from whom they come, are expressly mentioned). Isa. 66:21, where, under the names of Priests and Levites to be continued under the gospel, are meant evangelical pastors, who therefore are by office to bless the people.

To take care of the poor.

And he hath also a ruling power over the flock as a pastor.

Teacher or Doctor

The scripture doth hold out the name and title of teacher, as well as of the pastor.

Who is also a minister of the word, as well as the pastor, and hath power of administration of the sacraments.

The Lord having given different gifts, and divers exercises according to these gifts, in the ministry of the word: though these different gifts may meet in, and accordingly be exercised by, one and the same minister; yet, where be several ministers in the same congregation, they may be designed to several employments, according to the different gifts in which each of them doth most excel. And he that doth more excel in exposition of scripture, in teaching sound doctrine, and in convincing gainsayers, than he doth in application, and is accordingly employed therein, may be called a teacher, or doctor, (the places alleged by the notation of the word do prove the proposition). Nevertheless, where is but one minister in a particular congregation, he is to perform, as far as he is able, the whole work of the ministry.

A teacher, or doctor, is of most excellent use in schools and universities: as of old in the schools of the prophets, and at Jerusalem, where Gamaliel and others taught as doctors.

Other Church-Governors

As there were in the Jewish church elders of the people joined with the priests and Levites in the government of the Church; so Christ, who hath instituted government, and governors ecclesiastical in the Church, hath furnished some in his Church, beside the ministers of the word, with gifts for government, and with commission to execute the same when called thereunto, who are to join with the minister in the government of the Church. Which officers reformed churches commonly call Elders.

Deacons

The scripture doth hold out deacons as distinct officers in the Church.

Whose office is perpetual. To whose office it belongs not to preach the word, or administer the sacraments, but to take special care in distributing to the necessities of the poor.

Of particular Congregations

It is lawful and expedient that there be fixed congregations, that is, a certain company of Christians to meet in one assembly ordinarily for public worship. When believers multiply to such a number, that they cannot conveniently meet in one place, it is lawful and expedient that they should be divided into distinct and fixed congregations, for the better administration of such ordinances as belong unto them, and the discharge of mutual duties.

The ordinary way of dividing Christians into distinct congregations, and most expedient for edification, is by the respective bounds of their dwellings.

First, Because they who dwell together, being bound to all kind of moral duties one to another, have the better opportunity thereby to discharge them; which moral tie is perpetual; for Christ came not to destroy the law, but to fulfil it.

Secondly, The communion of saints must be so ordered as may stand with the most convenient use of the ordinances, and discharge of duties, without respect of persons.

Thirdly, The pastor and people must so nearly cohabit together, as that they may mutually perform their duties each to other with most conveniency.

In this company some must be set apart to bear office.

Of the Officers of a particular Congregation

For officers in a single congregation, there ought to be one at the least, both to labour in the word and doctrine, and to rule.

It is also requisite that there should be others to join in government.

And likewise it is requisite that there be others to take special care for the relief of the poor.

The number of each of which is to be proportioned according to the condition of the congregation.

These officers are to meet together at convenient and set times, for the well-ordering of the affairs of that congregation, each according to his office.

It is most expedient that, in these meetings, one whose office is to labour in the word and doctrine, do moderate in their proceedings.

Of the Ordinances in a particular Congregation

The ordinances in a single congregation are, prayer, thanksgiving, and singing of psalms, the word read, (although there follow no immediate explication of what is read,) the word expounded and applied, catechising, the sacraments administered, collection made for the poor, dismissing the people with a blessing.

Of Church-Government, and the several sorts of Assemblies for the same

Christ hath instituted a government, and governors ecclesiastical in the Church: to that purpose, the apostles did immediately receive the keys from the hand of Jesus Christ, and did use and exercise them in all the churches of the world upon all occasions.

And Christ hath since continually furnished some in his Church with gifts of government, and with commission to execute the same, when called thereunto.

It is lawful, and agreeable to the word of God, that the Church be governed by several sorts of assemblies, which are congregational, classical, and synodical.

Of the Power in common of all these Assemblies

It is lawful, and agreeable to the word of God, that the several assemblies before mentioned have power to convent, and call before them, any person within their several bounds, whom the ecclesiastical business which is before them doth concern.

They have power to hear and determine such causes and differences as do orderly come before them.

It is lawful, and agreeable to the word of God, that all the said assemblies have some power to dispense church-censures.

Of Congregational Assemblies, that is, the Meeting of the ruling Officers of a particular Congregation, for the Government thereof

The ruling officers of a particular congregation have power, authoritatively, to call before them any member of the congregation, as they shall see just occasion.

To enquire into the knowledge and spiritual estate of the several members of the congregation.

To admonish and rebuke.

Which three branches are proved by Heb. 13:17, 1 Thess. 5:12, 13, Ezek. 24:4.

Authoritative suspension from the Lord's table, of a person not yet cast out of the Church, is agreeable to scripture:

First, Because the ordinance itself must not be profaned.

Secondly, Because we are charged to withdraw from those that walk disorderly.

Thirdly, Because of the great sin and danger, both to him that comes unworthily, and also to the whole Church. And there was power and authority, under the Old Testament, to keep unclean persons from holy things.

The like power and authority, by way of analogy, continues under the New Testament.

The ruling officers of a particular congregation have power authoritatively to suspend from the Lord's table a person not yet cast out of the Church:

First, Because those who have authority to judge of, and admit, such as are fit to receive the sacrament, have authority to keep back such as shall be found unworthy.

Secondly, Because it is an ecclesiastical business of ordinary practice belonging to that congregation.

When congregations are divided and fixed, they need all mutual help one from another, both in regard of their intrinsical weaknesses and mutual dependence, as also in regard of enemies from without.

Of Classical Assemblies

The scripture doth hold out a presbytery in a church.

A presbytery consisteth of ministers of the word, and such other public officers as are agreeable to and warranted by the word of God to be church-governors, to join with the ministers in the government of the Church.

The scripture doth hold forth, that many particular congregations may be under one presbyterial government.

This proposition is proved by instances:

I *First,* Of the church of Jerusalem which consisted of more congregations than one, and all these congregation were under one presbyterial government.

This appeareth thus: If 1 *First,* The church of Jerusalem, consisted of more congregations than one, as is manifest:

(1) By the multitude of believers mentioned in divers; both before the dispersion of the believers there, by means of the persecution; and also after the dispersion.

(2) By the many apostles and other preachers in the church of Jerusalem. And if there were but one congregation there, then each apostle preached but seldom; which will not consist with Acts 6:2.

(3) The diversity of languages among the believers, mentioned both in the second and sixth chapters of the Acts, doth argue more congregations than one in that church.

2 *Secondly,* All those congregations were under one presbyterial government; because

(1) They were one church.

(2) The elders of the church are mentioned.

(3) The apostles did the ordinary acts of presbyters, as presbyters in that kirk; which proveth a presbyterial church before the dispersion, Acts 6.

(4) The several congregations in Jerusalem being one church, the elders of that church are mentioned as meeting together for acts of government; which proves that those several congregations were under one presbyterial government.

And whether these congregations were fixed or not fixed, in regard of officers or members, it is also one as to the truth of the proposition.

Nor doth there appear any material difference betwixt the several congregations in Jerusalem, and of the many congregations now in the ordinary condition of the Church, as to the point of fixedness required of officers or members.

3 *Thirdly*, Therefore the scripture doth hold forth, that many congregations may be under one presbyterial government.

II *Secondly*, By the instance of the church of Ephesus; for,

1 *First*, That there were more congregations than one in the church of Ephesus, appears by Acts 20:31, where is mention of Paul's continuance at Ephesus in preaching for the space of three years; and Acts 19:18, 19, 20, where the special effect of the word is mentioned; and ver. 10. and 17. of the same chapter, where is a distinction of Jews and Greeks; and 1 Cor. 16:8, 9. where is a reason of Paul's stay at Ephesus until Pentecost; and ver. 19. where is mention of a particular church in the house of Aquila and Priscilla, then at Ephesus, as appears, Acts 17:19, 24, 26. All which laid together, doth prove that the multitudes of believers did make more congregations than one in the church of Ephesus.

2 *Secondly*, That there were many elders over these many congregations, as one flock, appeareth.

3 *Thirdly*, That these many congregations were one Church, and that they were under one presbyterial government, appeareth.

Of Synodical Assemblies

The scripture doth hold out another sort of assemblies for the government of the Church, beside classical and congregational, all which we call *Synodical*.

Pastors and teachers, and other church-governors, (as also other fit persons, when it shall be deemed expedient,) are members of those assemblies which we call *Synodical*, where they have a lawful calling thereunto.

Synodical assemblies may lawfully be of several sorts, as provincial, national, and oecumenical.

It is lawful, and agreeable to the word of God, that there be a subordination of congregational, classical, provincial, and national assemblies, for the government of the Church.

Of Ordination of Ministers

Under the head of ordination of ministers is to be considered, either the doctrine of ordination, or the power of it.

Touching the Doctrine of Ordination

No man ought to take upon him the office of a minister of the word without a lawful calling.

Ordination is always to be continued in the Church.

Ordination is the solemn setting apart of a person to some public church office.

Every minister of the word is to be ordained by imposition of hands, and prayer, with fasting, by those preaching presbyters to whom it doth belong.

It is agreeable to the word of God, and very expedient, that such as are to be ordained ministers, be designed to some particular church, or other ministerial charge.

He that is to be ordained minister, must be duly qualified, both for life and ministerial abilities, according to the rules of the apostle.

He is to be examined and approved by those by whom he is to be ordained.

No man is to be ordained a minister for a particular congregation, if they of that congregation can show just cause of exception against him.

Touching the Power of Ordination

Ordination is the act of a presbytery.

The power of ordering the whole work of ordination is in the whole presbytery, which, when it is over more congregations than one, whether those congregations be fixed or not fixed, in regard of officers or members, it is indifferent as to the point of ordination.

It is very requisite, that no single congregation, that can conveniently associate, do assume to itself all and sole power in ordination:

1 Because there is no example in scripture that any single congregation, which might conveniently associate, did assume to itself all and sole power in ordination; neither is there any rule which may warrant such a practice.

2 Because there is in scripture example of an ordination in a presbytery over divers congregations; as in the church of Jerusalem, where were many congregations: these many congregations were under one presbytery, and this presbytery did ordain.

The preaching presbyters orderly associated, either in cities or neighbouring villages, are those to whom the imposition of hands doth appertain, for those congregations within their bounds respectively.

Concerning the Doctrinal Part of Ordination of Ministers

1 No man ought to take upon him the office of a minister of the word without a lawful calling.

2 Ordination is always to be continued in the Church.

3 Ordination is the solemn setting apart of a person to some public church office.

4 Every minister of the word is to be ordained by imposition of hands, and prayer, with fasting, by those preaching presbyters to whom it doth belong.

5 The power of ordering the whole work of ordination is in the whole presbytery, which, when it is over more congregations than

one, whether those congregations be fixed or not fixed, in regard of officers or members, it is indifferent as to the point of ordination.

6 It is agreeable to the word, and very expedient, that such as are to be ordained ministers, to be designed to some particular church, or other ministerial charge.

7 He that is to be ordained minister, must be duly qualified, both for life and ministerial abilities, according to the rules of the apostle.

8 He is to be examined and approved by those by whom he is to be ordained.

9 No man is to be ordained a minister for a particular congregation, if they of that congregation can show just cause of exception against him.

10 Preaching presbyters orderly associated, either in cities or neighbouring villages, are those to whom the imposition of hands doth appertain, for those congregations within their bounds respectively.

11 In extraordinary cases, something extraordinary may be done, until a settled order may be had, yet keeping as near as possible may be to the rule.

12 There is at this time (as we humbly conceive) an extraordinary occasion for a way of ordination for the present supply of ministers.

The Directory for the Ordination of Ministers

It being manifest by the word of God, that no man ought to take upon himself the office of a minister of the gospel, until he be lawfully called and ordained thereunto; and, that the work of ordination is to be performed with all due care, wisdom, gravity, and solemnity, we humbly tender these directions, as requisite to be observed.

1 He that is to be ordained, being either nominated by the people, or otherwise commended to the presbytery, for any place, must address himself to the presbytery, and bring with him a testimonial of his taking the Covenant of the three kingdoms; of his diligence and proficiency in his studies; what degrees he hath taken in the

university, and what hath been the time of his abode there; and withal, of his age, which is to be twenty-four years; but especially, of his life and conversation.

2 Which being considered by the presbytery, they are to proceed to enquire touching the grace of God in him, and whether he be of such holiness of life as is requisite in a minister of the gospel; and to examine him touching his learning and sufficiency, and touching the evidences of his calling to the holy ministry; and, in particular, his fair and direct calling to that place.

The Rules for Examination are these:

(1) That the party examined be dealt withal in a brotherly way, with mildness of spirit, and with special respect to the gravity, modesty, and quality of every one.

(2) He shall be examined touching his skill in the original tongues, and his trial to be made by reading the Hebrew and Greek Testaments, and rendering some portion of some into Latin; and if he be defective in them, enquiry shall be made more strictly after his other learning, and whether he hath skill in logic and philosophy.

(3) What authors in divinity he hath read, and is best acquainted with; and trial shall be made in his knowledge of the grounds of religion, and of his ability to defend the orthodox doctrine contained in them against all unsound and erroneous opinions, especially these of the present age; of his skill in the sense and meaning of such places of scripture as shall be proposed unto him, in cases of conscience, and in the chronology of the scripture, and the ecclesiastical history.

(4) If he hath not before preached in public with approbation of such as are able to judge, he shall, at a competent time assigned him, expound before the presbytery such a place of scripture as shall be given him.

(5) He shall also, within a competent time, frame a discourse in Latin, upon such a common-place or controversy in divinity as shall be assigned to him, and exhibit to the presbytery such theses as express the sum thereof, and maintain a dispute upon them.

(6) He shall preach before the people, the presbytery, or some of the ministers of the word appointed by them, being present.

(7) The proportion of his gifts in relation to the place unto which he is called shall be considered.

(8) Beside the trial of his gifts in preaching, he shall undergo an examination in the premises two several days, and more, if the presbytery shall judge is necessary.

(9) And as for him that hath formerly been ordained a minister, and is to be removed to another charge, he shall bring a testimonial of his ordination, and of his abilities and conversation, whereupon his

fitness for that place shall be tried by his preaching there, and (if it shall be judged necessary) by a further examination of him.

3 In all which he being approved, he is to be sent to the church where he is to serve, there to preach three several days, and to converse with the people, that they may have trial of his gifts for their edification, and may have time and occasion to inquire into, and the better to know, his life and conversation.

4 In the last of these three days appointed for the trial of his gifts in preaching, there shall be sent from the presbytery to the congregation, a public intimation in writing, which shall be publicly read before the people, and after affixed to the church-door, to signify, that such a day a competent number of the members of that congregation, nominated by themselves, shall appear before the presbytery, to give their consent and approbation to such a man to be their minister; or otherwise, to put in, with all Christian discretion and meekness, what exceptions they have against him. And if, upon the day appointed, there be no just exception against him, but the people give their consent, then the presbytery shall proceed to ordination.

5 Upon the day appointed for ordination, which is to be performed in that church where he that is to be ordained is to serve, a solemn fast shall be kept by the congregation, that they may the more earnestly join in prayer for a blessing upon the ordinances of Christ, and the labours of his servant for their good. The presbytery shall come to the place, or at least three or four ministers of the word shall be sent thither from the presbytery; of which one appointed by the presbytery shall preach to the people concerning the office and duty of ministers of Christ, and how the people ought to receive them for their work's sake.

6 After the sermon, the minister who hath preached shall, in the face of the congregation, demand of him who is now to be ordained, concerning his faith in Christ Jesus, and his persuasion of the truth of the reformed religion, according to the scriptures; his sincere intentions and ends in desiring to enter into this calling; his diligence in praying, reading, meditating, preaching, ministering the sacraments, discipline, and doing all ministerial duties towards his charge; his zeal and faithfulness in maintaining the truth of the gospel, and unity of the Church, against error and schism; his care that himself and his family may be unblameable, and examples to

the flock; his willingness and humility, in meekness of spirit, to submit unto the admonitions of his brethren, and discipline of the Church; and his resolution to continue in his duty against all trouble and persecution.

7 In all which having declared himself, professed his willingness, and promised his endeavours, by the help of God; the minister likewise shall demand of the people concerning their willingness to receive and acknowledge him as the minister of Christ; and to obey and submit unto him, as having rule over them in the Lord; and to maintain, encourage, and assist him in all parts of his office.

8 Which being mutually promised by the people, the presbytery, or the ministers sent from them for ordination, shall solemnly set him apart to the office and work of the ministry, by laying their hands on him, which is to be accompanied with a short prayer or blessing, to this effect:

> Thankfully acknowledging the great mercy of God in sending Jesus Christ for the redemption of his people; and for his ascension to the right hand of God the Father, and thence pouring out his Spirit, and giving gifts to men, apostles, evangelists, prophets, pastors, and teachers; for the gathering and building up of his Church; and for fitting and inclining this man to this great work[1]: to entreat him to fit him with his Holy Spirit, to give him (who in his name we thus set apart to this holy service) to fulfil the work of his ministry in all things, that he may both save himself, and his people committed to his charge.

9 This or the like form of prayer and blessing being ended, let the minister who preached, briefly exhort him to consider of the greatness of his office and work, the danger of negligence both to himself and his people, the blessing which will accompany his faithfulness in this life, and that to come; and withal exhort the people to carry themselves to him, as to their minister in the Lord, according to their solemn promise made before. And so by prayer commending both him and his flock to the grace of God, after singing of a psalm, let the assembly be dismissed with a blessing.

10 If a minister be designed to a congregation, who hath been formerly ordained presbyter according to the form of ordination which hath been in the church of England, which we hold for

---

[1] Here let them impose hands on his head.

substance to be valid, and not to be disclaimed by any who have received it; then, there being a cautious proceeding in matters of examination, let him be admitted without any new ordination.

11 And in case any person already ordained minister in Scotland, or in any other reformed church, be designed to another congregation in England, he is to bring from that church to the presbytery here, within which that congregation is, a sufficient testimonial of his ordination, of his life and conversation while he lived with them, and of the causes of his removal; and to undergo such a trial of his fitness and sufficiency, and to have the same course held with him in other particulars, as it set down in the rule immediately going before, touching examination and admission.

12 That records be carefully kept in the several presbyteries, of the names of the persons ordained, with their testimonials, the time and place of their ordination, of the presbyters who did impose their hands upon them, and of the charge to which they are appointed.

13 That no money or gift, of what kind soever, shall be received from the person to be ordained, or from any on his behalf, for ordination, or ought else belonging to it, by any of the presbytery, or any appertaining to any of them, upon what pretence soever.

Thus far of ordinary Rules, and course of Ordination, in the ordinary way; that which concerns the extraordinary way, requisite to be now practised, followeth

1 In these present exigencies, which we cannot have any presbyteries formed up to their whole power and work, and that many ministers are to be ordained for the service of the armies and navy, and to many congregations where there is no minister at all; and where (by reason of the public troubles) the people cannot either themselves enquire and find out one who may be a faithful minister for them, or have any with safety sent unto them, for such a solemn trial as was before mentioned in the ordinary rules; especially, when there can be no presbytery near unto them, to whom they may address themselves, or which may come and send to them a fit man to be ordained in that congregation, and for that people; and yet notwithstanding, it is requisite that ministers be ordained for them by some, who, being set apart themselves for the work of the ministry, have power to join in the setting apart others, who are found fit and worthy. In those cases, until, by God's blessing,

the aforesaid difficulties may be in some good measure removed, let some godly ministers, in or about the city of London, be designed by public authority, who, being associated, may ordain ministers for the city and the vicinity, keeping as near to the ordinary rules fore-mentioned as possibly they may; and let this association be for no other intent or purpose, but only for the work of ordination.

2 Let the like association be made by the same authority in great towns, and the neighbouring parishes in the several counties, which are at the present quiet and undisturbed, to do the like for the part adjacent.

3 Let such as are chosen, or appointed for the service of the armies or navy, be ordained, as aforesaid, by the associated ministers of London, or some others in the country.

4 Let them do the like, when any man shall duly and lawfully be recommended to them for the ministry of any congregation, who cannot enjoy liberty to have a trial of his parts and abilities, and desire the help of such ministers so associated, for the better furnishing of them with such a person as by them shall be judged fit for the service of that church and people.

4. The Savoy Declaration, 1658

If the Westminster Confession and its related documents are the charter of Presbyterianism, then the Savoy Declaration might be regarded as a similar statement for Congregationalism. However, it has never been so well-known, even among Congregationalists.

The origins of the meeting of elders and messengers of the Congregational Churches in England at the Savoy Palace from 29 September to 12 October 1658 are obscure. Unlike the Westminster Assembly it was not summoned by Parliament. Oliver Cromwell had dissolved his last parliament in February 1658, and the Lord Protector himself died on 3 September. The suggestion for the meeting seems to have arisen from conversations between a number of ministers gathered for the annual University of Oxford Act in July 1658; and the arrangements for it were entrusted to the elders of the churches in and around London. Some two hundred elders and ministers assembled at the Savoy, though the names of only a handful are known: in all probability a majority were laymen. About 120 churches were represented.

The Declaration of Faith adopted by the meeting was substantially the Westminster Confession, as it had been amended by Parliament in 1647–48. Theologically, the most substantial changes are found in chapters 15 and 20, the latter of which (*Of the Gospel, and of the Extent of the Grace thereof*) is entirely new. Presbyteriansim is, of course, eschewed, and this emerges clearly in the Declaration on *The Institution of Churches, and the Order Appointed in them by Jesus Christ*. On the other hand, that declaration assumes that preachers would be publicly maintained (Article 14) and it also marks a shift away from the pure separatism of the early followers of Robert Browne at the end of the sixteenth century. This reflects the fact that the Savoy Declaration comes at the point when Congregationalism enjoyed its most favourable position in English history, comparable in many ways to the privileged position of New England Congregationalism. The Restoration of 1660 and the years of persecution which followed the Act of Uniformity of 1662 were not foreseen when the Declaration was drafted, though nowadays it is almost impossible to examine it without being aware of the sequel.

The Congregationalism reflected in the Declaration is that of John Cotton (1584–1652) and John Owen (1616–83), to whom the Preface is usually attributed. In the words of A.G. Matthews, the Savoy Declaration was 'the last of its race', reflecting a century of Reformed Confessions. Curiously it was not widely adopted among English Congregationalists in the following century, though it was in Massachusetts and Connecticut; and it was substantially adopted by the English Particular Baptists in 1677. When the Congregational Union was formed in 1832, its leaders preferred to draft a new declaration which reflected the influence of the eighteenth-century Evangelical Revival.

For further reading, see page 264.

Declaration of Faith

Preface

Confession of the faith that is in us, when justly called for, is so indispensable a due all owe to the glory of the sovereign God, that it is ranked among the duties of the first commandment, such as prayer is; and therefore by Paul yoked with faith it self, as necessary to salvation: With the heart man believeth unto righteousness, and with the mouth confession is made unto salvation. Our Lord Christ himself, when he was accused of his doctrine, considered simply as a matter of fact by preaching, refused to answer; because, as such, it lay upon evidence, and matter of testimony of others; unto whom therefore he refers himself: But when both the High Priest and Pilate expostulate his faith, and what he held himself to be; he without any demur at all, cheerfully makes declaration, That he was the Son of God; so to the High Priest: And that he was a king, and born to be a king: thus to Pilate; though upon the uttering of it his life lay at the stake: Which holy profession of his is celebrated for our example, I Tim. 6:13.

Confessions, when made by a company of professors of Christianity jointly meeting to that end, the most genuine and natural use of such confessions is, That under the same form of words, they express the substance of the same common salvation, or unity of their faith; whereby speaking the same things, they shew themselves perfectly joined in the same mind, and in the same judgment.

And accordingly such a transaction is to be looked upon but as a meet or fit medium or means whereby to express that their common faith and salvation, and no way is to be made use of as an imposition upon any: Whatever is of force or constraint in matters of this nature causeth them to degenerate from the name and nature of confessions, and turns them from being confessions of faith into exactions and impositions of faith.

And such common confessions of the orthodox faith, made in simplicity of heart by any such body of Christians, with concord among themselves, ought to be entertained by all others that love the truth as it is in Jesus, with an answerable rejoicing: For if the unanimous opinions and assertions but in some few points of religion, and that when by two churches, namely, that of Jerusalem, and the messengers of Antioch met, assisted by some of of the Apostles, were by the believers of those times received with so much joy, (as it is said, They rejoiced for the consolation) much more this is to be done, when the whole substance of faith, and form of wholesome words shall be declared by the messengers of a multitude of churches, though wanting those advantages of counsel and authority of the Apostles, which that assembly had.

Which acceptation is then more specially due, when these shall (to choose) utter and declare their faith, in the same substance for matter, yea, words, for the most part, that other churches and assemblies, reputed the most orthodox, have done before them: For upon such a correspondency, all may see that actually accomplished, which the Apostle did but exhort unto, and pray for, in those two more eminent Churches of the Corinthians and the Romans; (and so in them for all the Christians of his time) that both Jew and Gentile, that is, men of different persuasions, (as they were) might glorify God with one mind and with one mouth. And truly, the very turning of the Gentiles to the owning of the same faith, in the substance of it, with the Christian Jew (though differing in greater points than we do from our brethren) is presently after dignified by the Apostle with this style, That it is the confession of Jesus Christ himself; not as the object only, but as the author and maker thereof: I will confess to thee (saith Christ to God) among the Gentiles. So that in all such accords, Christ is the great and first confessor; and we, and all our faith uttered by us, are but the epistles, (as Paul) and confessions (as Isaiah there) of their Lord and ours; He, but expressing what is written in his heart, through their hearts and mouths, to the glory of God the Father: And shall not we all rejoice herein, when as Christ himself is said to do it upon this occasion: as it there also follows, I will sing unto thy Name.

Further, as the soundness and wholesomeness of the matter gives the vigour and life to such confessions, so the inward freeness, willingness and readiness of the spirits of the confessors do contribute the beauty and loveliness thereunto: as it is in prayer to God, so in confessions made to men. If two or three meet, do agree, it renders both, to either the more acceptable. The Spirit of Christ is in himself too free, great and generous a Spirit, to suffer himself to be used by any human arm, to whip men into belief; he drives not, but gently leads into all truth, and persuades men to dwell in the tents of like precious faith; which would lose of its preciousness and value, if that sparkle of freeness shone not in it: The character of his people is to be a willing people in the day of his power, (not man's) in the beauties of holiness, which are the assemblings of the saints: one glory of which assemblings in that first church, is said to have been, They met with one accord; which is there in that psalm prophesied of, in the instance of that first church, for all other that should succeed.

And as this great Spirit is in himself free, when, and how far, and in whom to work, so where and when he doth work, he carrieth it with the same freedom, and is said to be a free Spirit, as he both is, and works in us: And where this spirit of the Lord is, there is liberty.

Now, as to this confession of ours, besides, that a conspicuous conjunction to the particulars mentioned, hath appeared therein: There are also four remarkable attendants thereon, which added, might perhaps in the eyes of sober and indifferent spirits, give the whole of this transaction a room and rank amongst other many good and memorable things of this age; at least all set together, do cast as clear a gleam and manifestation of God's power and presence, as hath appeared in any such kind of confessions, made by so numerous a company these later years.

The first, is the temper, (or distemper rather) of the times, during which, these churches have been gathering, and which they have run through. All do (out of a general sense) complain that the times have been perilous, or difficult times; (as the Apostle foretold) and that in respect to danger from seducing spirits, more perilous then the hottest seasons of persecution. We have sailed through an æstuation,[1] fluxes and refluxes of great varieties of spirits, doctrines, opinions and occurrences; and especially in the matter of opinions, which have been accompanied in their several seasons, with powerful persuasions and temptations, to seduce those of our way. It is known men have taken the freedom (notwithstanding what authority hath interposed to the contrary) to vent and vend their own vain and accursed imaginations, contrary to the great and fixed truths of the Gospel, insomuch, as take the whole round and circle of delusions, the Devil hath in this small time, ran, it will be found, that every truth, of greater or lesser weight, hath by one or

---

[1]   i.e. feverish disturbance (*Ed.*)

other hand, at one time or another, been questioned and called to the bar amongst us, yea, and impleaded, under the pretext (which hath some degree of justice in it) that all should not be bound up to the traditions of former times, nor take religion upon trust.

Whence it hath come to pass, that many of the soundest professors were put upon a new search and disquisition of such truths, as they had taken for granted, and yet had lived upon the comfort of: to the end they might be able to convince others, and establish their own hearts against that darkness and unbelief, that is ready to close with error, or at least to doubt of the truth, when error is speciously presented. And hereupon we do professedly account it one of the greatest advantages gained out of the temptations of these times; yea the honour of the saints and ministers of these nations, That after they had sweetly been exercised in, and had improved practical and experimental truths, this should be their further lot, to examine and discuss, and indeed, anew to learn over every doctrinal truth, both out of the Scriptures, and also with a fresh taste thereof in their own hearts; which is no other than what the Apostle exhorts to, Try all things, hold fast that which is good. Conversion unto God at first, what is it else than a savoury and affectionate application, and the bringing home to the heart with spiritual light and life, all truths that are necessary to salvation, together with other lesser truths? all which we had afore conversion taken in but notionally from common education and tradition.

Now that after this first gust those who have been thus converted should be put upon a new probation and search out of the Scriptures, not only of all principles explicitly ingredients to conversion; (unto which the Apostle referreth the Galatians when they had diverted from them) but of all other superstructures as well as fundamentals; and together therewith, anew to experiment the power and sweetness of all these in their own souls: What is this but tried faith indeed? and equivalent to a new conversion unto the truth? An anchor that is proved to be sure and stedfast, that will certainly hold in all contrary storms: This was the eminent seal and commendation which those holy Apostles that lived and wrote last; Peter, John and Jude; in their epistles did set and give to the Christians of the latter part of those primitive times. And besides, it is clear and evident by all the other epistles, from first to last, that it cost the Apostles as much, and far more care and pains to preserve them they had converted, in the truth, than they had taken to turn

66

them thereunto first: And it is in itself as great a work and instance of the power of God, that keeps, yea, guards us through faith unto salvation.

Secondly, let this be added, (or superadded rather) to give full weight and measure, even to running over, that we have all along this season, held forth (though quarrelled with for it by our brethren) this great principle of these times, That amongst all Christian states and churches, there ought to be vouchsafed a forbearance and mutual indulgence unto saints of all persuasions, that keep unto, and hold fast the necessary foundations of faith and holiness, in all other matters extrafundamental, whether of faith or order.

This to have been our constant principle, we are not ashamed to confess to the whole Christian world. Wherein yet we desire we may be understood, not as if in the abstract we stood indifferent to falsehood or truth, or were careless whether faith or error, in any truths but fundamental, did obtain or not, so we had our liberty in our petty and smaller differences: or as if to make sure of that, we had cut out this wide cloak for it: No, we profess that the whole, and every particle of that faith delivered to the saints, (the substance of which we have according to our light here professed) is, as to the propagation and furtherance of it by all gospel-means, as precious to us as our lives; or what can be supposed dear to us; and in our sphere we have endeavoured to promote them accordingly: But yet withal, we have and do contend, (and if we had all the power which any, or all of our brethren of differing opinions have desired to have over us, or others, we should freely grant it unto them all) we have and do contend for this, That in the concrete, the persons of all such gracious saints, they and their errors, as they are in them, when they are but such errors as do and may stand with communion with Christ, though they should not repent of them, as not being convinced of them to the end of their days; that those, with their errors (that are purely spiritual, and intrench and overthrow not civil societies), as concrete with their persons, should for Christ's sake be born withal by all Christians in the world; and they notwithstanding be permitted to enjoy all ordinances and spiritual privileges according to their light, as freely as any other of their brethren that pretend to the greatest orthodoxy; as having as equal, and as fair a right in and unto Christ, and all the holy things of Christ, that any other can challenge to themselves.

And this doth afford a full and invincible testimony on our behalf, in that while we have so earnestly contended for this just liberty of saints in all the churches of Christ, we ourselves have had no need of it: that is as to the matter of the profession of faith which we have maintained together with others: and of this, this subsequent confession of faith gives sufficient evidence. So as we have the confidence in Christ, to utter in the words of those two great Apostles, That we have stood fast in the liberty wherewith Christ hath made us free (in the behalf of others, rather than ourselves) and having been free, have not made use of our liberty for a cloak of error or maliciousness in ourselves: And yet, lo, whereas from the beginning of the rearing of these churches, that of the Apostle hath been (by some) prophesied of us, and applied to us, That while we promised (unto others) liberty, we ourselves would become servants of corruption, and be brought in bondage to all sorts of fancies and imaginations: yet the whole world may now see after the experience of many years ran through (and it is manifest by this confession) that the great and gracious God hath not only kept us in that common unity of the faith and knowledge of the Son of God, which the whole community of saints have and shall in their generations come unto, but also in the same truths, both small and great, that are built thereupon, that any other of the best and more pure Reformed Churches in their best times (which were their first times) have arrived unto: This confession withal holding forth a professed opposition unto the common errors and heresies of these times.

These two considerations have been taken from the seasons we have gone through.

Thirdly, let the space of time itself, or days, wherein from first to last the whole of this confession was framed and consented to by the whole of us, be duly considered by sober and ingenuous spirits: the whole of days in which we had meetings about it, (set aside the two Lord's days, and the first day's meeting, in which we considered and debated what to pitch upon) were but eleven days, part of which also was spent by some of us in prayer, others in consulting; and in the end all agreeing. We mention this small circumstance but to this end, (which still adds unto the former) That it gives demonstration, not of our freeness and willingness only, but of our readiness and preparedness unto so great a work; which otherwise, and in other assemblies, hath ordinarily taken up long and great debates, as in such a variety of matters of such concernment, may well be supposed to fall out. And this is no other than what the Apostle Peter exhorts unto, Be ready always to give an answer to every man that asketh you a reason or account of the hope that is in you. The Apostle Paul saith of the spiritual truths of the gospel, That God hath prepared them for those that love him. The inward and innate constitution of the new creature being in itself such as is suited to all those truths, as congenial thereunto: But although there be this mutual adaptness between these two, yet such is the mixture of ignorance, darkness and unbelief, carnal reason, preoccupation of judgment, interest of parties, wantonness in opinion, proud adhering to our own persuasions, and perverse oppositions and averseness to agree with others, and a multitude of such like distempers common to believing man: All which are not only mixed with, but at times, (especially in such times as have passed over our heads) are ready to overcloud our judgments, and do cause our eyes to be double, and sometimes prevail as well as lusts, and do bias our wills and affections: And such is their mixture, that although there may be existent an habitual preparedness in men's spirits, yet not always a present readiness [is] to be found, specially not in such a various multitude of men, to make a solemn and deliberate profession of all truths, it being as great a work to find the spirits of the just (perhaps the best) of saints, ready for every truth, as to be prepared for every good work.

It is therefore to be looked at as a great and special work of the Holy Ghost, that so numerous a company of ministers, and other principal brethren, should so readily, speedily and jointly give up themselves unto such a whole body of truths that are after godliness.

This argues they had not their faith to seek; but, as it said of Ezra, that they were ready scribes, and (as Christ) instructed unto the kingdom of heaven, being as the good householders of so many families of Christ, bringing forth of their store and treasury new and old. It shews these truths had been familiar to them, and they acquainted with them, as with their daily food and provision, (as Christ's allusion there insinuates) in a word, that so they had preached, and that so their people had believed, as the Apostle speaks upon one like particular occasion. And the Apostle Paul considers (in cases of this nature) the suddenness or length of time, either one way or the other; whether it were in men's forsaking or learning of the truth. Thus the suddenness in the Galatians case in leaving the truth, he makes a wonder of it: I marvel that you are so soon, (that is, in so short a time) removed from the true gospel unto another. Again on the contrary, in the Hebrews, he aggravates their backwardness, That when for the time you ought to be teachers, you had need that one teach you the very first principles of the oracles of God. The parable contrary to both these having fallen out in this transaction, may have some ingredient and weight with ingenuous spirits in its kind, according to the proportion is put upon either of these forementioned in their adverse kind, and obtain the like special observation.

This accord of ours hath fallen out without having held any correspondence together, or prepared consultation, by which we might come to be advised of one another's minds. We allege not this as a matter of commendation in us; no, we acknowledge it to have been a great neglect: And accordingly one of the first proposals for union amongst us was that there might be a constant correspondence held among the churches for counsel and mutual edification, so for time to come to prevent the like omission.

We confess that from the first, every, or at least the generality of our churches have been in a manner like so many ships (though holding forth the same general colours) launched singly, and sailing apart and alone in the vast ocean of these tumultuating times, and they exposed to every wind of doctrine, under no other conduct than the Word and Spirit and their particular elders and principal brethren, without associations among ourselves, or so much as holding out common lights to others, whereby to know where we were.

But yet whilest we thus confess to our own shame this neglect, let all acknowledge, that God hath ordered it for his high and greater glory, in that his singular care and power should have so watched over each of these, as that all should be found to have steered their course by the same chart, and to have been bound for one and the same port, and that upon this general search now made, that the same holy and blessed truths of all sorts, which are current and warrantable amongst all the other churches of Christ in the world, should be found to be our lading.

The whole, and every of these things when put together, do cause us (whatever men of prejudiced and opposite spirits may find out to slight them) with a holy admiration, to say, That this is no other than the Lord's doing; and which we with thanksgiving do take from his hand as a special token upon us for good, and doth show that God is faithful and upright towards those that are planted in his house: And that as the faith was but once for all, and intentionally first delivered unto the saints; so the saints, when not abiding scattered, but gathered under their respective pastors according to God's heart into an house, and churches unto the living God, such together are, as Paul forespake it, the most steady and firm pillar and seat of truth that God hath anywhere appointed to himself on earth, where his truth is best conserved, and publicly held forth; there being in such assemblies weekly a rich dwelling of the Word amongst them, that is, a daily open house kept by the means of those good householders, their teachers and other instructers respectively appropriated to them, whom Christ in the virtue of his ascension, continues to give as gifts to his people, himself dwelling amongst them; to the end that by this, as the most sure standing permanent means, the saints might be perfected, till we all (even all the saints in present and future ages) do come by this constant and daily ordinance of his unto the unity of the faith and knowledge of the Son of God unto a perfect man, unto the measure of the stature of the fulness of Christ (which though growing on by parts and piecemeal, will yet appear complete, when that great and general assembly shall be gathered, then when this world is ended, and these dispensations have had their fulness and period) and so that henceforth (such a provision being made for us) we be no more children tossed to and fro, and carried about with every wind of doctrine.

And finally, this doth give a fresh and recent demonstration, that the great Apostle and High-priest of our profession is indeed ascended into heaven, and continues there with power and care, faithful as a son over his own house, whose house are we, if we hold fast the confidence and the rejoicing of the hope firm unto the end: and shews that he will, as he hath promised, be with his own institutions to the end of the world.

It is true, that many sad miscarriages, divisions, breaches, fallings off from holy ordinances of God, have along this time of temptation, (especially in the beginning of it) been found in some of our churches; and no wonder, if what hath been said be fully considered: Many reasons might further be given hereof, that would be a sufficient apology, without the help of a retortion upon other churches (that promised themselves peace) how that more destroying ruptures have befallen them, and that in a wider sphere and compass;

which though it should not justify us, yet may serve to stop others mouths.

Let Rome glory of the peace in, and obedience of her children, against the Reformed Churches for their divisions that occurred (especially in the first rearing of them) whilst we all know the causes of their dull and stupid peace to have been carnal interests, wordly correspondencies, and coalitions strengthened by gratifications of all sorts of men by that religion, the principles of blind devotion, traditional faith, ecclesiastical tyranny, by which she keeps her children in bondage to this day. We are also certain, that the very same prejudice that from hence they would cast upon the Reformed (if they were just) do lie as fully against those pure churches raised up by the Apostles themselves in those first times: for as we have heard of their patience, sufferings, consolations, and the transcending gifts poured out, and graces shining in them, so we have heard complaints of their divisions too, for the forsakings of their assemblies, as the custom or manner of some was (which later were in that respect *felones de se*, and needed no other delivering up to Satan as their punishment, than what they executed upon themselves). We read of the shipwreck also of faith and a good conscience, and overthrowings of the faith of some; and still but of some, not all, nor the most: which is one piece of an apology the Apostle again and again inserts to future ages, and through mercy we have the same to make.

And truly we take the confidence professedly to say, that these temptations common to the purest churches of saints separated from the mixture of the world, though they grieve us (for who is offended and we burn not?) yet they do not at all stumble us, as to the truth of our way, had they been many more: We say it again, these stumble us no more (as to that point) than it doth offend us against the power of religion itself, to have seen, and to see daily in particular persons called out and separated from the world by an effectual work of conversion, that they for a while do suffer under disquietments, vexations, turmoils, unsettlements of spirit, that they are tossed with tempests and horrid temptations, such as they had not in their former estate, whilst they walked according to the course of this world: For Peter hath sufficiently instructed us whose business it is to raise such storms, even the Devil's; and also whose design it is, that after they have suffered a while, thereby they shall be settled, perfected, stablished, that have so suffered, even the

God of all grace. And look what course of dispensation God holds to saints personally, he doth the like to bodies of saints in churches, and the Devil the same for his part too: And that consolatory maxim of the Apostle, God shall tread down Satan under your feet shortly, which Paul uttereth concerning the Church of Rome, shows how both God and Satan have this very hand therein; for he speaks that very thing in reference unto their divisions, as the coherence clearly manifests; and so you have both designs expressed at once.

Yea, we are not a little induced to think, that the divisions, breaches, etc, of those primitive churches would not have been so frequent among the people themselves, and not the elders only, had not the freedom, liberties and rights of the members (the brethren, we mean) been stated and exercised in those churches, the same which we maintain and contend for to be in ours.

Yea (which perhaps may seem more strange to many) had not those churches been constituted by members enlightened further than with notional and traditional knowledge, by a new and more powerful light of the Holy Ghost, wherein they had been made partakers of the Holy Ghost, and the heavenly gift, and their hearts had tasted the good Word of God, and the powers of the world to come, and of such members at lowest, there had not fallen out those kinds of divisions among them.

For experience hath shown, that the most common sort of mere doctrinal professors (such as the most are nowadays) whose highest elevation is but freedom from moral scandal joined with devotion to Christ through mere education, such as in many Turks is found towards Mahomet, that these finding and feeling themselves not much concerned in the active part of religion, so that may have the honour (especially upon a reformation of a new refinement) that themselves are approved members, admitted to the Lord's Supper, and their children to the ordinance of Baptism; they regard not other matters (as Gallio did not) but do easily and readily give up themselves unto their guides, being like dead fishes carried with the common stream; whereas those that have a further renewed light by a work of the Holy Ghost, whether saving or temporary, are upon the quite contrary grounds apt to be busy about, and inquisitive into, what they are to receive and practise, or wherein their consciences are professedly concerned and involved: And thereupon they take the freedom to examine and try the spirits, whether of God or no: And from hence are more apt to dissatisfaction, and from thence to run into division, and many of such proving to be enlightened but with a temporary, not saving faith (who have such a work of the Spirit upon them, and profession in them, as will and doth approve itself to the judgment of saints, and ought to be so judged, until they be otherwise discovered) who at long run, prove hypocrites through indulgence unto lusts, and then out of their lusts persist to hold up these divisions unto breach of, or departings from churches, and the ordinances of God, and God is even with them for it, they waxing worse and worse, deceiving and being deceived; and even many of those that are sincere, through a mixture of darkness and erroneousness in their judgments, are for a season apt out of conscience to be led away with the error of others, which lie in wait to deceive.

Insomuch as the Apostle upon the example of those first times, foreseeing also the like events in following generations upon the like causes, hath been bold to set this down as a ruled case, that likewise in other churches so constituted and *de facto* emprivileged as that of the Church of Corinth was (which single church, in the sacred records about it, is the completest mirror of church constitution, order and government, and events thereupon ensuing, of any one church whatever that we have story of) his maxim is, there must also be divisions amongst you; he setly inserts an [also][2] in the case, as that which had been in his own observation, and that which would be ἐπὶ τὸ πολὺ the fate of other churches like thereunto, so prophesieth he: And he speaks this as peremptorily as he doth elsewhere in that other, We must through many tribulations enter into the Kingdom of Heaven: Yea, and that all that will live godly in Christ Jesus shall suffer persecution: There is a [must] upon both alike, and we bless God, that we have run through both, and do say, and we say no more; That as it was then, so it is now, in both respects.

However, such hath been the powerful hand of God's providence in these, which have been the worst of our trials, That out of an approved experience and observation of the issue, we are able to add that other part of the Apostle's prediction. That therefore such rents must be, they they which are approved may be made manifest among you; which holy issue God (as having aimed at it therein)

---

2   The brackets are in original, as also round 'must' below (*Ed.*).

doth frequently and certainly bring about in churches as he doth bring upon them that other fate of division. Let them therefore look unto it, that are the authors of such disturbances, as the Apostle warneth, Gal. 5:10. The experiment is this, That we have seen, and do daily see, that multitudes of holy and precious souls, and (in the Holy Ghost's word) approved saints, have been, and are the more rooted and grounded by means of these shakings, and do continue to cleave the faster to Christ, and the purity of his ordinances, and value them the more by this cost God hath put them to for the enjoying of them, who having been planted in the house of the Lord have flourished in the courts of our God, in these evil times, to show that the Lord is upright. And this experimented event from out of such divisions, hath more confirmed us and is a louder apology for us, than all that our opposites are able from our breaches to allege to prejudice us.

We will add a few words for conclusion, and give a more particular account of this our declaration. In drawing up this Confession of Faith, we have had before us the Articles of Religion, approved and passed by both Houses of Parliament [June 20, 1648], after advice had with an assembly of Divines, called together by them for that purpose. To which Confession, for the substance of it, we fully assent, as do our brethren of New England, and the churches also of Scotland, as each in their general synods have testified.

A few things we have added for obviating some erroneous opinions, that have been more broadly and boldly here of late maintained by the asserters, than in former times; and made some other additions and alterations in method, here and there, and some clearer explanations, as we found occasion.

We have endeavoured throughout, to hold to such truths in this our confession, as are more properly terms matters of faith; and what is of church order, we dispose in certain propositions by itself. To this course we are led by the example of the honourable Houses of Parliament, observing what was established, and what omitted by them in that Confession the Assembly presented to them. Who thought it not convenient to have matters of discipline and church government put into a confession of faith, especially such particulars thereof, as then were, and still are controverted and under dispute by men orthodox and sound in faith. The 30th chapter therefore of that Confession, as it was presented to them by the Assembly, which is 'Of Church Censures' their use, kinds, and in whom placed. As also chapter 31 'Of Synods and Councils' by whom to be called, of what force in their decrees and determinations. And the 4th paragraph of the 20th chapter which determines what opinions and practices disturb the peace of the Church, and how such disturbers ought to be proceeded against by the censures of the Church, and punished by the civil magistrate. Also a great part of the 24th chapter 'Of Marriage and Divorce'. These were such doubtful assertions, and so unsuitable to a confession of faith, as the honourable Houses in their great wisdom thought fit to lay them aside: There being nothing that tends more to heighten dissentings among brethren, than to determine and adopt the matter of their difference, under so high a title, as to be an article of our faith: So that there are two whole chapters, and some paragraphs in other chapters in their Confession, that we have upon this account omitted; and the rather do we give this notice, because that copy of the Parliaments, followed by us, is in few men's hands; the other as it came from the Assembly, being approved of in Scotland, was printed and hastened [i]nto the world [August 1647] before the Parliament had declared their resolutions about it; which was not till June 20, 1648 and yet hath been, and continueth to be the copy (ordinarily) only sold, printed and reprinted for these eleven years.

After the 19th chapter 'Of the Law' we have added a chapter 'Of the Gospel', it being a title that may not well be omitted in a confession of faith: In which chapter, what is dispersed, and by intimation in the Assembly's Confession with some little addition, is here brought together, and more fully under one head.

That there are not Scriptures annexed as in some Confessions (though in divers others it's otherwise) we give the same account as did the reverend Assembly in the same case: which was this; The Confession being large, and so framed, as to meet with the common errors, if the Scriptures should have been alleged with any clearness, and by showing where the strength of the proof lieth, it would have required a volume.

We say, further, it being our utmost end in this (as it is indeed of a Confession) humbly to give an account what we hold and assert in these matters; that others, especially the churches of Christ, may judge of us accordingly. This we aimed at, and not so much to instruct others, or convince gainsayers. These are the proper works of other institutions of Christ, and are to be done in the strength of express Scripture. A Confession is an ordinance of another nature.

What we have laid down and asserted about churches and their government, we humbly conceive to be the order which Christ himself hath appointed to be observed, we have endeavoured to follow Scripture-light; and those also that went before us according to that rule, desirous of nearest uniformity with reforming churches, as with our brethren in New England, so with others, that differ from them and us.

The models and platforms of this subject laid down by learned men, and practised by churches, are various: We do not judge it brotherly, or grateful, to insist upon comparisons as some have done; but this experience teacheth, That the variety, and possibly the disputes and emulations arising thence, have much strengthened, if not fixed, this unhappy persuasion in the minds of some learned and good men, namely, that there is no settled order laid down in Scripture; but it's left to the prudence of the Christian magistrate, to compose or make choice of such a form as is most suitable and consistent with their civil government. Where this opinion is entertained in the persuasion of governors, there, churches asserting their power and order to be *jure divino*, and the appointment of Jesus Christ, can have no better nor more honourable entertainment, than a toleration or permission.

Yet therein there is this remarkable advantage to all parties that differ, about what in government is of Christ's appointment; in that such magistrates have a far greater latitude in conscience, to tolerate and permit the several forms of each so bound up in their persuasion, than they have to submit unto what the magistrate shall impose: And thereupon the magistrate exercising an indulgency and forbearance, with protection and encouragement to the people of God, so differing from him, and amongst themselves; doth therein discharge as great a faithfulness to Christ, and love to his people, as can any way be supposed and expected from any Christian magistrate, of what persuasion soever he is. And where this clemency from governors is showed to any sort of persons or churches of Christ upon such a principle, it will in equity produce this just effect, that all that so differ from him, and amongst themselves, standing in equal and alike difference from the principle of such a magistrate, he is equally free to give a like liberty to them, one as well as the other.

This faithfulness in our governors we do with thankfulness to God acknowledge, and to their everlasting honour, which appeared much in the late Reformation. The hierarchy, common-prayer-book, and all other things grievous to God's people, being removed, they made choice of an Assembly of learned men, to advise what government and order is meet to be established in the room of these things; and because it was known there were different opinions (as always hath been among godly men) about forms of church government, there was by the ordinance first sent forth to call an Assembly, not only a choice made of persons of several persuasions to sit as members there, but liberty given to a lesser number, if dissenting, to report their judgments and reasons, as well and as freely as the major part.

Hereupon the honourable House of Commons (an indulgence we hope will never be forgotten) finding by papers received from them, that the members of the assembly were not like to compose differences amongst themselves, so as to join in the same rule for church government, did order further as followeth:

> That a Committee of Lords and Commons, &c, do take into consideration the differences of the opinions in the Assembly of Divines in point of church-government, and to endeavour a union if it be possible; and in case that cannot be done, to endeavour the finding out some way, how far tender consciences, who cannot in all things submit to the same rule which shall be established, may be born with according to the Word, and as may stand with the public peace.

By all which it is evident the Parliament purposed not to establish the rule of church government with such vigor,[3] as might not permit and bear with a practice different from what they had established: In persons and churches of different principles, if occasion were. And this Christian clemency and indulgence in our governors, hath been the foundation of that freedom and liberty, in the managing of church affairs, which our brethren as well as we, that differ from them, do now, and have many years enjoyed.

---

3   1659 ed has 'rigor' (Ed.)

The honourable Houses by several ordinances of Parliament after much consultation, having settled rules for church government [Ordinance of March 14, 1645], and such an ecclesiastical order as they judged would best join with the laws and government of the kingdom, did publish them, requiring the practice thereof throughout the nation; and in particular, by the ministers of the Province of London. But (upon the former reason, or the like charitable consideration) these rules were not imposed by them under any penalty or rigorous enforcement, though frequently urged thereunto by some.

Our reverend brethren of the Province of London, having considered of these ordinances, and the church government laid down in them, declared their opinions to be, that there is not a complete rule in those ordinances; also, that there are many necessary things not yet established, and some things wherein their consciences are not so fully satisfied. These brethren in the same paper, [Considerations and Cautions from Sion College, June 19, 1646], have published also their joint resolution to practise in all things according to the rule of the Word, and according to these ordinances, so far as they conceive them correspond to it, and in so doing they trust they shall not grieve the spirit of the truly godly, nor give any just occasion to them that are contrary minded, to blame their proceedings.

We humbly conceive (that we being dissatisfied in these things as our brethren) the like liberty was intended by the honourable Houses, and may be taken by us of the Congregational way (without blame or grief to the spirits of those brethren at least) to resolve, or rather to continue in the same resolution and practice in these matters, which indeed were our practices in times of greatest opposition, and before this reformation was begun.

And as our brethren, the ministers of London, drew up and published their opinions and apprehensions about church government into an entire system; so we now give the like public account of our consciences, and the rules by which we have constantly practised hitherto; which we have here drawn up, and do present. Whereby it will appear how much, or how little we differ in these things from our Presbyterian brethren.

And we trust there is no just cause why any man, either for our differing from the present settlement, it being out of conscience, and not out of contempt, or our differences one from another, being not wilful, should charge either of us with that odious reproach of schism. And indeed, if not for our differing from the state-settlement, much less because we differ from our brethren, our differences being in some lesser things and circumstances, only, as themselves acknowledge. And let it be further considered, that we have not broken from them or their order by these differences (but rather they from us) and in that respect we less deserve their censure; our practice being no other than what it was in our breaking from Episcopacy, and long before Presbytery, or any such form as now they are in, was taken up by them; and we will not say how probable it is that the yoke of Episcopacy had been upon our neck to this day, if some such way (as formerly, and now is, and hath been termed schism) had not with much suffering been then practised and since continued in.

For novelty, wherewith we are likewise both charged by the enemies of both, it is true, in respect of the public and open profession, either of presbytery or independency, this nation hath been a stranger to each way, it's possible ever since it hath been Christian; though for ourselves we are able to trace the footsteps of an independent Congregational way in the ancientest customs of the churches, as also in the writings of our soundest Protestant Divines, *Puritanis. Ang.* by Dr Ames near 50 years since,[4] as the opinions of Whitehead, Gilby, Fox, Dearing, Greenham, Cartwright, Fenne, Fulk, Whitaker, Rainold, Perkins etc. and (that which we are much satisfied in) a full concurrence throughout in all the substantial parts of church governments, with our reverend brethren the old Puritan non-conformists, who being instant in prayer and much sufferings, prevailed with the Lord, and we reap with joy, what they sowed in tears. Our brethren also that are for presbyterial subordinations, profess what is of weight against novelty for their way.

And now therefore seeing the Lord, in whose hand is the heart of princes, hath put into the hearts of our governors to tolerate and permit (as they have done many years) persons of each persuasion, to enjoy their consciences, though neither come up to the rule established by authority: And that which is more, to give us both protection, and the same encouragement that the most devoted conformists in those former superstitious times enjoyed,

---

[4] *Puritanismus Anglicanus*, Frankfurt 1610, a Latin translation of W. Bradshaw's *English Puritanism*, with a preface by William Ames (*Ed*).

yea, and by a public law to establish this liberty for time to come; and yet further, in the midst of our fears, to set over us a prince that owns this establishment, and cordially resolves to secure our churches in the enjoyment of these liberties, if we abuse them not to the disturbance of the civil peace.

This should be a very great engagement upon the hearts of all, though of different persuasions, to endeavour our utmost, jointly to promote the honour and prosperity of such a government and governors by whatsoever means, which in our callings as ministers of the gospel, and as churches of Jesus Christ the Prince of peace, we are any way able to; as also to be peaceably disposed one towards another, and with mutual toleration to love as brethren, notwithstanding such differences, remembering as it's very equal we should, the differences that are between Presbyterians and Independents, being differences between fellow-servants, and neither of them having authority given from God or man, to impose their opinions, one more than the other. That our governors after so solemn an establishment, should thus bear with us both, in our greater differences from their rule, and after this, for any of us to take a fellow-servant by the throat, upon the account of a lesser reckoning, and nothing due to him upon it: is to forget, at least not to exercise, that compassion and tenderness we have found, where we had less ground to challenge or expect it.

Our prayer unto God is, That whereto we have already attained, we all may walk by the same rule, and that wherein we are otherwise minded, God would reveal it to us in his due time.

Chapter 1
Of the Holy Scripture

1 Although the light of nature, and the works of creation and providence, do so far manifest the goodness, wisdom and power of God, as to leave men inexcusable; yet are they not sufficient to give that knowledge of God and of his will, which is necessary unto salvation: therefore it pleased the Lord at sundry times, and in divers manners, to reveal himself, and to declare that his will unto his Church; and afterwards for the better preserving and propagating of the truth, and for the more sure establishment and comfort of the

Church against the corruption of the flesh, and the malice of Satan and of the world, to commit the same wholly unto writing: which maketh the holy Scripture to be most necessary; those former ways of God's revealing his will unto his people, being now ceased.

2 Under the name of holy Scripture, or the Word of God written, are now contained all the Books of the Old and New Testament; which are these:

Of the Old Testament

Genesis
Exodus
Leviticus
Numbers
Deuteronomy
Joshua
Judges
Ruth
I. Samuel
II. Samuel
I. Kings
II. Kings
I. Chronicles
II. Chronicles
Ezra
Nehemiah
Esther
Job
Psalms
Proverbs.

Ecclesiastes
The Song of Songs
Isaiah
Jeremiah
Lamentations
Ezekiel
Daniel
Hosea
Joel
Amos
Obadiah
Jonah
Micah
Nahum
Habakkuk
Zephaniah
Haggai
Zechariah
Malachi

Of the New Testament

The Gospels according to
    Matthew
    Mark
    Luke
    John
The Acts of the Apostles
Paul's Epistles to the Romans
Corinthians I
Corinthians II
Galatians
Ephesians
Philippians
Colossians
Thessalonians I

Thessalonians II
To Timothy I
To Timothy II
To Titus
To Philemon
The Epistle to the Hebrews
The Epistle of James
The First and Second
    Epistles of Peter
The First, Second and
    Third Epistles of John
The Epistle of Jude
The Revelation

All which are given by the inspiration of God to be the rule of faith and life.

3 The Books commonly called Apocrypha, not being of divine inspiration, are no part of the canon of the Scripture; and therefore are of no authority in the Church of God, nor to be any otherwise approved or made use of, than other human writings.

4 The authority of the holy Scripture, for which it ought to be believed and obeyed, dependeth not upon the testimony of any man or church; but wholly upon God (who is truth itself) the Author thereof: and therefore it is to be received, because it is the Word of God.

5 We may be moved and induced by the testimony of the Church to an high and reverent esteem of the holy Scripture; and the heavenliness of the matter, the efficacy of the doctrine, the majesty of the style, the consent of all the parts, the scope of the whole (which is, to give all glory to God), the full discovery it makes of the only way of man's salvation, the many other incomparable excellencies, and the entire perfection thereof, are arguments whereby it doth abundantly evidence itself to be the Word of God; yet notwithstanding, our full persuasion and assurance of the infallible truth and divine authority thereof, is from the inward work of the Holy Spirit, bearing witness by and with the Word in our hearts.

6 The whole counsel of God concerning all things necessary for his own glory, man's salvation, faith and life, is either expressly set down in Scripture, or by good and necessary consequence may be deduced from Scripture; unto which nothing at any time is to be added, whether by new revelations of the Spirit, or traditions of men. Nevertheless we acknowledge the inward illumination of the Spirit of God to be necessary for the saving understanding of such things as are revealed in the Word: and that there are some circumstances concerning the worship of God and government of the Church, common to human actions and societies, which are to be ordered by the light of nature and Christian prudence, according to the general rules of the Word, which are always to be observed.

7 All things in Scripture are not alike plain in themselves, nor alike clear unto all: yet those things which are necessary to be known, believed and observed for salvation, are so clearly propounded and opened in some place of Scripture or other, that not only the learned, but the unlearned, in a due use of the ordinary means, may attain unto a sufficient understanding of them.

8 The Old Testament in Hebrew (which was the native language of the people of God of old) and the New Testament in Greek (which

at the time of writing of it was most generally known to the nations) being immediately inspired by God, and by his singular care and providence kept pure in all ages, are therefore authentical; so as in all controversies of religion the Church is finally to appeal unto them. but because these original tongues are not known to all the people of God, who have right unto and interest in the Scriptures, and are commanded in the fear of God to read and search them; therefore they are to be translated into the vulgar language of every nation unto which they come, that the Word of God dwelling plentifully in all, they may worship him in an acceptable manner, and through patience and comfort of the Scriptures may have hope.

9 The infallible rule of interpretation of Scripture, is the Scripture itself; and therefore when there is a question about the true and full sense of any Scripture (which is not manifold, but one) it must be searched and known by other places, that speak more clearly.

10 The supreme judge by which all controversies of religion are to be determined, and all decrees of councils, opinions of ancient writers, doctrines of men and private spirits, are to be examined, and in whose sentence we are to rest, can be no other, but the holy Scripture delivered by the Spirit; into which Scripture so delivered, our faith is finally resolved.

Chapter 2
Of God and Of the Holy Trinity

1 There is but one only living and true God; who is infinite in being and perfection, a most pure Spirit, without body, parts or passions, immutable, immense, eternal, incomprehensible, almighty, most wise, most holy, most free, most absolute, working all things according to the counsel of his own immutable and most righteous will, for his own glory, most loving, gracious, merciful, long-suffering, abundant in goodness and truth, forgiving iniquity, transgression and sin, the rewarder of them that diligently seek him; and withal most just and terrible in his judgments, hating all sin, and who will by no means clear the guilty.

2 God hath all life, glory, goodness, blessedness, in and of himself; and is alone, in, and unto himself, all-sufficient, not standing in need of any creatures, which he hath made, nor deriving any glory from them, but only manifesting his own glory in, by, unto, and upon them: He is

the alone fountain of all being, of who, through whom, and to whom are all things; and hath most sovereign dominion over them, to do by them, for them, or upon them, whatsoever himself pleaseth. In his sight all things are open and manifest, his knowledge is infinite, infallible, and independent upon the creature, so as nothing is to him contingent or uncertain. He is most holy in all his counsels, in all his works, and in all his commands. To him is due from angels and men, and every other creature, whatsoever worship, service or obedience, as creatures, they owe unto the Creator, and whatever he is further pleased to require of them.

3 In the unity of the God-head there be three Persons, of one substance, power and eternity. God the Father, God the Son, and God the Holy Ghost. The Father is of none, neither begotten, nor proceeding; the Son is eternally begotten of the Father; the Holy Ghost eternally proceeding from the Father and the Son. Which doctrine of the Trinity is the foundation of all our communion with God, and comfortable dependence upon him.

Chapter 3
Of God's Eternal Decree

1 God from all eternity did by the most wise and holy counsel of his own will, freely and unchangeably ordain whatsoever comes to pass: yet so, as thereby neither is God the author of sin, nor is violence offered to the will of the creatures, nor is the liberty or contingency of second causes taken away, but rather established.

2 Although God knows whatsoever may or can come to pass upon all supposed conditions, yet hath he not decreed any thing, because he foresaw it as future, or as that which would come to pass upon such conditions.

3 By the decree of God for the manifestation of his glory, some men and angels are predestinated unto everlasting life, and other foreordained to everlasting death.

4 These angels and men thus predestinated, and fore ordained, are particularly and unchangeably designed, and their number is so certain and definite, that it cannot be either increased or diminished.

5 Those of mankind that are predestinated unto life, God, before the foundation of the world was laid, according to his eternal and immutable purpose, and the secret counsel and good pleasure of his

will, hath chosen in Christ unto everlasting glory, out of his mere free grace and love, without any foresight of faith or good works, or perseverance in either of them, or any other thing in the creature, as conditions or causes moving him thereunto, and all to the praise of his glorious grace.

6 As God hath appointed the elect unto glory, so hath he by the eternal and most free purpose of his will foreordained all the means thereunto. Wherefore they who are elected, being fallen in Adam, are redeemed by Christ, are effectually called unto faith in Christ by his Spirit working in due season, are justified, adopted, sanctified, and kept by his power, through faith, unto salvation. Neither are any other redeemed by Christ, or effectually called, justified, adopted, sanctified and saved, but the elect only.

7 The rest of mankind God was pleased, according to the unsearchable counsel of his own will, whereby he extendeth or withholdeth mercy, as he pleaseth, for the glory of his sovereign power over his creatures, to pass by and to ordain them to dishonour and wrath for their sin, to the praise of his glorious justice.

8 The doctrine of this high mystery of predestination is to be handled with special prudence and care, that men attending the will of God revealed in his Word, and yielding obedience thereunto, may from the certainty of their effectual vocation, be assured of their eternal election. So shall this doctrine afford matter of praise, reverence and admiration of God, and of humility, diligence, and abundant consolation to all that sincerely obey the Gospel.

Chapter 4
Of Creation

1 It pleased God the Father, Son and Holy Ghost, for the manifestation of the glory of his eternal power, wisdom and goodness, in the beginning, to create or make out of nothing the world, and all things therein, whether visible or invisible, in the space of six days, and all very good.

2 After God had made all other creatures, he created man, male and female, with reasonable and immortal souls, endued with knowledge, righteousness and true holiness, after his own image, having the law of God written in their hearts, and power to fulfil it; and yet under

a possibilty of transgressing, being left to the liberty of their own will, which was subject unto change. Besides this law written in their hearts, they received a command not to eat of the tree of the knowledge of good and evil; which while they kept, they were happy in their communion with God, and had dominion over the creatures.

Chapter 5
Of Providence

1 God the great Creator of all things, doth uphold, direct, dispose and govern all creatures, actions and things from the greatest even to the least by his most wise and holy providence, according to his infallible foreknowledge, and the free and immutable counsel of his own will, to the praise of the glory of his wisdom, power, justice, goodness and mercy.

2 Although in relation to the foreknowledge and decree of God, the first cause, all things come to pass immutably and infallibly; yet by the same providence he ordereth them to fall out according to the nature of second causes, either necessarily, freely, or contingently.

3 God in his ordinary providence maketh use of means, yet is free to work without, above, and against them at his pleasure.

4 The almighty power, unsearchable wisdom, and infinite goodness of God, so far manifest themselves in his providence, in that his determinate counsel extendeth itself even to the first fall, and all other sins of angels and men (and that not by a bare permission) which also he most wisely and powerfully boundeth, and otherwise ordereth and governeth in a manifold dispensation to his own most holy ends; yet so, as the sinfulness thereof proceedeth only from the creature, and not from God, who being most holy and righteous, neither is, nor can be the author or approver of sin.

5 The most wise, righteous and gracious God doth oftentimes leave for a season his own children to manifold temptations, and the corruption of their own hearts, to chastise them for their former sins, or to discover unto them the hidden strength of corruption, and deceitfulness of their hearts, that they may be humbled; and to raise them to a more close and constant dependence for their support upon himself, and to make them more watchful against all future occasions of sin, and for sundry other just and holy ends.

6 As for those wicked and ungodly men, whom God as a righteous judge, for former sins, doth blind and harden, from them he not only withholdeth his grace, whereby they might have been enlightened in their understandings, and wrought upon in their hearts; but sometimes also withdraweth the gifts which they had, and exposeth them to such objects, as their corruption makes occasions of sin; and withal gives them over to their own lusts, the temptations of the world, and the power of Satan; whereby it comes to pass that they harden themselves, even under those means which God useth for the softening of others.

7 As the providence of God doth in general reach to all creatures, so after a most special manner it taketh care of his Church, and disposeth all things to the good thereof.

Chapter 6
Of the Fall of Man, of Sin, and of the Punishment thereof

1 God having made a covenant of works and life, thereupon, with our first parents and all their posterity in them, they being seduced by the subtlety and temptation of Satan did wilfully transgress the law of their creation, and break the covenant in eating the forbidden fruit.

2 By this sin they, and we in them, fell from original righteousness and communion with God, and so became dead in sin, and wholly defiled in all the faculties and parts of soul and body.

3 They being the root, and by God's appointment standing in the room and stead of all mankind, the guilt of this sin was imputed, and corrupted nature conveyed to all their posterity descending from them by ordinary generation.

4 From this original corruption, whereby we are utterly indisposed, disabled and made opposite to all good, and wholly inclined to all evil, do proceed all actual transgressions.

5 This corruption of nature during this life, doth remain in those that are regenerated; and although it be through Christ pardoned and mortified, yet both itself and all the motions thereof are truly and properly sin.

6 Every sin, both original and actual, being a transgression of the rightous law of God, and contrary thereunto, doth in its own nature bring guilt upon the sinner, whereby he is bound over to the wrath of God, and curse of the law, and so made subject to death, with all miseries, spiritual, temporal and eternal.

Chapter 7
Of God's Covenant with Man

1 The distance between God and the creature is so great, that although reasonable creatures do owe obedience unto him as their Creator, yet they could never have attained the reward of life, but by some voluntary condescension on God's part, which he hath been pleased to express by way of covenant.

2 The first covenant made with man, was a covenant of works, wherein life was promised to Adam, and in him to his posterity, upon condition of perfect and personal obedience.

3 Man by his fall having made himself incapable of life by that covenant, the Lord was pleased to make a second, commonly called the covenant of grace; wherein he freely offereth unto sinners life and salvation by Jesus Christ, requiring of them faith in him that they may be saved, and promising to give unto all those that are ordained unto life, his Holy Spirit, to make them willing and able to believe.

4 This covenant of grace is frequently set forth in the Scripture by the name of a testament, in reference to the death of Jesus Christ the testator, and to the everlasting inheritance, with all things belonging to it, therein bequeathed.

5 Although this covenant hath been differently and variously administered in respect of ordinances and institutions in the time of the law, and since the coming of Christ in the flesh; yet for the substance and efficacy of it, to all its spiritual and saving ends, it is one and the same; upon the account of which various dispensations, it is called the Old and New Testament.

Chapter 8
Of Christ the Mediator

1 It pleased God, in his eternal purpose, to choose and ordain the Lord Jesus his only begotten Son, according to a covenant made between them both, to be the Mediator between God and man; the Prophet, Priest and King, the Head and Saviour of his Church, the Heir of all things and Judge of the world; unto whom he did from all eternity give a people to be his seed, and to be by him in time redeemed, called, justified, sanctified, and glorified.

2 The Son of God, the second person in the Trinity, being very and eternal God, of one substance and equal with the Father, did, when the fulness of time was come, take upon him man's nature, with all the essential properties and common infirmities thereof, yet without sin, being conceived by the power of the Holy Ghost, in the womb of the Virgin Mary, of her substance: So that two whole perfect and distinct natures, the Godhead and the manhood, were inseparably joined together in one person, without conversion, composition, or confusion; which person is very God and very man, yet one Christ, the only Mediator between God and man.

3 The Lord Jesus in his human nature, thus united to the divine in the person of the Son, was sanctified and anointed with the Holy Spirit above measure, having in him all the treasures of wisdom and knowledge, in whom it pleased the Father that all fulness should dwell; to the end that being holy, harmless, undefiled, and full of grace and truth, he might be thoroughly furnished to execute the office of a Mediator and Surety; which office he took not unto himself, but was thereunto called by his Father, who also put all power and judgment into his hand, and gave him commandment to execute the same.

4 This office the Lord Jesus did most willingly undertake; which that he might discharge, he was made under the law, and did perfectly fulfil it, and underwent the punishment due to us, which we should have borne and suffered, being made sin and a curse for us, enduring most grievous torments immediately from God in his soul, and most painful sufferings in his body, was crucified, and died; was buried, and remained under the power of death, yet saw no corruption. On the third day he arose from the dead with the same body in which he suffered, with which also he ascended into heaven, and there sitteth at the right hand of his Father, making intercession, and shall return to judge men and angels at the end of the world.

5 The Lord Jesus by his perfect obedience and sacrifice of himself, which he through the eternal Spirit, once offered up unto God, hath fully satisfied the justice of God, and purchased not only reconciliation, but an everlasting inheritance in the kingdom of heaven, for all those whom the Father hath given unto him.

6 Although the work of redemption was not actually wrought by Christ, till after his incarnation; yet the virtue, efficacy and benefits thereof were communicated to the elect in all ages, successively from the beginning of the world, in and by those promises, types and sacrifices wherein he was revealed and signified to be the seed of the

woman, which should bruise the serpent's head, and the lamb slain from the beginning of the world, being yesterday and today the same, and for ever.

7 Christ in the work of mediation acteth according to both natures; by each nature doing that which is proper to itself; yet by reason of the unity of the person, that which is proper to one nature, is sometimes in Scripture attributed to the person denominated by the other nature.

8 To all those for whom Christ hath purchased redemption, he doth certainly and effectually apply and communicate the same; making intercession for them; and revealing unto them in and by the Word, the mysteries of salvation; effectually persuading them by his Spirit to believe and obey, and governing their hearts by his Word and Spirit; overcoming all their enemies by his almighty power and wisdom, and in such manner and ways as are most consonant to his most wonderful and unsearchable dispensation.

Chapter 9
Of Free-Will

1 God hath endued the will of man with that natural liberty and power of acting upon choice that it is neither forced, nor by any absolute necessity of nature determined to do good or evil.

2 Man in his state of innocency had freedom and power to will and to do that which was good and well-pleasing to God; but yet mutably, so that he might fall from it.

3 Man by his fall into a state of sin, hath wholly lost all ability of will to any spiritual good accompanying salvation; so as a natural man being altogether averse from that good, and dead in sin, is not able by his own strength to convert himself, or to prepare himself thereunto.

4 When God converts a sinner, and translates him into the state of grace, he freeth him from his natural bondage under sin, and by his grace alone enables him freely to will and to do that which is spiritually good; yet so as that, by reason of his remaining corruption, he doth not perfectly nor only will that which is good, but doth also will that which is evil.

5 The will of man is made perfectly and immutably free to do good alone in the state of glory only.

Chapter 10
Of Effectual Calling

1 All those whom God hath predestinated unto life, and those only, he is pleased in his appointed and accepted time effectually to call by his Word and Spirit, out of that state of sin and death in which they are by nature, to grace and salvation by Jesus Christ; enlightening their minds spiritually and savingly to understand the things of God, taking away their heart of stone, and giving unto them an heart of flesh; renewing their wills, and by his almighty power determining them to that which is good; and effectually drawing them to Jesus Christ; yet so, as they come most freely, being made willing by his grace.

2 This effectual call is of God's free and special grace alone, not from any thing at all foreseen in man, who is altogether passive therein, until being quickened and renewed by the Holy Spirit he is thereby enabled to answer this call, and to embrace the grace offered and conveyed in it.

3 Elect infants dying in infancy, are regenerated and saved by Christ, who worketh when, and where, and how he pleaseth; so also are all other elect persons who are incapable of being outwardly called by the ministry of the Word.

4 Others not elected, although they may be called by the ministry of the Word, and may have some common operations of the Spirit, yet not being effectually drawn by the Father, they neither do nor can come unto Christ, and therefore cannot be saved: much less can men not professing the Christian religion, be saved in any other way whatsoever, be they never so diligent to frame their lives according to the light of nature, and the law of that religion they do profess: and to assert and maintain that they may, is very pernicious, and to be detested.

Chapter 11
Of Justification

1 Those whom God effectually calleth, he also freely justifieth; not by infusing righteousness into them, but by pardoning their sins, and by accounting and accepting their persons as righteous; not for anything wrought in them, or done by them, but for Christ's sake

alone; nor by imputing faith itself, the act of believing, or any other evangelical obedience to them, as their righteousness; but by imputing Christ's active obedience to the whole law, and passive obedience in his death for their whole and sole righteousness, they receiving and resting on him and his righteousness by faith; which faith they have not of themselves, it is the gift of God.

2 Faith thus receiving and resting on Christ, and his righteousness, is the alone instrument of justification; yet it is not alone in the person justified, but is ever accompanied with all other saving graces, and is no dead faith, but worketh by love.

3 Christ by his obedience and death did fully discharge the debt of all those that are justified, and did by the sacrifice of himself, in the blood of his cross, undergoing in their stead the penalty due unto them make a proper, real, and full satisfaction to God's justice in their behalf. Yet in as much as he was given by the Father for them, and his obedience and satisfaction accepted in their stead, and both freely, not for any thing in them, their justification is only of free grace, that both the exact justice and rich grace of God might be glorified in the justification of sinners.

4 God did from all eternity decree to justify all the elect, and Christ did in the fulness of time die for their sins, and rise again for their justification; nevertheless, they are not justified personally, until the Holy Spirit doth in due time actually apply Christ unto them.

5 God doth continue to forgive the sins of those that are justified; and although they can never fall from the state of justification, yet they may by their sins fall under God's fatherly displeasure; and in that condition they have not usually the light of his countenance restored unto them, until they humble themselves, confess their sins, beg pardon, and renew their faith and repentance.

6 The justification of believers under the Old Testament, was in all these respects one and the same with the justification of believers under the New Testament.

Chapter 12
Of Adoption

1 All those that are justified, God vouchsafeth in and for his only Son Jesus Christ to make partakers of the grace of adoption, by which they are taken into the number, and enjoy the liberties and privileges of the

children of God, have his name put upon them, receive the Spirit of adoption; have access to the throne of grace with boldness, are enabled to cry, Abba Father; are pitied, protected, provided for, and chastened by him as by a father; yet never cast off, but sealed to the day of redemption, and inherit the promises as heirs of everlasting salvation.

Chapter 13
Of Sanctification

1 They that are united to Christ, effectually called and regenerated, having a new heart and a new spirit created in them, through the virtue of Christ's death and resurrection, are also further sanctified really and personally through the same virtue, by his Word and Spirit dwelling in them; the dominion of the whole body of sin is destroyed and the several lusts thereof are more and more weakened, and mortified, and they more and more quickened, and strengthened in all saving graces, to the practice of all true holiness, without which no man shall see the Lord.

2 This sanctification is throughout in the whole man, yet imperfect in this life; there abideth still some remnants of corruption in every part; whence ariseth a continual and irreconcilable war, the flesh lusting against the Spirit, and the Spirit against the flesh.

3 In which war, although the remaining corruption for a time may much prevail, yet through the continual supply of strength from the sanctifying Spirit of Christ, the regenerate part doth overcome, and so the saints grow in grace, perfecting holiness in the fear of God.

Chapter 14
Of Saving Faith

1 The grace of faith, whereby the elect are enabled to believe to the saving of their souls, is the work of the Spirit of Christ in their hearts, and is ordinarily wrought by the ministry of the Word; by which also, and by the administration of the seals, prayer, and other means, it is increased and strengthened.

2 By this faith a Christian believeth to be true whatsoever is revealed in the Word, for the authority of God himself speaking therein, and

acteth differently upon that which each particular passage thereof containeth; yielding obedience to the commands, trembling at the threatenings, and embracing the promises of God for this life, and that which is to come. But the principal acts of saving faith are, accepting, receiving, and resting upon Christ alone, for justification, sanctification, and eternal life, by virtue of the covenant of grace.

3 This faith, although it be different in degrees, and may be weak or strong, yet it is in the least degree of it different in the kind or nature of it (as is all other saving grace) from the faith and common grace of temporary believers; and therefore, though it may be many times assailed and weakened, yet it gets the victory, growing up in many to the attainment of a full assurance through Christ, who is both the author and finisher of our faith.

Chapter 15
Of Repentance Unto Life and Salvation

1 Such of the elect as are converted at riper years, having sometime lived in the state of nature, and therein served divers lusts and pleasures, God in their effectual calling giveth them repentance unto life.

2 Whereas there is none that doth good, and sinneth not, and the best of men may through the power and deceitfulness of their corruptions dwelling in them, with the prevalency of temptation, fall into great sins and provocations; God hath in the covenant of grace mercifully provided, that believers so sinning and falling, be renewed through repentance unto salvation.

3 This saving repentance is an evangelical grace, whereby a person being by the Holy Ghost made sensible of the manifold evils of his sin, doth by faith in Christ humble himself for it with godly sorrow, detestation of it, and self-abhorrence, praying for pardon and strength of grace, with a purpose, and endeavour by supplies of the Spirit, to walk before God unto all well-pleasing in all things.

4 As repentance is to be continued through the whole course of our lives, upon the account of the body of death, and the motions thereof; so it is every man's duty to repent of his particular known sins particularly.

5 Such is the provision which God hath made through Christ in the covenant of grace, for the preservation of believers unto salvation, that

although there is no sin so small, but it deserves damnation; yet there is no sin so great, that it shall bring damnation on them who truly repent; which makes the constant preaching of repentance necessary.

Chapter 16
Of Good Works

1 Good works are only such as God hath commanded in his holy word, and not such as without the warrant thereof are devised by men out of blind zeal, or upon pretence of good intentions.

2 These good works done in obedience to God's commandments, are the fruits and evidences of a true and lively faith; and by them believers manifest their thankfulness, strengthen their assurance, edify their brethren, adorn the profession of the gospel, stop the mouths of the adversaries, and glorify God, whose workmanship they are, created in Christ Jesus thereunto; that having their fruit unto holiness, they may have the end, eternal life.

3 Their ability to do good works is not at all of themselves, but wholly from the Spirit of Christ. And that they may be enabled thereunto, besides the graces they have already received, there is required an actual influence of the same Holy Spirit to work in them to will and to do of his good pleasure; yet are they not hereupon to grow negligent, as if they were not bound to perform any duty unless upon a special motion of the Spirit; but they ought to be diligent in stirring up the grace of God that is in them.

4 They who in their obedience attain to the greatest height which is possible in this life, are so far from being able to supererogate, and to do more than God requires, as that they fall short of much which in duty they are bound to do.

5 We cannot by our best works merit pardon of sin, or eternal life at the hand of God, by reason of the great disproportion that is between them and the glory to come; and the infinite distance that is between us and God, whom by them we can neither profit, nor satisfy for the debt of our former sins; but when we have done all we can, we have done but our duty, and are unprofitable servants; and because, as they are good, they proceed from the Spirit, and as they are wrought by us, they are defiled and mixed with so much weakness and imperfection, that they cannot endure the severity of God's judgment.

6 Yet notwithstanding, the persons of believers being accepted through Christ, their good works also are accepted in him; not as though they were in this life wholly unblameable and unreproveable in God's sight; but that he looking upon them in his Son is pleased to accept and reward that which is sincere, although accompanied with many weaknesses and imperfections.

7 Works done by unregenerate men, although for the matter of them they may be things which God commands, and of good use both to themselves and to others; yet because they proceed not from a heart purified by faith; nor are done in a right manner, according to the Word; nor to a right end, the glory of God; they are therefore sinful, and cannot please God, nor make a man meet to receive grace from God; and yet their neglect of them is more sinful, and displeasing unto God.

Chapter 17
Of the Perseverance of the Saints

1 They whom God hath accepted in his Beloved, effectually called and sanctified by his Spirit, can neither totally nor finally fall away from the state of grace; but shall certainly persevere therein to the end, and be eternally saved.

2 This perseverance of the saints depends not upon their own free will, but upon the immutability of the decree of election; from the free and unchangeable love of God the Father; upon the efficacy of the merit and intercession of Jesus Christ, and union with him; the oath of God; the abiding of his Spirit; and of the seed of God within them; and the nature of the covenant of grace; from all which ariseth also the certainty and infallibility thereof.

3 And though they may, through the temptation of Satan, and of the world, the prevalency of corruption remaining in them, and the neglect of the means of their preservation, fall into grievous sins; and for a time continue therein, whereby they incur God's displeasure, and grieve his Holy Spirit; come to have their graces and comforts impaired; have their hearts hardened, and their consciences wounded; hurt and scandalize others, and bring temporal judgments upon themselves; yet they are and shall be kept by the power of God through faith unto salvation.

Chapter 18
Of the Assurance of Grace and Salvation

1 Although temporary believers and other unregenerate men may vainly deceive themselves with false hopes, and carnal presumptions of being in the favour of God, and state of salvation, which hope of theirs shall perish; yet such as truly believe in the Lord Jesus, and love him in sincerity, endeavouring to walk in all good conscience before him, may in this life be certainly assured that they are in the state of grace, and may rejoice in the hope of the glory of God, which hope shall never make them ashamed.

2 This certainly is not a bare conjectural and probable persuasion, grounded upon a fallible hope; but an infallible assurance of faith, founded on the blood and righteousness of Christ, revealed in the gospel, and also upon the inward evidence of those graces unto which promises are made, and on the immediate witness of the Spirit, testifying our adoption, and as a fruit thereof, leaving the heart more humble and holy.

3 This infallible assurance doth not so belong to the essence of faith, but that a true believer may wait long, and conflict with many difficulties before he be partaker of it; yet being enabled by the Spirit to know the things which are freely given him of God, he may, without extraordinary revelation, in the right use of ordinary means attain thereunto. And therefore it is the duty of every one to give all diligence to make his calling and election sure; that thereby his heart may be enlarged in peace and joy in the Holy Ghost, in love and thankfulness to God, and in strength and cheerfulness in the duties of obedience, the proper fruits of this assurance; so far is it from inclining men to looseness.

4 True believers may have the assurance of their salvation divers ways shaken, diminished and intermitted; as by negligence in preserving of it; by falling into some special sin, which woundeth the conscience, and grieveth the Spirit; by some sudden or vehement temptation; by God's withdrawing the light of his countenance; suffering even such as fear him to walk in darkness, and to have no light; yet are they neither utterly destitute of that seed of God, and life of faith, that love of Christ and the brethren, that sincerity of heart and conscience of duty, out of which by the operation of the Spirit this assurance may in due time be revived, and by the which in the meantime they are supported from utter despair.

Chapter 19
Of the Law of God

1 God gave to Adam a law of universal obedience written in his heart, and a particular precept of not eating the fruit of the tree of knowledge of good and evil, as a covenant of works, by which he bound him and all his posterity to personal, entire, exact and perpetual obedience; promised life upon the fulfilling, and threatened death upon the breach of it; and endued him with power and ability to keep it.

2 This law, so written in the heart, continued to be a perfect rule of righteousness after the fall of man; and was delivered by God upon mount Sinai in ten commandments, and written in two tables; the four first commandments containing our duty towards God, and the other six our duty to man.

3 Beside this law, commonly called moral, God was pleased to give to the people of Israel ceremonial laws, containing several typical ordinances; partly of worship, prefiguring Christ, his graces, actions, sufferings and benefits, and partly holding forth divers instructions of moral duties. All which ceremonial laws being appointed only to the time of reformation, are by Jesus Christ the true Messiah and only lawgiver, who was furnished with power from the Father for that end, abrogated and taken away.

4 To them also he gave sundry judicial laws, which expired together with the state of that people, not obliging any now by virtue of that institution, their general equity only being still of moral use.

5 The moral law doth for ever bind all, as well justified persons as others, to the obedience thereof; and that not only in regard of the matter contained in it, but also in respect of the authority of God the Creator, who gave it; neither doth Christ in the gospel any way dissolve, but much strengthen this obligation.

6 Although true believers be not under the law, as a covenant of works, to be thereby justified or condemned; yet it is of great use to them as well as to others, in that, as a rule of life, informing them of the will of God, and their duty, it directs and binds them to walk accordingly; discovering also the sinful pollutions of their nature, hearts and lives; so as examining themselves thereby, they may come to further conviction of, humiliation for, and hatred against sin; together with a clearer sight of the need they have of Christ, and the perfection of his obedience. It is likewise of use to the regenerate, to

restrain their corruptions, in that it forbids sin; and the threatenings of it serve to show what even their sins deserve, and what afflictions in this life they may expect for them, although freed from the curse thereof threatened in the law. The promises of it in like manner show them God's approbation of obedience, and what blessings they may expect upon the performance thereof, although not as due to them by the law, as a covenant of works; so as a man's doing good, and refraining from evil, because the law encourageth to the one, and deterreth from the other, is no evidence of his being under the law, and not under grace.

7 Neither are the forementioned uses of the law contrary to the grace of the gospel, but do sweetly comply with it; the Spirit of Christ subduing and enabling the will of man to do that freely and cheerfully, which the will of God revealed in the law required to be done.

Chapter 20
Of the Gospel, and of the Extent of the Grace thereof

1 The covenant of works being broken by sin, and made unprofitable unto life, God was pleased to give unto the elect the promise of Christ, the seed of the woman, as the means of calling them, and begetting in them faith and repentance; in this promise the gospel, as to the substance of it, was revealed, and was therein effectual for the conversion and salvation of sinners.

2 This promise of Christ, and salvation by him, is revealed only in and by the Word of God; neither do the works of creation or providence, with the light of nature, make discovery of Christ, or of grace by him, so much as in a general or obscure way; much less that men destitute of the revelation of him by the promise or gospel, should be enabled thereby to attain saving faith or repentance.

3 The revelation of the gospel unto sinners, made in divers times, and by sundry parts, with the addition of promises and precepts for the obedience required therein, as to the nations and persons to whom it is granted, is merely of the sovereign will and good pleasure of God, not being annexed by virtue of any promise to the due improvement of men's natural abilities, by virtue of common light received without it, which none ever did make or can so do. And therefore in all ages the preaching of the gospel hath been granted unto persons and nations,

as to the extent or straitening of it, in great variety, according to the counsel of the will of God.

4 Although the gospel be the only outward means of revealing Christ and saving grace, and is as such abundantly sufficient thereunto; yet that men who are dead in trespasses, may be born again, quickened or regenerated, there is moreover necessary an effectual, irresistible work of the Holy Ghost upon the whole soul, for the producing in them a new spiritual life, without which no other means are sufficient for their conversion unto God.

Chapter 21
Of Christian Liberty, and Liberty of Conscience

1 The liberty which Christ hath purchased for believers under the gospel, consists in their freedom from the guilt of sin, the condemning wrath of God, the rigour and curse of the law; and in their being delivered from this present evil world, bondage to Satan, and dominion of sin, from the evil of afflictions, the fear and sting of death, the victory of the grave, and everlasting damnation; as also in their free access to God, and their yielding obedience unto him, not out of slavish fear, but a childlike love and willing mind. All which were common also to believers under the law, for the substance of them; but under the New Testament the liberty of Christians is further enlarged in their freedom from the yoke of the ceremonial law, the whole legal administration of the covenant of grace, to which the Jewish church was subjected; and in greater boldness of access to the throne of grace, and in fuller communications of the free Spirit of God, than believers under the law did ordinarily partake of.

2 God alone is lord of the conscience, and hath left it free from the doctrines and commandments of men which are in any thing contrary to his Word, or not contained in it; so that to believe such doctrines, or to obey such commands out of conscience, is to betray true liberty of conscience; and the requiring of an implicit faith, and an absolute and blind obedience, is to destroy liberty of conscience, and reason also.

3 They who upon pretence of Christian liberty do practise any sin, or cherish any lust, as they do thereby pervert the main design of the grace of the gospel to their own destruction; so they wholly destroy the end of Christian liberty, which is, that being delivered out of the hands

of our enemies, we might serve the Lord without fear, in holiness and righteousness before him all the days of our life.

Chapter 22
Of Religious Worship, and the Sabbath-Day

1 The light of nature showeth that there is a God, who hath lordship and sovereignty over all, is just, good, and doth good unto all, and is therefore to be feared, loved, praised, called upon, trusted in, and served with all the heart, and all the soul, and with all the might. But the acceptable way of worshipping the true God is instituted by himself, and so limited by his own revealed will, that he may not be worshipped according to the imaginations and devices of men, or the suggestions of Satan, under any visible representations, or any other way not prescribed in the holy Scripture.

2 Religious worship is to be given to God the Father, Son, and Holy Ghost, and to him alone; not to angels, saints, or any other creatures; and since the fall, not without a Mediator, nor in the mediation of any other but of Christ alone.

3 Prayer, with thanksgiving, being one special part of natural worship, is by God required of all men; but that it may be accepted, it is to be made in the name of the Son by the help of his Spirit, according to his will, with understanding, reverence, humility, fervency, faith, love, and perseverance; and when with others in a known tongue.

4 Prayer is to be made for things lawful, and for all sorts of men living, or that shall live hereafter; but not for the dead, nor for those of whom it may be known that they have sinned the sin unto death.

5 The reading of the Scriptures, preaching, and hearing the Word of God, singing of psalms; as also the administration of baptism and the Lord's Supper, are all parts of religious worship of God, to be performed in obedience unto God with understanding, faith, reverence, and godly fear. Solemn humiliations, with fastings and thanksgivings upon special occasions, are in their several times and seasons to be used in a holy and religious manner.

6 Neither prayer, nor any other part of religious worship, is now under the gospel either tied unto, or made more acceptable by any place in which it is performed, or towards which it is directed; but God is to be worshipped everywhere in spirit and in truth, as in private

families daily, and in secret each one by himself, so more solemnly in the public assemblies, which are not carelessly nor wilfully to be neglected, or forsaken, when God by his Word or providence calleth thereunto.

7 As it is of the law of nature, that in general a proportion of time by God's appointment be set apart for the worship of God; so by his Word in a positive, moral, and perpetual commandment, binding all men in all ages, he hath particularly appointed one day in seven for a Sabbath to be kept holy unto him; which from the beginning of the world to the resurrection of Christ, was the last day of the week; and from the resurrection of Christ was changed into the first day of the week, which in Scripture is called the Lord's Day, and is to be continued to the end of the world as the Christian Sabbath, the observation of the last day of the week being abolished.

8 This Sabbath is then kept holy unto the Lord, when men after a due preparing of their hearts, and ordering their common affairs beforehand, do not only observe an holy rest all the day from their own works, words, and thoughts about their wordly employments and recreations; but also are taken up the whole time in the public and private exercises of his worship, and in the duties of necessity and mercy.

Chapter 23
Of Lawful Oaths and Vows

1 A lawful oath is a part of religious worship, wherein the person swearing in truth, righteousness and judgment, solemnly calleth God to witness what he asserteth or promiseth, and to judge him according to the truth or falsehood of what he sweareth.

2 The name of God only is that by which men ought to swear, and therein it is to be used with all holy fear and reverence. Therefore to swear vainly, or rashly, by that glorious or dreadful name, or to swear at all by any other thing, is sinful and to be abhorred. Yet as in matters of weight and moment an oath is warranted by the Word of God under the New Testament, as well as under the Old; so a lawful oath, being imposed by lawful authority in such matters, ought to be taken.

3 Whosoever taketh an oath, warranted by the Word of God, ought duly to consider the weightiness of so solemn an act, and therein to

avouch nothing but what he is fully persuaded is the truth; neither may any man bind himself by oath to any thing, but what is good and just, and what he believeth so to be, and what he is able and resolved to perform. Yet it is a sin to refuse an oath touching any thing that is good and just, being lawfully imposed by authority.

4 An oath is to be taken in the plain and common sense of the words, without equivocation or mental reservation. It cannot oblige to sin, but in any thing not sinful, being taken it binds to performance, although to a man's own hurt; nor is it to be violated, although made to heretics and infidels.

5 A vow, which is not to be made to any creature, but God alone, is of the like nature with a promissory oath, and ought to be made with the like religious care, and to be performed with the like faithfulness.

6 Popish monastical vows of perpetual single life, professed poverty, and regular obedience, are so far from being degrees of higher perfection, that they are superstitious and sinful snares, in which no Christian may entangle himself.

Chapter 24
Of the Civil Magistrate

1 God the supreme Lord and King of all the world, hath ordained civil magistrates to be under him, over the people for his own glory and the public good; and to this end hath armed them with the power of the sword, for the defence and encouragement of them that do good, and for the punishment of evil-doers.

2 It is lawful for Christians to accept and execute the office of a magistrate, when called thereunto; in the management whereof, as they ought specially to maintain justice and peace, according to the wholesome laws of each commonwealth; so for that end they may lawfully now under the New Testament wage war upon just and necessary occasion.

3 Although the magistrate is bound to encourage, promote, and protect the professors and profession of the gospel, and to manage and order civil administrations in a due subserviency to the interest of Christ in the world, and to that end to take care that men of corrupt minds and conversations do not licentiously publish and divulge blasphemy and errors, in their own nature subverting the faith and

inevitably destroying the souls of them that receive them; yet in such differences about the doctrines of the gospel, or ways of the worship of God, as may befall men exercising a good conscience, manifesting it in their conversation, and holding the foundation, not disturbing others in their ways or worship that differ from them; there is no warrant for the magistrate under the gospel to abridge them of their liberty.

4 It is the duty of people to pray for magistrates, to honour their persons, to pay them tribute and other dues, to obey their lawful commands, and to be subject to their authority for conscience sake. Infidelity, or difference in religion, doth not make void the magistrate's just and legal authority, nor free the people from their obedience to him; from which ecclesiastical persons are not exempted, much less hath the Pope any power or jurisdiction over them in their dominions, or over any of their people, and least of all to deprive them of their dominions or lives, if he shall judge them to be heretics, or upon any other pretence whatsoever.

Chapter 25
Of Marriage

1 Marriage is to be between one man and one woman; neither is it lawful for any man to have more than one wife, nor for any woman to have more than one husband at the same time.

2 Marriage was ordained for the mutual help of husband and wife; for the increase of mankind with a legitimate issue, and of the Church with an holy seed, and for preventing of uncleanness.

3 It is lawful for all sorts of people to marry, who are able with judgment to give their consent. Yet it is the duty of Christians to marry in the Lord; and therefore such as profess the true reformed religion, should not marry with infidels, Papists, or other idolaters; neither should such as are godly, be unequally yoked by marrying with such as are wicked in their life, or maintain damnable heresies.

4 Marriage ought not to be within the degrees of consanguity or affinity forbidden in the Word; nor can such incestuous marriages ever be made lawful by any man, or consent of parties, so as those

persons may live together as man and wife.

Chapter 26
Of the Church

1 The catholic or universal Church, which is invisible, consists of the whole number of the elect, that have been, are, or shall be gathered into one under Christ, the Head thereof, and is the Spouse, the Body, the fulness of him that filleth all in all.

2 The whole body of men throughout the world, professing the faith of the gospel and obedience unto God by Christ according to it, not destroying their own profession by any errors everting the foundation, or unholiness of conversation, are, and may be called the visible catholic Church of Christ; although as such it is not entrusted with the administration of any ordinances, or have any officers to rule or govern in, or over the whole body.

3 The purest churches under heaven are subject both to mixture and error, and some have so degenerated as to become no churches of Christ, but synagogues of Satan: nevertheless Christ always hath had, and ever shall have, a visible kingdom in this world, to the end thereof, of such as believe in him, and make profession of his name.

4 There is no other Head of the Church but the Lord Jesus Christ; nor can the Pope of Rome in any sense be head thereof; but is that antichrist, that man of sin, and son of perdition, that exalteth himself in the Church against Christ, and all that is called God, whom the Lord shall destroy with the brightness of his coming.

5 As the Lord in his care and love towards his Church, hath in his infinite wise providence exercised it with great variety in all ages, for the good of them that love him, and his own glory; so according to his promise, we expect that in the latter days, antichrist being destroyed, the Jews called, and the adversaries of the kingdom of his dear Son broken, the churches of Christ being enlarged, and edified through a free and plentiful communication of light and grace, shall enjoy in this world a more quiet, peaceable and glorious condition than they have enjoyed.

Chapter 27
Of the Communion of Saints

1 All saints that are united to Jesus Christ their Head, by his Spirit and faith, although they are not made thereby one person with him, have fellowship in his graces, sufferings, death, resurrection and glory; and being united to one another in love, they have communion in each others gifts and graces, and are obliged to the performance of such duties, public and private, as do conduce to their mutual good, both in the inward and outward man.

2 All saints are bound to maintain an holy fellowship and communion in the worship of God, and in performing such other spiritual services as tend to their mutual edification; as also in relieving each other in outward things, according to their several abilities and necessities: which communion, though especially to be exercised by them in the relations wherein they stand, whether in families or churches, yet as God offereth opportunity, is to be extended unto all those who in every place call upon the Name of the Lord Jesus.

Chapter 28
Of the Sacraments

1 Sacraments are holy signs and seals of the covenant of grace, immediately instituted by Christ, to represent him and his benefits, and to confirm our interest in him, and solemnly to engage us to the service of God in Christ, according to his Word.

2 There is in every sacrament a spiritual relation, or sacramental union, between the sign and the thing signified; whence it comes to pass that the names and effects of the one are attributed to the other.

3 The grace which is exhibited in or by the sacraments rightly used, is not conferred by any power in them; neither doth the efficacy of a sacrament depend upon the piety or intention of him that doth administer it, but upon the work of the Spirit, and the word of institution; which contains, together with a precept authorising the use thereof, a promise of benefit to worthy receivers.

4 There be only two sacraments ordained by Christ our Lord in the gospel, that is to say, Baptism and the Lord's Supper; neither of which may be dispensed by any but a minister of the Word lawfully called.

5 The Sacraments of the Old Testament, in regard of the spiritual things, thereby signified and exhibited, were for substance the same with those of the New.

Chapter 29
Of Baptism

1 Baptism is a sacrament of the New Testament, ordained by Jesus Christ to be unto the party baptised a sign and seal of the covenant of grace, of his ingrafting into Christ, of regeneration, of remission of sins, and of his giving up unto God through Jesus Christ to walk in newness of life; which ordinance is by Christ's own appointment to be continued in his Church until the end of the world.

2 The outward element to be used in this ordinance, is water, wherewith the party is to be baptised in the name of the Father, and of the Son, and of the Holy Ghost, by a minister of the gospel lawfully called.

3 Dipping of the person into the water is not necessary; but baptism is rightly administered by pouring or sprinkling water upon the person.

4 Not only those that do actually profess faith in and obedience unto Christ, but also the infants of one or both believing parents are to be baptised, and those only.

5 Although it be a great sin to contemn or neglect this ordinance, yet grace and salvation are not so inseparably annexed unto it, as that

no person can be regenerated or saved without it; or that all that are baptised are undoubtedly regenerated.

6 The efficacy of baptism is not tied to that moment of time wherein it is administered; yet notwithstanding, by the right use of this ordinance, the grace promised is not only offered, but really exhibited and conferred by the Holy Ghost to such (whether of age or infants) as that grace belongeth unto, according to the counsel of God's own will in his appointed time.

7 Baptism is but once to be administered to any person.

Chapter 30
Of the Lord's Supper

1 Our Lord Jesus in the night wherein he was betrayed, instituted the sacrament of his body and blood, called the Lord's Supper, to be observed in his churches to the end of the world, for the perpetual remembrance, and showing forth of the sacrifice of himself in his death, the sealing of all benefits thereof unto true believers, their spiritual nourishment, and growth in him, their further engagement in and to all duties which they owe unto him, and to be a bond and pledge of their communion with him, and with each other.

2 In this sacrament Christ is not offered up to his Father, nor any real sacrifice made at all for remission of sin of the quick or dead, but only a memorial of that one offering up of himself upon the cross once for all, and a spiritual oblation of all possible praise unto God for the same; so that the Popish sacrifice of the mass (as they call it) is most abominable, injurious to Christ's own only sacrifice, the alone propitiation for all the sins of the elect.

3 The Lord Jesus hath in this ordinance appointed his ministers to pray and bless the elements of bread and wine, and thereby to set them apart from a common to an holy use; and to take and break the bread, to take the cup, and (they communicating also themselves) to give both to the communicants; but to none who are not then present in the congregation.

4 Private masses, or receiving the sacrament by a priest, or any other, alone; as likewise the denial of the cup to the people; worshipping the elements, the lifting them up, or carrying them about for adoration, and the reserving them for any pretended religious use;

are contrary to the nature of this sacrament, and to the institution of Christ.

5 The outward elements in this sacrament duly set apart to the uses ordained by Christ, have such relation to him crucified, as that truly, yet sacramentally only, they are sometimes called by the name of the things they represent, to wit, and body and blood of Christ; albeit, in substance and nature, they still remain truly and only bread and wine as they were before.

6 The doctrine which maintains a change of the substance of bread and wine into the substance of Christ's body and blood (commonly called Transubstantiation) by consecration of a priest, or by any other way, is repugnant not to Scripture alone, but even to common sense and reason; overthroweth the nature of the sacrament; and hath been and is the cause of manifold superstitions, yea, of gross idolatries.

7 Worthy receivers outwardly partaking of the visible elements in this sacrament, do then also inwardly by faith, really and indeed, yet not carnally and corporally, but spiritually, receive and feed upon Christ crucified, and all benefits of his death; the body and blood of Christ being then not corporally or carnally in, with, or under the bread or wine; yet as really, but spiritually present to the faith of believers in that ordinance, as the elements themselves are to their outward senses.

8 All ignorant and ungodly persons, as they are unfit to enjoy communion with Christ, so are they unworthy of the Lord's table, and cannot without great sin against him, while they remain such, partake of these holy mysteries, or be admitted thereunto; yea, whosoever shall receive unworthily, are guilty of the body of blood of the Lord, eating and drinking judgment to themselves.

Chapter 31
Of the State of Man after Death, and of the Resurrection of the Dead

1 The bodies of men after death return to dust, and see corruption; but their souls (which neither die nor sleep) having an immortal subsistence, immediately return to God who gave them. The souls of the righteous being then made perfect in holiness, are received

into the highest heavens, where they behold the face of God in light and glory, waiting for the full redemption of their bodies: and the souls of the wicked are cast into hell, where they remain in torment and utter darkness, reserved to the judgment of the great day: Besides these two places for souls separated from their bodies, the Scripture acknowledgeth none.

2 At the last day such as are found alive shall not die, but be changed; and all the dead shall be raised up with the self-same bodies, and none other, although with different qualities, which shall be united again to their souls for ever.

3 The bodies of the unjust shall by the power of Christ be raised to dishonour, the bodies of the just, by his Spirit unto honour, and to be made comfortable to his own glorious body.

Chapter 32
Of the Last Judgment

1 God hath appointed a day wherein he will judge the world in righteousness by Jesus Christ, to whom all power and judgment is given of the Father. In which day, not only the apostate angels shall be judged, but likewise all persons that have lived upon earth shall appear before the tribunal to Christ, to give an account of their thoughts, words and deeds, and to receive according to what they have done in the body, whether good or evil.

2 The end of God's appointing this day is for the manifestation of the glory of his mercy in the eternal salvation of the elect, and of his justice in the damnation of the reprobate, who are wicked and disobedient. For then shall the righteous go into everlasting life, and receive that fulness of joy and glory, with everlasting reward in the presence of the Lord; but the wicked who know not God, and obey not the gospel of Jesus Christ, shall be cast into eternal torments, and be punished with everlasting destruction from the presence of the Lord, and from the glory of his power.

3 As Christ would have us to be certainly persuaded that there shall be a judgment, both to deter all men from sin, and for the greater consolation of the godly in their adversity; so will he have that day unknown to men, that they may shake off all carnal security, and be always watchful, because they know not at what hour

the Lord will come, and may be ever prepared to say, Come Lord Jesus, come quickly, Amen.

The Institution of Churches and the Order Appointed in them by Jesus Christ

1 By the appointment of the Father all power for the calling, institution, order, or government of the Church, is invested in a supreme and sovereign manner in the Lord Jesus Christ, as King and Head thereof.

2 In the execution of this power wherewith he is so entrusted, the Lord Jesus calleth out of the world unto communion with himself, those that are given unto him by his Father, that they may walk before him in all the ways of obedience, which he prescribeth to them in his Word.

3 Those thus called (through the ministry of the Word by his Spirit) he commandeth to walk together in particular societies or churches, for their mutual edification, and the due performance of that public worship, which he requireth of them in this world.

4 To each of these churches thus gathered, according to his mind declared in his Word, he hath given all that power and authority, which is any way needful for their carrying on that order in worship and discipline, which he hath instituted for them to observe, with commands and rules for the due and right exerting and executing of that power.

5 These particular churches thus appointed by the authority of Christ, and entrusted with power from him for the ends before expressed, are each of them as unto those ends, the seat of that power which he is pleased to communicate to his saints or subjects in this world, so that as such they receive it immediately from himself.

6 Besides these particular churches, there is not instituted by Christ any church more extensive or catholic entrusted with power for the administration of his ordinances, or the execution of any authority in his name.

7 A particular church gathered and completed according to the mind of Christ, consists of officers and members. The Lord Christ having given to his called ones (united according to his appointment

in church-order) liberty and power to choose persons fitted by the Holy Ghost for that purpose, to be over them, and to minister to them in the Lord.

8 The members of these churches are saints by calling, visibly manifesting and evidencing (in and by their profession and walking) their obedience unto that call of Christ; who, being further known to each other by their confession of the faith wrought in them by the power of God, declared by themselves or otherwise manifested, do willingly consent to walk together according to the appointment of Christ; giving up themselves to the Lord, and to one another by the will of God in professed subjection to the ordinances of the gospel.

9 The officers appointed by Christ, to be chosen and set apart by the church so called, and gathered for the peculiar administration of ordinances, and execution of power and duty which he entrusts them with, or calls them to, to be continued to the end of the world, are pastors, teachers, elders and deacons.

10 Churches thus gathered and assembling for the worship of God, are thereby visible and public, and their assemblies (in whatever place they are,) according as they have liberty or opportunity) are therefore church or public assemblies.

11 The way appointed by Christ for the calling of any person, fitted and gifted by the Holy Ghost, unto the office of pastor, teacher or elder in a church, is, that he be chosen thereunto by the common suffrage of the church itself, and solemnly set apart by fasting and prayer, with imposition of hands of the eldership of that church, if there be any before constituted therein. And of a deacon, that he be chosen by the like suffrage, and set apart by prayer, and the like imposition of hands.

12 The essence of this call of a pastor, teacher or elder unto office, consists in the election of the church, together with his acceptation of it, and separation by fasting and prayer. And those who are so chosen, though not set apart by imposition of hands, are rightly constituted ministers of Jesus Christ, in whose name and authority they exercise the ministry to them so committed. The calling of deacons consisteth in the like election and acceptation with separation by prayer.

13 Although it be incumbent on the pastors and teachers of the churches to be instant in preaching the Word, by way of office; yet the work of preaching the Word is not so peculiarly confined to them, but that others also gifted and fitted by the Holy Ghost for

it, and approved (being by lawful ways and means in the providence of God called thereunto) may publicly, ordinarily and constantly perform it; so that they give themselves up thereunto.

14 However, they who are engaged in the work of public preaching, and enjoy the public maintenance upon that account, are not thereby obliged to dispense the seals to any other than such as (being saints by calling, and gathered according to the order of the gospel) they stand related to, as pastors or teachers. yet ought they not to neglect others living within their parochial bounds, but besides their constant public preaching to them, they ought to enquire after their profiting by the Word, instructing them in, and pressing upon them (whether young or old) the great doctrines of the gospel, even personally and particularly, so far as their strength and time will admit.

15 Ordination alone without the election of precedent consent of the church, by those who formerly have been ordained by virtue of that power they have received by their ordination, doth not constitute any person a church-officer, or communicate office-power to him.

16 A church furnished with officers (according to the mind of Christ) hath full power to administer all his ordinances; and where there is want of any one or more officers required, that officer, or those which are in the church, may administer all the ordinances proper to their particular duty and offices; but where there are no teaching officers, none may administer the seals, nor can the church authorise any so to do.

17 In the carrying on of church-administrations, no person ought to be added to the church, but by the consent of the church itself; that so love (without dissimulation) may be preserved between all the members thereof.

18 Whereas the Lord Jesus Christ hath appointed and instituted as a means of edification, that those who walk not according to the rules and laws appointed by him (in respect of faith and life, so that just offence doth arise to the church thereby) be censured in his name and authority. Every church hath power in itself to exercise and execute all those censures appointed by him in the way and order prescribed in the gospel.

19 The censures so appointed by Christ, are admonition and excommunication. And whereas some offences are or may be known only to some, it is appointed by Christ, that those to

whom they are so known, do first admonish the offender in private: in public offences where any sin, before all. Or in case of non-amendment upon private admonition, the offence being related to the church, and the offender not manifesting his repentance, he is to be duly admonished in the name of Christ by the whole church, by the ministry of the elders of the church; and if this censure prevail not for his repentance, then he is to be cast out by excommunication with the consent of the church.

20 As all believers are bound to join themselves to particular churches, when and where they have opportunity so to do, so none are to be admitted unto the privileges of the churches, who do not submit themselves to the rule of Christ in the censures for the government of them.

21 This being the way prescribed by Christ in case of offence, no church-members upon any offences taken by them, having performed their duty required of them in this matter, ought to disturb any church-order, or absent themselves from the public assemblies, or the administration of any ordinances upon that pretence, but to wait upon Christ in the further proceeding of the church.

22 The power of censures being seated by Christ in a particular church, is to be exercised only towards particular members of each church respectively as such; and there is no power given by him unto any synods or ecclesiastical assemblies to excommunicate, or by their public edicts to threaten excommunication, or other church-censures against churches, magistrates, or their people upon any account, no man being obnoxious to that censure, but upon his personal miscarriage, as a member of a particular church.

23 Although the church is a society of men, assembling for the celebration of the ordinances according to the appointment of Christ, yet every society assembling for that end or purpose, upon the account of cohabitation within any civil precincts and bounds, is not thereby constituted a church, seeing there may be wanting among them, what is essentially required thereunto; and therefore a believer living with others in such a precinct, may join himself with any church for his edification.

24 For the avoiding of differences that may otherwise arise, for the greater solemnity in the celebration of the ordinances of Christ, and the opening a way for the larger usefulness of the gifts and graces of the Holy Ghost; saints living in one city or town, or within such distances as that they may conveniently assemble

for divine worship, ought rather to join in one church for their mutual strengthening and edification, than to set up many distinct societies.

25 As all churches and all the members of them are bound to pray continually for the good or prosperity of all the churches of Christ in all places, and upon all occasions to further it; (every one within the bounds of their places and callings, in the exercise of their gifts and graces). So the churches themselves (when planted by the providence of God, so as they may have opportunity and advantage for it) ought to hold communion amongst themselves for their peace, increase of love, and mutual edification.

26 In cases of difficulties or differences, either in point of doctrine or in administrations, wherein either the churches in general are concerned, or any one church in their peace, union, and edification, or any member or members of any church are injured in, or by any proceeding in censures, not agreeable to truth and order: it is according to the mind of Christ, that many churches holding communion together, do by their messengers meet in a synod or council, to consider and give their advice in, or about that matter in difference, to be reported to all the churches concerned. Howbeit, these synods so assembled are not entrusted with any church-power, properly so called, or with any jurisdiction over the churches themselves, to exercise any censures, either over any churches or persons, or to impose their determinations on the churches or officers.

27 Besides these occasional synods or councils, there are not instituted by Christ any stated synods in a fixed combination of churches, or their officers in lesser or greater assemblies; nor are there any synods appointed by Christ in a way of subordination to one another.

28 Persons that are joined in church-fellowship, ought not lightly or without just cause to withdraw themselves from the communion of the church whereunto they are so joined. Nevertheless, where any person cannot continue in any church without his sin, either for want of the administration of any ordinances instituted by Christ, or by his being deprived of his due privileges, or compelled to anything in practice not warranted by the Word, or in case of persecution, or upon the account of conveniency of habitation; he consulting with the church, or the officer or officers thereof, may peaceably depart from the communion of the church, wherewith he hath so walked, to join himself with some other church, where he

may enjoy the ordinances in the purity of the same, for his edification and consolation.

29 Such reforming churches as consist of persons sound in the faith and of conversation becoming the gospel, ought not to refuse the communion of each other, so far as may consist with their own principles respectively, though they walk not in all things according to the same rules of church-order.

30 Churches gathered and walking according to the mind of Christ, judging other churches (though less pure) to be true churches, may receive unto occasional communion with them, such members of those churches as are credibly testified to be godly, and live without offence.

5. Thomas Campbell's *Declaration and Address*, 1809

It is not easy to find a document from the history of Churches of Christ that corresponds to the Westminster Confession or the Savoy Declaration. Certainly no comparable declaration was ever produced on the British side of the Atlantic. The text which came closest to occupying an equivalent position of authority in the British Churches was Thomas Campbell's *Declaration and Address* of 1809.

For most of their history Disciples or Churches of Christ have been suspicious of creeds and confessions of faith. What began as a reaction against the use of confessions as tests of fellowship turned to complete rejection of all creeds in the middle period of their history in the later nineteenth century. Under the influence of the modern ecumenical movement in the twentieth century that attitude softened to one which recognised the usefulness for certain purposes of such statements. The position taken up in the preface to the Savoy Declaration would be congenial – that a confession, 'is to be looked upon but as a meet or fit medium or means whereby to express that their common faith and salvation, and no way is to be made use of as an imposition upon any'.

Thomas Campbell (1763-1854) was a minister of the Secession Presbyterian Church in Ahorey, near Armagh, until his emigration to the United States in 1807. Whilst in Ireland he worked to develop fellowship among the divided groups in the Secession Church and he was a member of the Evangelical Society of Ulster. When he arrived in Pennsylvania, he welcomed other Presbyterians to communion in his church, but discovered that this incurred censure. He therefore withdrew from the Associate Presbytery of Chartiers and formed the Christian Association of Washington, Pennsylvania. This was one of the two main sources from which the movement subsequently known as Disciples or Churches of Christ developed. The other was that which gathered around another group of Presbyterians under the leadership of Barton Stone in Kentucky.

The *Declaration and Address* was prepared by Campbell in the summer of 1809 to set out the aims of the Christian Association. The Declaration sets out the principles: that Christians must make their own judgment on the basis of Scripture; that the Divine Word alone, not any human interpretation of it, is binding; that unity and peace need to be restored to the Church; and that this can only be done by a return to the Divine Word as rule, the Holy Spirit as teacher and guide, and Christ as salvation. The Address develops these themes, articulating them in thirteen Propositions, which have often been quoted amongst Churches of Christ subsequently. The Appendix defends this position against misinterpretation, and particularly against charges of latitutidinariansim.

Thomas Campbell was a moderate Calvinist who took for granted the essential truths of the Westminster Confession. His main concern was that the Narrative and Testimony of the Secession Church, which defined the reasons for separating from the Church of Scotland, was being given an unwarranted status. He was also influenced by the Evangelical Revival and was anxious that the Gospel should be widely preached. The *Declaration and Address*, with its emphasis on Christian Unity and the means to attain it, is a different type of document from the two preceding ones. It was never formally adopted by Churches of Christ in Great Britain and Ireland, but they looked to it as an expression of their essential concerns.

For further reading, see page 265.

The Christian Association of Washington, PA., USA

At a meeting held at Buffalo, August 17, 1809, consisting of persons
of different religious denominations; most of them in an unsettled
state as to a fixed gospel ministry; it was unanimously agreed, upon
the considerations, and for the purposes herein after declared, to form
themselves into a religious association, designated as above – which
they accordingly did, and appointed twenty-one of their number to
meet and confer together; and, with the assistance of Mr. Thomas
Campbell, minister of the gospel, to determine upon the proper
means to carry into effect the important ends of their association:
the result of which conference was the following declaration and
address, agreed upon and ordered to be printed at the expense and
for the benefit of the society, September 7, 1809.

Declaration

From the series of events which have taken place in the churches
for many years past, especially in this western country, as well as
from what we know in general of the present state of things in
the Christian world, we are persuaded that it is high time for us
not only to think, but also to act, for ourselves; to see with our
own eyes, and to take all our measures directly and immediately
from the Divine Standard. To this alone we feel ourselves divinely
bound to be conformed, as by this alone we must be judged. We are
also persuaded that, as no man can be *judged* for his brother, so no
man can *judge* for his brother; but that every man must be allowed
to judge for himself, as every man must bear his own judgment,
must give an account of himself to God. We are also of opinion
that, as the divine word is equally binding upon all, so all lie under
an equal obligation to be bound by it, and it alone; and not by any
human interpretation of it: and that, therefore, no man has a right
to judge his brother, except in so far as he manifestly violates the
express letter of the law; also that every such judgment is an express
violation of the law of Christ, a daring usurpation of His throne,
and a gross intrusion upon the rights and liberties of His subjects.
We are therefore of opinion that we should beware of such things;
and that, knowing the judgment of God against them that commit
such things, we should neither do the same ourselves, nor have

pleasure in them that do them. Moreover, being well aware from sad experience of the heinous nature, and pernicious tendency of religious controversy among Christians, tired and sick of the bitter jarrings and janglings of a party spirit, we would desire to be at rest; and, were it possible, we would also desire to adopt and recommend such measures as would give rest to our brethren throughout all the churches as would restore unity, peace, and purity, to the whole Church of God. This desirable rest, however, we utterly despair either to find for ourselves, or to be able to recommend to our brethren, by continuing amidst the diversity and rancour of party contentions, the veering uncertainty and clashings of human opinions: nor indeed, can we reasonably expect to find it anywhere, but in Christ and His simple word which is the same yesterday, and today, and forever. Our desire, therefore, for ourselves and our brethren would be, that, rejecting human opinions and the inventions of men as of any authority, or as having any place in the Church of God, we might forever cease from farther contentions about such things; returning to, and holding fast by, the original standard; taking the divine word alone for our rule; the Holy Spirit for our teacher and guide, to lead us into all truth; and Christ alone, as exhibited in the word, for our salvation, that, by so doing, we may be at peace among ourselves, follow peace with all men, and holiness, without which no man shall see the Lord. Impressed with these sentiments, we have resolved as follows:

I That we form ourselves into a religious association under the denomination of the Christian Association of Washington for the sole purpose of promoting simple, evangelical Christianity, free from all mixture of human opinions and inventions of men.

II That each member, according to ability, cheerfully and liberally subscribe a certain specified sum, to be paid half yearly, for the purpose of raising a fund to support a pure Gospel Ministry that shall reduce to practice that whole form of doctrine, worship, discipline, and government, expressly revealed and enjoined in the word of God; and also for supplying the poor with the Holy Scriptures.

III That this society consider it a duty, and shall use all proper means in its power, to encourage the formation of similar associations and shall for this purpose hold itself in readiness, upon application, to correspond with, and render all possible assistance to, such as may desire to associate for the same desirable and important purposes.

IV That this society by no means considers itself a church, nor does at all assume to itself the powers peculiar to such a society; nor do the members, as such, consider themselves as standing connected in that relation; nor as at all associated for the peculiar purposes of church association, but merely as voluntary advocates for church reformation; and, as possessing the powers common to all individuals who may please to associate, in a peaceable and orderly manner, for any lawful purpose: namely, the disposal of their time, counsel and property, as they may see cause.

V That this society, formed for the sole purpose of promoting simple, evangelical Christianity, shall, to the utmost of its power, countenance and support such ministers, and such only, as exhibit a manifest conformity to the original standard in conversation and doctrine, in zeal and diligence; only such as reduce to practice that simple, original form of Christianity expressly exhibited upon the sacred page; without attempting to inculcate anything of human authority, of private opinion, or inventions of men, as having any place in the constitution, faith, or worship of the Christian Church or anything as matter of Christian faith, or duty, for which there cannot be expressly produced a 'thus saith the Lord', either in express terms, or by approved precedent.

VI That a standing committee of twenty-one members of unexceptionable moral character, inclusive of the secretary and treasurer, be chosen annually to superintend the interests and transact the business, of the society; and that said committee be invested with full powers to act and do, in the name and behalf of their constituents, whatever the society had previously determined, for the purpose of carrying into effect the entire object of its institution; and that in case of any emergency, unprovided for in the existing determinations of the society, said committee be empowered to call a *pro re nota* meeting for that purpose.

VII That this society meet at least twice a year, viz. on the first Thursday of May and of November, and that the collectors appointed to receive the half-yearly quotas of the promised subscriptions, be in readiness, at or before each meeting, to make their returns to the treasurer, that he may be able to report upon the state of the funds. The next meeting to be held at Washington on the first Thursday of November next.

VIII That each meeting of the society be opened with a sermon, the constitution and address read, and a collection lifted for the benefit of the society, and that all communications of a public nature be laid before the society at its half-yearly meetings.

IX That this society, relying upon the all-sufficiency of the Church's Head, and, through His grace, looking with an eye of confidence to the generous liberality of the sincere friends of genuine Christianity, holds itself engaged to afford a competent support to such ministers as the Lord may graciously dispose to assist, at the request and by invitation of the society, in promoting a pure, evangelical reformation, by the simple preaching of the everlasting gospel, and the administration of its ordinances in an exact conformity to the Divine Standard as aforesaid and that, therefore, whatever the friends of the institution shall please to contribute toward the support of ministers in connexion with this society who may be sent forth to preach at considerable distances, the same shall be gratefully received and acknowledged as a donation to its funds.

Address

To all that love our Lord Jesus Christ in sincerity, throughout all the Churches, the following Address is most respectfully submitted.

Dearly beloved brethren, that it is the grand design and native tendency of our holy religion to reconcile and unite man to God and to each other, in truth and love, to the glory of God and their own present and eternal good, will not, we presume, be denied by any of the genuine subjects of Christianity. The nativity of its Divine Author was announced from heaven by a host of angels, with high acclamations of 'glory to God in the highest, and on earth, peace and good will toward men'. The whole tenor of that divine book which contains its institutes, in all its gracious declarations, precepts, ordinances and holy examples, most expressly and powerfully inculcates this. In so far, then, as this holy unity and unanimity in faith and love is attained, just in the same degree, is the glory of God and the happiness of man promoted and secured. Impressed with those sentiments, and at the same time grievously affected with those sad divisions which have so awfully interfered

123

with the benign and gracious intention of our holy religion by exciting its professed subjects to bite and devour one another, we cannot suppose ourselves justifiable in withholding the mite of our sincere and humble endeavours to heal and remove them.

What awful and distressing effects have those sad divisions produced! what adversions, what reproaches, what backbitings, what evil surmisings, what angry contentions, what enmities, what excommunications, and even persecutions! And indeed, this must in some measure continue to be the case so long as those schisms exist, for, said the Apostle, where envying and strife is, *there* is confusion and every evil work. What dreary effects of these accursed divisions are to be seen, even in this highly favoured country, where the sword of the civil magistrate has not, as yet, learned to serve at the altar. Have we not seen congregations broken to pieces, neighbourhoods of professing Christians first thrown into confusion by party contentions and, in the end, entirely deprived of gospel ordinances; while in the meantime, large settlements and tracts of country remain to this day entirely destitute of a gospel ministry; many of them in little better than a state of heathenism, the churches being either so weakened with divisions that they cannot send them ministers or, the people so divided among themselves that they will not receive them? Several at the same time who live at the door of a preached gospel, dare not in conscience go to hear it, and, of course, enjoy little more advantage in that respect, than if living in the midst of heathens. How seldom do many in those circumstances enjoy the dispensation of the Lord's Supper, that great ordinance of unity and love! How sadly, also, does this broken and confused state of things interfere with that spiritual intercourse amongst Christians, one with another, which is so essential to their edification and comfort in the midst of a present evil world, so divided in sentiment, and, of course, living at such distances, that but few of the same opinion or party, can conveniently and frequently assemble for religious purposes, or enjoy a due frequency of ministerial attentions. And even where things are in a better state with respect to settled churches, how is the tone of discipline relaxed under the influence of a party spirit, many being afraid to exercise it with due strictness, lest their people should leave them and, under the cloak of some specious pretence, find refuge in the bosom of another party; while, lamentable to be told, so corrupt is the Church with those accursed divisions, that there are but few so base as not to find admission into some professing party or other. Thus, in a great measure, is that scriptural purity of communion banished from the Church of God, upon the due preservation of which, much of her comfort, glory, and usefulness depend. To complete the dread result of our woeful divisions, one evil yet remains of a very awful nature: the divine displeasure justly provoked with this sad perversion of the gospel of peace, the Lord withholds His gracious influential presence from His ordinances and, not unfrequently, gives up the contentious authors and abettors of religious discord to fall into grievous scandals, or visits them with judgments, as he did the house of Eli. Thus, while professing Christians bite and devour one another, they are consumed one of another, or fall a prey to the righteous judgment of God. Meantime the truly religious of all parties are grieved, the weak stumbled, the graceless and profane hardened, the mouths of infidels opened to blaspheme religion; and thus the only thing under heaven, divinely efficacious to promote and secure the present spiritual and eternal good of man, even the gospel of the blessed Jesus, is reduced to contempt; while multitudes deprived of the gospel ministry, as has been observed, fall an easy pray to seducers and so become the dupes of almost unheard of delusions. Are not such the visible effects of our sad divisions even in this otherwise happy country? Say, dear brethren, are not these things so? Is it not then your incumbent duty to endeavour, by all scriptural means, to have those evils remedied? Who will say, that it is not? And does it not peculiarly belong to *you*, who occupy the place of gospel ministers, to be leaders in this laudable undertaking? Much depends upon *your* hearty concurrence and zealous endeavours. The favourable opportunity which Divine Providence has put into your hands, in this happy country, for the accomplishment of so great a good is, in itself, a consideration of no small encouragement. A country happily exempted from the baneful influence of a civil establishment of any peculiar form of Christianity, from under the direct influence of the anti-Christian hierarchy, and, at the same time, from any formal connexion with the devoted nations that have given their strength and power unto the beast; in which, of course, no adequate reformation can be accomplished, until the word of God is fulfilled, and the vials of His wrath poured out upon them. Happy exemption, indeed, from being the object of such awful judgments. Still more happy will it be for us, if we duly esteem and improve those great advantages, for the high and valuable ends for which they are manifestly given; and sure where much is given, much also will be required. Can the Lord expect, or require, anything less, from a people in such unhampered circumstances, from a people so liberally furnished with all means and mercies, than a thorough reformation in all things civil and religious, according to his word? Why should we suppose it? And would not such an improvement of our precious privileges be equally conducive to the glory of God and our own present and everlasting good? The auspicious phenomena of the times furnish collateral arguments of a very encouraging nature, that our dutiful and pious endeavours shall not be in vain in the Lord. Is it not the day of the Lord's vengeance upon the anti-Christian world; the year of recompences for the controversy of Zion? Surely then the time to favour her is come; even the set time. And is it not said that Zion shall be built in troublous times? Have not greater efforts been made, and more done, for the promulgation of the gospel among the nations, since the commencement of the French revolution than had been for many centuries prior to that event? And have not the churches both in Europe and America, since that period discovered a more than usual concern for the removal of contentions, for the healing of divisions, for the restoration of a Christian and brotherly intercourse one with another, and for the promotion of each other's spiritual good; as the printed documents, upon those subjects, amply testify? Should *we* not, then, be excited by these considerations to concur with all our might, to help forward this good work, that what yet remains to be done may be fully accomplished? And what! Though the well meant endeavours after union have not, in some instances, entirely succeeded to this wish of all parties, should this dissuade us from the attempt? Indeed, should Christians cease to contend earnestly for the sacred articles of faith and duty once delivered to the saints, on account of the opposition and scanty success which, in many instances attend their faithful and honest endeavours, the divine cause of truth and righteousness might have, long ago, been relinquished. And is there any thing more formidable in the Goliath-schism, than in many other evils which Christians have to combat? Or, has the Captain of Salvation sounded a desist from pursuing, or proclaimed a truce with, this deadly enemy that is sheathing its sword in the very bowels of His Church, rending and mangling His mystical body into pieces? Has He said to His servants let it alone? If not, where is the warrant for a cessation of endeavours to have it removed? On the other hand, are we not the better instructed by sage experience, how to proceed in this business, having before our eyes the inadvertencies and mistakes of others, which have hitherto, in many instances, prevented the desired success? Thus, taught by experience, and happily furnished with the accumulated instructions of those that have gone before us, earnestly labouring in this good cause, let us take unto ourselves the whole armour of God, and having our feet shod with the preparation of the gospel of peace, let us stand fast by this important duty, with all perseverance. Let none that love the peace of Zion be discouraged, much less offended, because that an object of such magnitude does not, in the first instance, come forth recommended by the express suffrage of the mighty or the many. This consideration, if duly weighed, will neither give offence, nor yield discouragement, to any, that considers the nature of the thing in question, in connexion with what has already been suggested. Is it not a matter of universal right, a duty equally belonging to every citizen of Zion, to seek her good? In this respect, no one can claim a preference above his fellows, as to any peculiar, much less exclusive, obligation. And, as for authority, it can have no place in this business; for surely none can suppose themselves invested with a divine right, as to any thing peculiarly belonging to them, to call the attention of their brethren to this dutiful and important undertaking. For our part, we entertain no such arrogant presumption; nor are we inclined to impute the thought to any of our brethren, that this work should be let alone till such time as they may think proper to come forward, and sanction the attempt by their invitation and example. It is an open field, an extensive work, to which all are equally welcome, equally invited.

Should we speak of competency, viewing the greatness of the object and the manifold difficulties which lie in the way of its accomplishment, we would readily exclaim, with the Apostle, Who is sufficient for these things! But, upon recollecting ourselves, neither would *we* be discouraged, persuaded with him, that, as the work in which we are engaged, so likewise *our* sufficiency, is of God. But, after all, both the mighty and the many are with us. The Lord himself, and all that are truly His people, are declaredly on our side. The prayers of all the churches, nay, the prayers of Christ Himself, (John 17:20, 23) and of all that have ascended to His heavenly

127

kingdom, are with us. The blessing out of Zion is pronounced upon our undertaking. 'Pray for the peace of Jerusalem, they shall prosper that love thee.' With such encouragements as these, what should deter us from the heavenly enterprise, or render hopeless the attempt of accomplishing, in due time, an entire union of all the churches in faith and practice, according to the word of God? Not that we judge ourselves competent to effect such a thing; we utterly disclaim the thought: but we judge it our bounden duty to make the attempt, by using all due means in our power to promote it; and also that we have sufficient reason to rest assured that our humble and well-meant endeavours shall not be in vain in the Lord.

The cause that we advocate is not our own peculiar, nor the cause of any party, considered as such; it is a common cause, the cause of Christ and our brethren of all denominations. All that we presume, then, is to do what we humbly conceive to be *our* duty, in connexion with our brethren, to all of whom it equally belongs, as to us, to exert themselves for this blessed purpose. And as we have no just reason to doubt the concurrence of our brethren to accomplish an object so desirable in itself and fraught with such happy consequences, so neither can we look forward to that happy event, which will forever put an end to our hapless divisions, and restore to the Church its primitive unity, purity and prosperity, but in the pleasing prospect of their hearty and dutiful concurrence.

Dearly beloved brethren, why should *we* deem it a thing incredible that the Church of Christ in this highly favoured country should resume that original unity, peace and purity, which belongs to its constitution, and constitutes its glory? Or, is there any thing that can be justly deemed necessary for this desirable purpose, but to conform to the model and adopt the practice of the primitive Church, expressly exhibited in the New Testament? Whatever alterations this might produce in any or all of the churches, should, we think, neither be deemed inadmissable or ineligible. Surely such alteration would be every way for the better and not for the worse; unless we should suppose the divinely inspired rule to be faulty, or defective. Were we, then, in our church constitution and managements, to exhibit a complete conformity to the Apostolic Church, would we not be in that respect, as perfect as Christ intended we should be? And should not this suffice us?

It is, to us, a pleasing consideration that all the churches of Christ, which mutually acknowledge each other as such, are not only agreed in the great doctrines of faith and holiness, but are also materially agreed, as to the positive ordinances of Gospel institution; so that our differences, at most, are about the things in which the kingdom of God does not consist, that is, about matters of private opinion, or human invention. What a pity, that the kingdom of God should be divided about such things! Who, then, would not be the first amongst us to give up with human inventions in the worship of God, and to cease from imposing his private opinions upon his brethren, that our breaches might *thus* be healed? Who would not willingly conform to the original pattern laid down in the New Testament, for *this* happy purpose? Our dear brethren, of all denominations, will please to consider, that we have our educational prejudices and particular customs to struggle with as well as they. But this we do sincerely declare, that there is nothing we have hitherto received as matter of faith or practice which is not expressly taught and enjoined in the word of God, either in express terms, or approved precedent, that we would not heartily relinquish, that so we might return to the original constitutional unity of the Christian Church, and, in this happy unity, enjoy full communion with all our brethren, in peace and charity. The like dutiful condescension we candidly expect of all that are seriously impressed with a sense of the duty they owe to God, to each other and to their perishing fellow-brethren of mankind. To this we call, we invite, our brethren of all denominations, by all the sacred motives which we have avouched as the impulsive reasons of our thus addressing them.

You are all, dear brethren, equally included as the object of our love and esteem. With you all we desire to unite in the bonds of an entire Christian unity, Christ alone being the head, the centre; his word the rule; an explicit belief of, and manifest comformity to it in all things, *the terms*. More than this you will not require of us; and less we cannot require of you; nor indeed, can we reasonably suppose, any would desire it; for what good purpose would it serve? We dare neither assume, nor purpose, the trite indefinite distinction between essentials and non-essentials in matters of revealed truth and duty; firmly persuaded, that, whatever may be their comparative importance, simply considered, the high obligation of the Divine Authority revealing, or enjoining them, renders the belief, or performance of them, absolutely essential to us, in so far as we know them. And to be ignorant of anything God has revealed, can

129

neither be our duty, nor our privilege. We humbly presume then, dear brethren, you can have no relevant objection to meet us upon this ground. And, we again beseech you, let it be known, that it is the invitation but of a few; by your accessions we shall be many; and whether few or many, in the first instance, it is all one with respect to the event, which must ultimately await the full information, and hearty concurrence, of all. Besides, whatever is to be done, must begin, sometime, somewhere; and no matter where, nor by whom, if the Lord puts his hand to the work, it must surely prosper. And has he not been graciously pleased, upon many signal occasions, to bring to pass the greatest events from very small beginnings, and even by means the most unlikely? Duty then is ours; but events belong to God.

We hope then, what we urge, will neither be deemed an unreasonable nor an unseasonable undertaking. Why should it be thought unseasonable? Can any time be assigned, while things continue as they are, that would prove more favourable for such an attempt, or what could be supposed to make it so? Might it be the approximation of parties to a greater nearness, in point of public profession and similarly of customs? Or, might it be expected from a gradual decline of bigotry? As to the former, it is a well known fact, that where the difference is least, the opposition is always managed with a degree of vehemence, inversely proportioned to the merits of the cause. With respect to the latter, though we are happy to say that, in some cases and places and, we hope, universally, bigotry is upon the decline, yet we are not warranted either by the past or present, to act upon that supposition. We have, as yet, by this means, seen no such effect produced; nor indeed could we reasonably expect it; for there will always be multitudes of weak persons in the church, and these are generally most subject to bigotry; add to this, that, while divisions exist, there will always be found interested men, who will not fail to support them: nor can we at all suppose that Satan will be idle to improve an advantage so important to the interests of his kingdom. And, let it be further observed upon the whole, that, in matters of similar importance to our secular interests, we would by no means content ourselves with such kind of reasoning. We might further add that, the attempt here suggested not being of a partial, but of general nature, it can have no just tendency to excite the jealousy, or hurt the feelings, of any party. On the contrary, every effort towards a permanent scriptural unity amongst the churches upon the solid basis of universally acknowledged, and self-evident truths, must have the happiest tendency to enlighten and conciliate, by thus manifesting to each other their mutual charity, and zeal for the truth: 'Whom I loved in the truth,' saith the Apostle, 'and not I only, but also all they that have known the truth; for the truth's sake, which is in us, and shall be with us forever.' Indeed, if no such divine and adequate basis of union can be fairly exhibited as will meet the approbation of every upright and intelligent Christian, nor such mode of procedure adopted in favour of the weak as will not oppress their consciences, then the accomplishment of this grand object upon principle, must be forever impossible. There would, upon this supposition, remain no other way of accomplishing it, but merely by voluntary compromise and good natured accommodation. That such a thing, however, will be accomplished, one way or other, will not be questioned by any that allow themselves to believe that the commands and prayers of our Lord Jesus Christ will not utterly prove ineffectual. Whatever way, then, it is to be effected, whether upon the solid basis of divinely revealed truth, or the good natured principle of Christian forbearance and gracious condescension, is it not equally practicable, equally eligible to us, as ever it can be to any; unless we should suppose ourselves destitute of that Christian temper and discernment, which is essentially necessary to qualify us to do the will of our gracious Redeemer, Whose expressed command to His people is that there be no division among them, but that they all walk by the same rule, speak the same thing, and be perfectly joined together in the same mind, and in the same judgment? We believe, then, it is as practicable as it is eligible. Let us attempt it. 'Up and be doing, and the Lord will be with you.'

Are we not all praying for that happy event, when there shall be but one fold, as there is but one Chief Shepherd? What! shall we pray for a thing and not strive to obtain it! not use the necessary means to have it accomplished! What said the Lord to Moses upon a piece of conduct somewhat similar? 'Why criest thou unto Me? Speak unto the children of Israel that they go forward, but lift thou up thy rod, and stretch out thine hand.' Let the ministers of Jesus but embrace this exhortation, put their hand to the work and encourage the people to go forward upon the firm ground of obvious truth, to unite in the bonds of an entire Christian unity, and who will venture to say that it would not soon be accomplished? 'Cast ye up, cast ye up, prepare the way, take up the stumbling block out of the way of My people,' saith your God. To you, therefore, it peculiarly belongs, as the professed and acknowledged leaders of the people, to go before them in this good work, to remove human opinions and the inventions of men out of the way; by carefully separating this chaff from the pure wheat of primary and authentic revelation; casting out that assumed authority, that enacting and decreeing power, by which those things have been imposed and established. To the ministerial department then do we look with anxiety. Ministers of Jesus, we can neither be ignorant of, nor unaffected with, the divisions and corruptions of His Church. His dying commands, His last and ardent prayers for the visible unity of His professing people, will not suffer you to be indifferent in this matter. You will not, you cannot, therefore, be silent, upon a subject of such vast importance to His personal glory and the happiness of His people, consistently you cannot; for silence gives consent. You will rather lift up your voice like a trumpet to expose the heinous nature and dreadful consequences of those unnatural and anti-Christian divisions which have so rent and ruined the church of God. Thus, in justice to your station and character, honoured of the Lord, would we hopefully anticipate your zealous and faithful efforts to heal the breaches of Zion; that God's dear children might dwell together in unity and love. But if otherwise – **** we forebear to utter it. See Mal. 2:1-10.

Oh! that ministers and people would but consider, that there are no divisions in the grave; nor in that world which lies beyond it: there our divisions must come to an end. We must all unite there. Would to God we could find in our hearts to put an end to our short-lived divisions here, that so we might leave a blessing behind us, even a happy and united church! What gratification, what utility, in the meantime, can our divisions afford either to ministers or people? Should they be perpetuated till the day of judgment, would they convert one sinner from the error of his ways, or save a soul from death? Have they any tendency to hide the multitude of sins that are so dishonourable to God and hurtful to His people? Do they not rather irritate and produce them? How innumerable and highly aggravated are the sins they have produced and are, at this day, producing, both amongst professors and profane. We entreat, we beseech you then, dear brethren, by all those considerations, to concur in this blessed and dutiful attempt. What is the work of all, must be done by all. Such was the work of the tabernacle in the wilderness. Such is the work to which you are called; not by the authority of man, but by Jesus Christ and God the Father, who raised Him from the dead. By this authority are you called to raise up the tabernacle of David, that is fallen down amongst us, and to set it up upon its own base. This you cannot do, while you run every man to his own house, and consult only the interest of his own party. Till you associate, consult, and advise together, and in a friendly and Christian manner explore the subject, nothing can be done. We would therefore, with all due deference and submission, call the attention of our brethren to the obvious and important duty of association. Unite with us in the common cause of simple, evangelical Christianity. In this glorious cause we are ready to unite with you. United we shall prevail. It is the cause of Christ, and of our brethren throughout all the churches, of catholic unity, peace, and purity, a cause that must finally prosper in spite of all opposition. Let us unite to promote it. Come forward then, dear brethren and help with us. do not suffer yourselves to be lulled asleep by that syren song of the slothful and reluctant professor, 'The time is not yet come, the time is not come, saith he, the time that the Lord's house should be built.' Believe him not. Do ye not discern the signs of the times? 'Have not the two witnesses arisen from their state of political death, from under the long proscription of ages? Have they not stood upon their feet, in the presence and to the consternation and terror of their enemies? Has not their resurrection been accompanied with a great earthquake? Has not the tenth part of the great city been thrown down by it? Has not this event aroused the nations to indignation? Have they not been angry, yea very angry? Therefore, O Lord, is Thy wrath come upon them, and the time of the dead that they should be avenged, and that thou shouldest give reward to thy servants, the Prophets, and to them that fear thy name, both small and great; and that thou shouldest destroy them that have destroyed the earth.' Who amongst us has not heard the report of these things, of these lightnings and thunderings, and voices of this tremendous earthquake and great hail; of these awful convulsions and revolutions that have dashed and are dashing to pieces the nations like a potter's vessel? Yea, have not the remote vibrations of this dreadful shock been felt even by us, whom Providence has graciously placed at so great a distance? What shall we say to these things? Is it time for us to sit still in our corruptions and divisions, when the Lord by His word and providence, is so loudly and expressly calling us to repentance and reformation? 'Awake, awake; put on thy strength, O Zion, put on thy beautiful garments, O Jerusalem the holy city; for henceforth there shall no more come unto thee the uncircumcised and the unclean. Shake thyself from the dust, O Jerusalem; arise, loose thyself from the *bands* of thy neck, O captive daughter of Zion.' Resume that precious, that dear bought liberty, wherewith Christ has made His people free; a liberty from subjection to any authority but His own, in matters of religion. 'Call no man father, no man master upon earth; for one is your master, even Christ, and all ye are brethren.' Stand fast therefore in this precious liberty, and be not entangled again with the yoke of bondage. For the vindication of this precious liberty have we declared ourselves hearty and willing advocates. For this benign and dutiful purpose have we associated, that by so doing, we might contribute the mite of our humble endeavours to promote it, and thus invite our brethren to do the same. As the first fruits of our efforts for this blessed purpose we respectfully present to their consideration the following propositions, relying upon their charity and candour that they will neither despise, nor misconstrue, our humble and adventurous attempt. If they should in any measure serve, as a preliminary, to open up the way to a permanent scriptural unity amongst the friends and lovers of truth and peace throughout the churches, we shall greatly rejoice at it. We by no means pretend to dictate: and could we propose any thing more evident, consistent, and adequate, it should be at their service. Their pious and dutiful attention to an object of such magnitude will induce them to communicate to us their emendations; and thus what is sown in weakness, will be raised up in power; for certainly the collective graces that are conferred upon the church, if duly united and brought to bear upon any point of commanded duty, would be amply sufficient for the right and successful performance of it. 'For to one is given by the spirit the word of wisdom; to another the word of knowledge by the same spirit; to another faith by the same spirit; to another the discerning of spirits; but the manifestation of the spirit is given to every man to profit withal. As every man, therefore, hath received the gift, even so minister the same one to another as good stewards of the manifold grace of God.' In the face then of such instructions, and with such assurances of an all-sufficiency of divine grace, as the Church has received from her exalted Head, we can neither justly doubt the concurrence of her genuine members, nor yet their ability, when dutifully acting together, to accomplish any thing that is necessary for His glory and their own good; and certainly their visible unity in truth and holiness, in faith and love, is of all things, the most conducive to both these, if we may credit the dying commands and prayers of our gracious Lord. In a matter, therefore, of such confessed importance, our Christian brethren, however unhappily distinguished by party names, will not, cannot, withhold their helping hand. We are as heartily willing to be their debtors, as they are indispensably bound to be our benefactors. Come, then, dear brethren, we most humbly beseech you, cause your light to shine upon our weak beginnings, that we may see to work by it. Evince your zeal for the glory of Christ, and the spiritual welfare of your fellow-Christians, by your hearty and zealous co-operation to promote the unity, purity and prosperity of His church.

Let none imagine that the subjoined propositions are at all intended as an overture towards a new creed, or standard, for the church, or, as in any wise designed to be made a term of communion; nothing can be farther away from our intention. They are merely designed for opening up the way, that we may come fairly and firmly to original ground upon clear and certain premises, and take up things just as the Apostles left them, that, thus disentangled from the accruing embarrassments of intervening ages, we may stand with evidence upon the same ground on which the Church stood at the beginning. Having said so much to solicit and prevent mistake, we submit as follows:

Proposition 1   That the Church of Christ upon earth is essentially, intentionally, and constitutionally one, consisting of all those in every place that profess their faith in Christ and obedience to Him in all things according to the scriptures, and that manifest the same by their tempers and conduct, and of none else, as none else can be truly and properly called Christians.

2   That although the Church of Christ upon earth must necessarily exist in particular and distinct societies, locally separate one from other, yet there ought to be no schisms, no uncharitable divisions among them. They ought to receive each other as Christ Jesus hath also received them to the glory of God. And for this purpose, they

ought all to walk by the same rule, to mind and speak the same thing and to be perfectly joined together in the same mind and the same judgment.

3   That in order to this, nothing ought to be inculcated upon Christians as articles of faith, nor required of them as terms of communion, but what is expressly taught and enjoined upon them in the word of God. Nor ought anything be admitted as of divine obligation in their church constitution and managements, but what is expressly enjoined by the authority of our Lord Jesus Christ and His Apostles upon the New Testament Church, either in expressed terms, or by approved precedent.

4   That although the scriptures of the Old and New Testament are inseparably connected, making together but one perfect and entire revelation of the Divine will, for the edification and salvation of the Church, and therefore in that respect cannot be separated, yet as to what directly and properly belongs to their immediate object, the New Testament is as perfect a constitution for the worship, discipline and government of the New Testament Church, and as perfect a rule for the particular duties of its members, as the Old Testament was for the worship, discipline and government of the Old Testament Church, and the particular duties of its members.

5   That with respect to the commands and ordinances of our Lord Jesus Christ, where the scriptures are silent, as to the express time or manner of performance, if any such there be, no human authority has power to interfere, in order to supply the supposed deficiency, by making laws for the Church; nor can any thing more be required of Christians in such cases, but only that they *so* observe these commands and ordinances, as will evidently answer the declared and obvious end of their institution. Much less has any human authority power to impose new commands or ordinances upon the Church, which our Lord Jesus Christ has not enjoined. Nothing ought to be received into the faith or worship of the Church, or be made a term of communion amongst Christians, that is not as old as the New Testament.

6   That although inferences and deductions from scripture premises, when fairly inferred, may be truly called the doctrine of God's

holy word, yet are they not formally binding upon the consciences of Christians farther than they perceive the connexion, and evidently see that they are so; for their faith must not stand in the wisdom of men, but in the power and veracity of God. Therefore no such deduction can be made terms of communion, but do properly belong to the after and progressive edification of the Church. Hence it is evident that no such deductions or inferential truths ought to have any place in the Church's confession.

7   That although doctrinal exhibitions of the great system of divine truths and defensive testimonies in opposition to prevailing errors, be highly expedient, and the more full and explicit they be for those purposes, the better, yet as these must be in a great measure the effect of human reasoning, and of course must contain many inferential truths, they ought not to be made terms of Christian communion; unless we suppose, what is contrary to fact, that none have a right to the communion of the Church but such as possess a very clear and decisive judgment, or are come to a very high degree of doctrinal information; whereas the Church from the beginning did, and ever will, consist of little children and young men as well as fathers.

8   That as it is not necessary that persons should have a particular knowledge or distinct apprehension of all divinely revealed truths in order to entitle them to a place in the Church, neither should they, for this purpose, be required to make a profession more extensive than their knowledge; but that, on the contrary, their having a due measure of scriptural self-knowledge respecting their lost and perishing condition by nature and practice, and of the way of salvation through Jesus Christ, accompanied with a profession of their faith in, and obedience to Him in all things according to His word, is all that is absolutely necessary to qualify them for admission to His Church.

9   That all that are enabled, through grace, to make such a profession, and to manifest the reality of it in their tempers and conduct, should consider each other as the precious saints of god, should love each other as brethren, children of the same family and Father, temples of the same Spirit, members of the same Body, subjects of the

same grace, objects of the same divine love, bought with the same price, and joint heirs of the same inheritance. Whom God hath thus joined together no man should dare to put asunder.

10   That division among Christians is a horrid evil, fraught with many evils. It is anti-Christian, as it destroys the visible unity of the Body of Christ; as if He were divided against Himself, excluding and excommunicating a part of Himself. It is anti-scriptural, as being strictly prohibited by His sovereign authority; a direct violation of His express command. It is anti-natural, as it excites Christians to condemn, to hate and oppose one another, who are bound by the highest and most endearing obligations to love each other as brethren, even as Christ has loved them. In a word, it is productive of confusion and of every evil work.

11   That, in some instances, a partial neglect of the expressly revealed will of God and, in others, an assumed authority for making the approbation of human opinions and human inventions a term of communion by introducing them into the constitution, faith, or worship, of the Church are, and have been, the immediate, obvious and universally acknowledged causes of all the corruptions and divisions that ever have taken place in the Church of God.

12   That all that is necessary to the highest state of perfection and purity of the Church upon earth is, that none be received as members but such as, having that due measure of scriptural self-knowledge described above, do profess their faith in Christ and obedience to Him in all things according to the scriptures; nor, secondly, that any be retained in her communion longer than they continue to manifest the reality of their profession by their tempers and conduct. Thirdly, that her ministers, duly and scripturally qualified, inculcate none other things than those very articles of faith and holiness expressly revealed and enjoined in the word of God. Lastly, that in all their administration they keep close by the observance of all divine ordinances, after the example of the primitive Church, exhibited in the New Testament, without any additions whatsoever of human opinions or inventions of men.

13   Lastly. That if any circumstantial, indispensably necessary to the observance of divine ordinances, be not found upon the page

of express revelation, such, and such only, as are absolutely necessary for this purpose should be adopted, under the title of human expedients, without any pretence to a more sacred origin; so that any subsequent alteration or difference in the observance of these things might produce no contention nor division in the Church.

From the nature and construction of these propositions it will evidently appear, that they are laid in a designed subserviency to the declared end of our association, and are exhibited for the express purpose of performing a duty of previous necessity; a duty loudly called for in existing circumstances at the hands of every one that would desire to promote the interests of Zion; a duty not only enjoined, as has been already observed from Isa. 57:14, but which is also there predicted of the faithful remnant as a thing in which they would voluntarily engage. 'He that putteth his trust in Me shall possess the land, and shall inherit My holy mountain; and shall say, cast ye up, cast ye up, prepare the way; take up the stumbling block out of the way of My people.'

To prepare the way for a permanent scriptural unity amongst Christians, by calling up to their consideration fundamental truths, directing their attention to first principles, clearing the way before them by removing the stumbling blocks, the rubbish of ages which has been thrown upon it and fencing it on each side, that in advancing towards the desired object, they may not miss the way through mistake, or inadvertency, by turning aside to the right hand or to the left, is, at least, the sincere intention of the above propositions. It remains with our brethren now to say how far they go toward answering this intention. Do they exhibit truths demonstrably evident in the light of scripture and right reason, so that, to deny any part of them, the contrary assertion would be manifestly absurd and inadmissible? Considered as a preliminary for the above purpose, are they adequate; so that if acted upon, they would infallibly lead to the desired issue? If evidently defective in either of these respects, let them be corrected and amended, till they become sufficiently evident, adequate and unexceptionable. In the meantime let them be examined with rigour, with all the rigour that justice, candour and charity will admit. If we have mistaken the way, we shall be glad to set right; but if, in the mean time, we have been happily led to suggest obvious and undeniable truths, which, if adopted and acted upon, would infallibly lead to the desired unity, and secure it when obtained, we hope it will be no objection, that they have not proceeded from a general council. It is not the voice of the multitude, but the voice of truth, that has power with the conscience, that can produce rational conviction and acceptable obedience. A conscience that awaits the decision of the multitude, that hangs in suspense for the casting vote of the majority, is a fit subject for the man of sin. This we are persuaded is the uniform sentiment of real Christians of every denomination. Would to God that all professors were such. Then should our eyes soon behold the prosperity of Zion. We should soon see Jerusalem a quiet habitation. Union in truth has been, and ever must be, the desire and prayer of all such. Union in Truth is our motto. The Divine word is our Standard. In the Lord's name do we display our banners. Our eyes are upon the promises, 'So shall they fear the name of the Lord from the west, and his glory from the rising of the sun.' 'When the enemy shall come in like a flood the spirit of the Lord shall lift up a standard against him.' Our humble desire is to be His standard bearers to fight under *His* banner, and with *His* weapons, 'which are not carnal, but mighty through God to the pulling down of strong holds'; even all these strong holds of division, those partition walls of separation, which, like the wall of Jericho, have been built up, as it were, to the very heavens, to separate God's people, to divide *His* flock and so to prevent them from entering into their promised rest, at least in so far as it respects this world. An enemy hath done this; but he shall not finally prevail; for 'the meek shall inherit the earth and shall delight themselves in the abundance of peace.' 'And the kingdom and dominion, even the greatness of the kingdom under the whole heaven, shall be given to the people of the saints of the Most High, and they shall possess it forever.' But this cannot be in their present broken and divided state, 'for a kingdom, or an house, divided against itself cannot stand, but cometh to desolation.' Now this has been the case with the Church for a long time. However, 'the Lord will not cast off his people, neither will he forsake his heritage, but judgment shall return unto righteousness, and all the upright in heart shall follow it.' To all such, and such alone, are our expectations directed. Come, then, ye blessed of the Lord, we have your prayers; let us also have your actual assistance. What, shall we pray for a thing and not strive to obtain it!

We call, we invite you again, by every consideration in these premises. You that are near, associate with us; you that are at too great a distance, associate as we have done. Let not the paucity of your number in any given district prove an insuperable discouragement. Remember Him that has said, 'if two of you shall agree on earth as touching anything that they shall ask, it shall be done for them of My Father which is in heaven: for where two or three are gathered together in My name, there am I in the midst of them.' With such a promise as this for the attainment of every possible and promised good, there is no room for discouragement. Come on, then, 'ye that fear the Lord keep not silence, and give him no rest till he make Jerusalem a joy and a praise in the earth.' Put on that noble resolution dictated by the prophet, saying, 'for Zion's sake will we not hold our peace, and for Jerusalem's sake we will not rest, until the righteousness thereof go forth as brightness, and the salvation thereof as a lamp that burneth.' Thus impressed, ye will find means to associate as such convenient distances as to meet, at least, once a month, to beseech the Lord to put an end to our lamentable divisions, to heal and unite His people, that His church may resume her original constitutional unity and purity and thus be exalted to the enjoyment of her promised prosperity, that the Jews may be speedily converted, and the fullness of the Gentiles brought in. Thus associated, you will be in a capacity to investigate the evil causes of our sad divisions, to consider and bewail their pernicious effects, and to mourn over them before the Lord, Who hath said, 'I will go and return to my place, till they acknowledge their offence and seek my face.' Alas! then, what reasonable prospect can we have of being delivered from those sad calamities which have so long afflicted the Church of God, while a party spirit, instead of bewailing, is everywhere justifying the bitter principle of these pernicious evils; by insisting upon the right of rejecting those, however unexceptionable in other respects, who cannot see with them in matters of private opinion, of human inference, that are nowhere expressly revealed or enjoined in the word of God? Thus associated, will the friends of peace, the advocates for Christian unity, be in a capacity to connect in large circles, where several of those smaller societies may meet semi-annually at a convenient centre, and thus avail themselves of their combined exertions for promoting the interests of the common cause. We hope that many of the Lord's ministers in all places will volunteer in this service, forasmuch as they know, it is His favourite work, the very desire of His soul.

Ye lovers of Jesus, and beloved of Him, however scattered in this cloudy and dark day, ye love the truth as it is in Jesus, if our hearts deceive us not; so do we. Ye desire union in Christ, with all them that love Him; so do we. Ye lament and bewail our sad divisions; so do we. Ye reject the doctrines and commandments of men that ye may keep the law of Christ; so do we. Ye believe the alone sufficiency of His word; so do we. Ye believe that the word itself ought to be our rule and not any human explication of it; so do we. Ye believe that no man has a right to judge, to exclude or reject, his professing Christian brother, except in so far as he stands condemned, or rejected, by the express letter of the law; so do we. Ye believe that the great fundamental law of unity and love ought not to be violated to make way for exalting human opinions to an equality with express revelation, by making them articles of faith and terms of communion; so do we. Ye sincere and impartial followers of Jesus, friends of truth and peace, we dare not, we cannot, think otherwise of you; it would be doing violence to your character; it would be inconsistent with your prayers and profession so to do. We shall therefore have *your* hearty concurrence. But if any of our dear brethren, from whom we should expect better things, should through weakness or prejudice be in any thing otherwise minded than we have ventured to suppose, we charitably hope that, in due time, God will reveal even this unto them. Only let such neither refuse to come to the light nor yet through prejudice, reject it, when it shines upon them. Let them rather seriously consider what we have thus most seriously and respectfully submitted to their consideration, weigh every sentiment in the balance of the sanctuary, as in the sight of God, with earnest prayer for and humble reliance upon His Spirit, and not in the spirit of self-sufficiency and party zeal; and in so doing, we rest assured, the consequence will be happy, both for their own, and the Church's peace. Let none imagine that, in so saying, we arrogate to ourselves a degree of intelligence superior to our brethren, much less superior to mistake; so far from this, our confidence is entirely founded upon the express scripture and matter of fact evidence of the things referred to; which may nevertheless, through inattention, or prejudice, fail to produce their proper effect; as has been the case with respect to some of the most evident truths in a thousand instances. But 'charity thinketh no evil' and we are far from surmising, though we must speak. To warn even against possible evils is certainly no breach of charity, as to be confident of the certainty of some things is no just argument of presumption. We by no means claim the approbation of our brethren as to any thing we have suggested for promoting the sacred cause of Christian unity, farther than it carries its own evidence along with it; but we humbly claim a fair investigation of the subject and solicit the assistance of our brethren for carrying into effect what we have thus weakly attempted. It is our consolation, in the mean time, that the desired event, as certain as it will be happy and glorious, admits of no dispute, however we may hesitate, or differ, about the proper means of promoting it. All we shall venture to say as to this, is that we trust we have taken the proper ground, at least; if we have not, we despair of finding it elsewhere. For if, holding fast in profession and practice whatever is expressly revealed and enjoined in the divine standard, does not, under the promised influence of the divine Spirit, prove an adequate basis for promoting and maintaining unity, peace and purity, we utterly despair of attaining those invaluable privileges by adopting the standard of any party. To advocate the cause of unity while espousing the interests of a party would appear as absurd, as for this country to take part with either of the belligerents in the present awful struggle, which has convulsed and is convulsing the nations, in order to maintain her neutrality and secure her peace. Nay, it would be adopting the very means by which the bewildered Church has, for hundreds of years past, been rending and dividing herself into fractions; for Christ's sake and for the truth's sake; though the first and foundation truth of our Christianity is union with Him, and the very next to it in order, union with each other in Him; 'that we receive each other, as Christ has also received us, to the glory of God.' 'For this is His commandment that we believe in His Son Jesus Christ, and love one another, as he gave us commandment. And he that keepeth His commandments dwelleth in Him, and He in him; and hereby we know that He dwelleth in us, by the spirit which He hath given us', even the spirit of faith, and of love, and of a sound mind. And surely this should suffice us. But how to love and receive our brother, as we believe and hope Christ has received both him and us, and yet refuse to hold communion with him is, we confess, a mystery too deep for us. If this be the way that Christ hath received us, then woe is unto us. We do not here intend a professed brother transgressing the expressed letter of the law, and refusing to be reclaimed. Whatever may be our charity in such a case, we have not sufficienty evidence that Christ hath received him, or that he hath received Christ as his teacher and Lord. To adopt means, then, apparently subversive of the very end proposed, means which the experience of ages has evinced successful only in overthrowing the visible interests of Christianity, in counteracting, as far as possible, the declared intention, the expressed command of its Divine Author, would appear in no wise a prudent measure for removing and preventing those evils. To maintain unity and purity has always been the plausible pretence of the compilers and abettors of human systems, and we believe in many instances their sincere intention: but have they at all answered the end? Confessedly, demonstrably, they have not, no not even in the several parties which have most strictly adopted them, much less to the catholic professing body. Instead of her catholic, constitutional unity and purity, what does the Church present us with, at this day, but a catalogue of sects and sectarian systems, each binding its respective party, by the most sacred and solemn engagements, to continue as it is to the end of the world; at least this is confessedly the case with many of them. What a sorry substitute these, for Christian unity and love! On the other hand, what a mercy is it, that no human obligation that man can come under is valid against the truth. When the Lord the healer, descends upon His people, to give them a discovery of the nature and tendency of those artificial bonds, wherewith they have suffered themselves to be bound in their dark and sleepy condition, they will no more be able to hold them in a state of sectarian bondage, than the withs and cords with which the Philistines bound Samson were able to retain him their prisoner; or, than the bonds of anti-Christ were, to hold in captivity the fathers of the Reformation. May the Lord soon open the eyes of His people to see these things in their true light, and excite them to come up out of their wilderness condition, out of this Babel of confusion, leaning upon their Beloved, and embracing each other in Him, holding fast the unity of the spirit in the bonds of peace. This gracious unity and unanimity in Jesus would afford the best external evidence of their union with Him and of their conjoint interest in the Father's love. 'By this shall all men know that ye are my disciples,' saith he, 'if ye have love one to another.' And 'this is My commandment that ye love one another as I have loved you; that ye also love one another.' And again, 'Holy Father, keep through Thine own name, those whom Thou has given Me that they may be one as We are,' even 'all that shall believe in Me, that they all may be one, as thou Father art in Me and I in Thee, that they also may be one in us; that the world may believe that Thou has sent Me. And the glory which thou gavest Me, I have given them, that they may be one, even as we are one; I in them and Thou in Me, that they may be made perfect in Me; and that the world may know that thou hast sent Me, and hast loved them, as thou hast loved Me.' May the Lord hasten it in His time. Farewell.

Peace be with all them that love our Lord Jesus Christ in sincerity. Amen.

Thos. Campbell, Secretary
Thos. Acheson, Treasurer

Appendix

To prevent mistakes, we beg to leave to subjoin the following explanations. As to what we have done, our reasons for so doing, and the grand object we would desire to see accomplished, all these, we presume, are sufficiently declared in the foregoing pages. As to what we intend to do in our associate capacity, though expressly and definitely declared, yet these, perhaps, might be liable to some misconstruction.

First, then, we beg leave to assure our brethren that we have no intention to interfere, either directly or indirectly, with the peace and order of the settled Churches, by directing any ministerial assis- tance with which the Lord may please to favour us to make inroads upon such; or by endeavouring to erect Churches out of Churches, to distract and divide congregations. We have no nostrum, no pecu- liar discovery of our own to propose to fellow-Christians, for the fancied importance of which they should become followers of us. We propose to patronize nothing but the inculcating of the express word of God, either as to matter of faith or practice, but every one that has a Bible, and can read it, can read this for himself. Therefore, we have nothing new.

Neither do we pretend to acknowledge persons to be ministers of Christ, and, at the same time, consider it our duty to forbid or discourage people to go to hear them, merely because they may hold some things disagreeable to us; much less to encourage their people to leave them on that account. And such do we esteem all who preach a free, unconditional salvation through the blood of Jesus to perishing sinners of every description, and who manifestly connect with this a life of holiness and pastoral diligence in the performance of all the duties of the sacred office, according to the Scriptures, of even all of whom, as to all appearance, it may be truly said to the objects of their charge: 'They seek not *yours* but *you.*' May the good Lord prosper all such, by whatever name they are called, and hasten that happy period when Zion's watchmen shall see eye to eye, and all be called by the same name. *Such*, then have nothing to fear from our associations, were our resources equal to our utmost wishes. But all others we esteem as hirelings, as idle shepherds, and should be glad to see the Lord's flock delivered from their mouth, according to his promise. Our principal and proper design, then, with respect to ministerial assistants, such as we have described in our fifth resolution, is to direct their attention to those place where there is manifest need for their labours; and many such places there are; would to God it were in our power to supply them.

As to creeds and confessions, although we may appear to our brethren to oppose them, yet this is to be understood only in so far as they oppose the unity of the Church, by containing sentiments not expressly revealed in the word of God; or, by the way of using them, become the instruments of a human or implicit faith, or oppress the weak of God's heritage. Where they are liable to none of these objections, we have nothing against them. It is the *abuse* and not the *lawful use* of such complications that we oppose. See Proposition 7.

Our intention, therefore, with respect to all the Churches of Christ, is perfectly amicable. We heartily wish their reformation, but by no means their hurt or confusion. Should any affect to say that our coming forward as we have done in advancing and publishing such things, has a manifest tendency to distract and divide the Churches, or to make a new party, we treat it as a confident and groundless assertion, and must suppose they have not duly considered, or, at least, not well understood the subject.

All we shall say to this at present, is, that the Divine word be not the standard of a party, then are we not a party principle, then are we not a party, for we have adopted no other. If to maintain its alone sufficiency be not a party principle, then we are not a party. If to justify this principle by our practice, in making a rule of it, and of *it alone*, and not of our own opinions, nor of those of others, be not a party principle, then are we not a party. If to propose and practice neither more or less than it expressly reveals and enjoying be not a partial business, then are we not a party. These are the very sentiments we have approved and recommended as a society formed for the express purpose of promoting Christian unity, in opposition to a party spirit.

Should any tell us that to do these things is impossible without the intervention of human reason and opinion, we humbly thank them for the discovery. But who ever thought otherwise? Were we not rational subjects, and of course capable of understanding and forming opinions, would it not evidently appear that, to us, revelation of any kind would be quite useless, even suppose it as evident as mathematics?

We pretend not, therefore, to divest ourselves of reason, that we may become quite inoffensive, and peaceable Christians; nor yet, of any of its proper and legitimate operations upon Divinely revealed truths. We only pretend to assert, what every one that pretends to reason must acknowledge, namely, that there is a manifest distinction between an express Scripture declaration, and the conclusion or inference which may be deduced from it; and that the former may be clearly understood, even where the latter is but imperfectly if at all perceived; and that we are at least as certain of the declaration as we can be of the conclusion we drew from it; and that after, all, the conclusion ought not to be exalted above the premises, so as to make void the declaration for the sake of establishing our own conclusion; and that, therefore, the express commands to preserve and maintain inviolate Christian unity and love, ought not to be set aside to make way for exalting our inferences above the express authority of God.

Our inference, upon the whole, is, that where a professing Christian brother opposes or refuses nothing either in faith or practice, for which there can be expressly produced a 'Thus saith the Lord,' that we ought not to reject him because he cannot see with our eyes as to matters of human inference, of private judgment. 'Through thy knowledge shall the weak brother perish? How walkest thou not charitably?' Thus we reason, thus we conclude, to make no conclusion of our own, nor of any other fallible fellow-creature, a rule of faith or duty to our brother. Whether we refuse reason, then, or abuse it, in our so doing, let our brethren judge. But, after all, we have only ventured to suggest what, in other words, the apostle has expressly taught; namely, that the strong ought to bear with the infirmities of the weak, and not to please themselves; that we ought to receive him that is weak in the faith, because God has received him. In a word, that we ought to receive one another, as Christ has also received us to the glory of God. We dare not, therefore, patronize the rejection of God's dear children, because they may not be able to see alike in matters of human inference – of private opinion; and such we esteem all things not expressly revealed and enjoined in the word of God. If otherwise, we know not what private opinion means.

On the other hand should our peaceful and affectionate overture for union in truth prove offensive to any of our brethren, or occasion disturbances in any of the Churches, the blame cannot be attached to us. We have only ventured to persuade, and, if possible, to excite to the performance of an important duty – a duty equally incumbent upon us all. Neither have we pretended to dictate to *them* what *they* should do. We have only proposed what appeared to us most likely to promote the desired event, humbly submitting the whole premises to their candid and impartial investigation, to be altered, corrected, and amended, as they see cause, or to adopt any other plan that may appear more just and exceptionable.

As for ourselves, we have taken all due care, in the meantime, to take no step that might throw a stumbling-block in the way, that might prove now, or at any future period, a barrier to prevent the accomplishment of that most desirable object, either by joining to support a party, or by patronizing anything as articles of faith or duty not expressly enjoined in the Divine standard; as we are sure, whatever alterations may take place, *that* will stand. That considerable alterations must and will take place, in the standards of all the sects, before that glorious object can be accomplished, no man, that duly considers the matter, can possibly doubt.

In so far, then, we have at least endeavoured to act consistently; and with the same consistency would desire to be instrumental in erecting as many Churches as possible throughout the desolate places of God's heritage, upon the same catholic foundation, being well persuaded that every such erection will not only in the issue prove an accession to the general cause, but will also, in the meantime, be a step toward it, and of course, will reap the first-fruits of that blissful harvest that will fill the face of the world with fruit. For if the first Christian Churches, walking in the fear of the Lord in holy unity and unanimity, enjoyed the comforts of the Holy Spirit, and were increased and edified, we have reason to believe that walking in their footsteps will everywhere and at all times insure the same blessed privileges. And it is in exact conformity to their recorded and approved example, that, we through grace, would be desirous to promote the erection of Churches; and this we believe to be quite practicable, if the legible and authentic records of *their* faith and practice be handed down to *us* upon the page of New Testament Scripture; but if otherwise, we cannot help it.

Yet, even in this case, might we not humbly presume that the Lord would take the will for the deed? for if there be first a willing mind, we are told, 'it is accepted according to what a man hath, and not according to what he hath not.'

It would appear, then, that sincerely and humbly adopting this model, with an entire reliance upon promised grace, we cannot, we shall not, be disappointed. By this, at least, we shall get rid of two great evils, which, we fear, are at this day grievously provoking the Lord to plead a controversy with the Churches, we mean the taking and giving of unjust offences; judging and rejecting each other in matters wherein the Lord hath not judged, in a flat contradiction to his expressly revealed will. But, according to the principle adopted, we can neither take offence at our brother for his private opinions, if he be content to hold them as such, nor yet offend him with ours, if he do not usurp the place of the lawgiver; and even suppose he should, in this case we judge him, not for his *opinions* but for his *presumption*. 'There is one Lawgiver, who is able to save and to destroy; who are thou that judgest another?'

But further, to prevent mistakes, we beg leave to explain our meaning in a sentence or two which might possibly be misunderstood. In the first page[1] we say, that no man has a right to judge his brother, except in so far as he manifestly violates the express letter of the law. By the law here, and elsewhere, when taken in this latitude, we mean that whole revelation of faith and duty expressly declared

---

[1] See p 120 (*Ed*).

in the Divine word, taken together, or in its due connection, upon every article, and not any detached sentence. We understand it as extending to all prohibitions, as well as to all requirements. 'Add thou not unto his words, lest he reprove thee, and thou be found a liar.' We dare, therefore, neither do nor receive anything as of a Divine obligation for which there cannot be expressly produced a 'Thus saith the Lord,' either in express terms or by approved precedent. According to this rule we judge and beyond it we dare not to go.

Taking this sentiment in connection with the last clause of the fifth resolution, we are to be understood, of all matters of faith and practice, of primary and universal obligation; that is to say, of express revelation; that nothing be inculcated, as such, for which there cannot be expressly produced a 'Thus saith the Lord,' as above, without, at the same time, interfering directly or indirectly with the private judgment of any individual, which does not expressly contradict the express letter of the law, or add to the number of its institutions. Every sincere and upright Christian will understand and do the will of God, in every instance, to the best of his skill and judgment, but in the application of the general rule to particular cases there may, and doubtless will, be some variety of opinion and practice. This, we see, was actually the case in the apostolic Churches, without any breach of Christian unity; and if this was the case at the erection of the Christian Church from among Jews and Gentiles, may we not reasonably expect that it will be the same at her restoration from under her long antichristian and sectarian desolations?

With a direct reference to this state of things, and, as we humbly think, in a perfect consistency with the foregoing explanations, have we expressed ourselves in the thirty-ninth page,[2] wherein we declare ourselves ready to relinquish whatever we have hitherto received as matter of faith or practice, not expressly taught and enjoined in the word of God, so that we and our brethren might, by this mutual concession, return together to the original constitutional unity of the Christian Church, and dwell together in peace and charity. By this proposed relinquishment we are to be understood, in the first

---

[2] See p 129 (*Ed*).

instance, of our manner of holding those things, and not simply of the things themselves; for no man can relinquish his opinions and practices till once convinced that they are wrong; and this he may not be immediately, even supposing they were so. One thing, however, he may do: when not bound by an express command, he need not impose them upon others, by anywise requiring their approbation; and when this is done, the things, to them, are as good as dead, yea, as good as buried, too, being thus removed out of the way.

Has not the apostle set us a noble example of this in his pious and charitable zeal for the comfort and edification of his brother, in declaring himself ready to forego his rights (not indeed to break commandments) rather than stumble, or offend his brother? And who knows not that the Hebrew Christians abstained from certain meats, observed certain days, kept the passover, circumcised their children, etc., etc., while no such things were practised by the Gentile converts, and yet no breach of unity while they charitably forebore one with the other. But had the Jews been expressly pro- hibited, or the Gentiles expressly enjoined, by the authority of Jesus, to observe these things, could they, in such a case, have lawfully exercised this forbearance? But where no express law is, there can be no formal, no intentional, transgression, even although its implicit and necessary consequences had forbid the thing, had they been discovered.

Upon the whole, we see one thing is evident: the Lord will bear with the weaknesses, the involuntary ignorances, and mistakes of his people, though not with their presumption. Ought they not, therefore, to bear with each other – 'to preserve the unity of the Spirit in the bond of peace; forbearing one with another in love?' What says the Scripture? We say, then, the declaration referred to is to be thus understood in the first instance; though we do not say but something further is intended. For certainly we may lawfully suspend both declaration and practice upon any subject, where the law is silent; when to do otherwise must prevent the accomplish- ment of an expressly commanded and highly important duty; and such, confessedly, is the thing in question. What says the apostle? 'All things are lawful for me; but all things edify not.'

It seems then, that among unlawful things which might be forborne – that is, we humbly conceive, things not expressly commanded – the governing principle of the apostle's conduct was the edification of his brethren of the Church of God. A Divine principle this, indeed! May the Lord God infuse it into all his people. Were all those non-preceptive opinions and practices which have been maintained and exalted to the destruction of the Church's unity, counterbalanced with the breach of the express law of Christ, and the black catalogue of mischiefs which have necessarily ensued, on which side, think you, would be the preponderance? When weighed in the balance with this monstrous complex evil, would they not all appeal lighter than vanity? Who, then, would not relinquish a cent to obtain a kingdom! And here let it be noted, that it is not the renunciation of an opinion or practice as sinful that is proposed or intended, but merely a cessation from the publishing or practising it, so as to give offence; a thing men are in the habit of doing every day for their private comfort or secular emolument, where the advantage is of infinitely less importance. Neither is there here any clashing of duties, as if to forbear was a sin and also to practise was sin; the thing to be forborne being a matter of private opinion, which, though not expressly forbidden, yet are we by no means expressly commanded to practice; whereas we are expressly commanded to endeavour to maintain the unity of the Spirit in the bond of peace. And what says the apostle to the doing in hand? 'Hast thou faith,' says he; 'have it to thyself before God. Happy is the man that condemneth not himself in the thing which he alloweth.'

It may be further added, that a still higher and more perfect degree of uniformity is intended, though neither in the first nor second instance, which are but so many steps toward it; namely: the utter abolition of those minor differences, which have been greatly increased, as well as continued, by our unhappy manner of treating them, in making them the subject of perpetual strife and contention. Many of the opinions which are now dividing the Church, had they been let alone, would have been long since dead and gone; but the constant insisting upon them, as articles of faith and terms of salvation, have so beaten them into the minds of men, that, in many instances, they would as soon deny the Bible itself as give up one of those opinions. Having thus embraced contentions and preferred divisions to that constitutional unity, peace, and charity so essential to Christianity, it would appear that the Lord, in righteous judgment, has abandoned his professing people to the awful scourge of those evils; as, in an instance somewhat similar, he formerly did his highly favoured Israel. 'My people,' says he, 'would not hearken to my voice. So I gave them up to their own hearts' lusts, and they walked in their own counsels.' 'Israel hath made many altars to sin: therefore altars shall be unto him to sin.'

Thus, then, are we to be consistently understood, as fully and fairly intending, on *our* part, what we have declared and proposed to our brethren, as, to *our* apprehension, incumbent upon *them* and *us*, for putting an end forever to our sad and lamentable schisms. Should any object and say that, after all, the fullest compliance with everything proposed and intended would not restore the Church to the desired unity, as there might remain differences of opinion and practice; let such but duly consider what properly belongs to the unity of the Church, and we are persuaded this objection will vanish. Does not the visible Scriptural unity of her public profession and practice, and, under this, in the manifest charity of her members, one toward another, and not in the unity of private opinion and practice of every individual? Was not this evidently the case in the apostles' days as has been already observed? If so, the objection falls to the ground. And here let it be noted (if the hint be at all necessary), that we are speaking of the unity of the church considered as a great, visible, professing body, consisting of many co-ordinate associations; each of these, in its aggregate or associate capacity, walking by the same rule, professing and practicing the same things. That this visible Scriptural unity be preserved without corruption, or breach of charity, throughout the whole, and in every particular worshipping society or Church, is the grand desideratum – the thing strictly enjoined and greatly to be desired. An agreement in the expressly revealed will of God is the adequate and firm foundation of this unity; ardent prayer, accompanied with prudent, peaceable, and persevering exertion, in the use of all Scriptural means for accomplishing it, are the things humbly suggested and earnestly recommended to our brethren. If we have mistaken the way, their charity will put us right; but if other wise, their fidelity to Christ and his cause will excite them to come forth speedily, to assist with us in the blessed work.

After all, should any impeach us with the vague charge of Latitudinarianism (let none be startled at this gigantic term), it will prove as feeble an opponent to the glorious cause in which we, however, weak and unworthy, are professedly engaged, as the Zamzummins did of old, to prevent the children of Lot from taking possession of their inheritance. If we take no greater latitude than the Divine law allows, either in judging of persons or doctrines – either in profession or practice (and this is the very thing we humbly propose and sincerely intend), may we not unreasonably hope that such a latitude will appear, to every upright Christian, perfectly innocent and unexceptional? If this be Latitudinarianism, it must be a good thing, and, therefore, the more we have of it the better; and may be it is, for we are told, 'the commandment is exceeding broad'; and we intend to go just as far as it will suffer us, but not one hair-breadth further; so, at least, says our profession. And surely it will be time enough to condemn our practice, when it appears manifestly inconsistent with the profession we have thus precisely and explicitly made. We here refer to the whole of the foregoing premises. But were this word as bad as it is long, were it stuffed with evil from beginning to end, may be it better belongs to those that brandish it so unmercifully at their neighbours, especially if they take a greater latitude than their neighbours do, or than the Divine law allows.

Let the case, then, be fairly submitted to all that know their Bible, to all that take upon them to see with their own eyes, to judge for themselves. And here let it be observed once for all, that it is only to such we direct our attention in the foregoing pages. As for those that either cannot or will not see and judge for themselves, they must be content to follow their leaders till they come to their eyesight, or determine to make use of the faculties and means of information which God has given them; with such, in the meantime, it would be useless to reason, seeing that they either confessedly cannot see, or have completely resigned themselves to the conduct of their leaders, and are therefore determined to hearken to none but them. If there be none such, however, we are happily deceived; but, if so, we are not only persons that are thus deceived; for this is the common fault objected by almost all the parties to each other, namely, that they either cannot or will not see; and it would be hard to think they were all mistaken; the fewer there be, however, of this description, the better.

To all those, then, that are disposed to see and think for themselves, to form their judgment by the Divine word itself, and not by any human explication of it, humbly relying upon and looking for the promised assistance of Divine teaching, and not barely trusting to their own understanding – to all such do we gladly commit our cause, being persuaded that, at least, they will give it a very serious and impartial consideration, as being truly desirous to know the truth. To you, then, we appeal, in the present instance, as we have also done from the beginning. Say, we beseech you, to whom does the charge of Latitudinarianism, when taken in a bad sense (for we have supposed it may be taken in a good sense), most truly and properly belong, whether to those that will neither add nor diminish anything as to matter of faith and duty, either to or from what is expressly revealed and enjoined in the holy Scriptures, or to those who pretend to go further than this, or to set aside some of its express declarations and injunctions, to make way for their own opinions, inferences, and conclusions? Whether to those who profess their willingness to hold communion with their acknowledged Christian brethren, when they neither manifestly oppose nor contradict anything expressly revealed and enjoined in the sacred standard, or to those who reject such, when professing to believe and practice whatever is expressly revealed and enjoined therein, without, at the same time, being *alleged* much less *found* guilty, of anything to the contrary, but instead of this asserting and declaring their hearty assent and consent to everything for which there can be expressly produced a 'Thus saith the Lord,' either in express terms or by approved precedent? To which of these, think you, does the odious charge of Latitudianariansim belong? Which of them takes the greatest latitude? Whether those that expressly judge and condemn where they have no express warrant for so doing, or those that absolutely refuse so to do? And we can assure our brethren, that such things are and have been done, to our own certain knowledge, and even where we least expect it; and that it is to this discovery, as much as to many other things, that we stand indebted for that thorough conviction of the evil state of things in the Churches, which has given rise to our association.

As for our part, we dare no longer give our assent to such proceedings; we dare no longer concur in expressly asserting or declaring anything in the name of the Lord, that he has not expressly declared in his holy word. And until such time as Christians come to see the evil of doing otherwise, we see no rational ground to hope that there can be either unity, peace, purity, or prosperity, in the Church of

God. Convinced of the truth of this, we would humbly desire to be instrumental in pointing out to our fellow-Christians the evils of such conduct. And if we might venture to give our opinion of such proceedings, we would not hesitate to say, that they appear to include three great evils – evils truly great in themselves, and at the same time productive of most evil consequences.

First, to determine expressly, in the name of the Lord, when the Lord has not expressly determined, appears to us a very great evil. (See Deut.18:20). 'The prophet that shall presume to speak a word in my name, which I have not commanded him to speak, even that prophet shall die.' The apostle Paul, no doubt, well aware of this, cautiously distinguishes between his own judgment and the express injunctions of the Lord. (see I Cor. 7:25 and 40). Though, at the same time, it appears that he was as well convinced of the truth and propriety of his declarations, and of the concurrence of the Holy Spirit with his judgment, as any of our modern determiners may be; for 'I think,' said he, 'that I have the Spirit of God': and we doubt much, if the best of them could honestly say more than this; yet we see that, with all this, he would not bind the Church with his conclusions; and, for this very reason, as he expressly tells us, because, as to the matter on hand, he had no commanding of the Lord. He spoke by permission, and not by commandment, as one that had obtained mercy to be faithful, and therefore would not forge his Master's name by affixing it to his own conclusions, saying, 'The Lord saith, when the Lord had not spoken.'

A second evil is, not only judging our brother to be absolutely wrong, because he differs from our opinions, but more especially, our judging him to be a transgressor of the law in so doing, and, of course, treating him as such by censuring or otherwise exposing him to contempt, or, at least, preferring ourselves before him in our own judgment, saying, as it were, Stand by, I am holier than thou.

A third and still more dreadful evil is, when we not only, in this kind of way, judge and set at naught our brother, but, moreover, proceed as a Church, acting and judging in the name of Christ, not only to determine that our brother is wrong because he differs from our determinations, but also, in connection with this, proceed so far as to determine the merits of the cause by rejecting him, or casting him out of the Church, as unworthy of a place in her communion, and thus, as far as in our power, cutting him off from the kingdom of heaven. In proceeding thus, we not only declare, that, in our judgment, our brother is in an error, which we may sometimes do in a perfect consistence with charity, but we also take upon us to judge, as acting in the name and by the authority of Christ, that his error cuts him off from salvation; that continuing such, he has no inheritance in the kingdom of Christ and of God. If not, what means our refusing him – our casting him out of the Church, which is the kingdom of God in this world?

For certainly, if a person have no right, according to the Divine word, to a place in the Church of God upon earth (which we say he has not, by thus rejecting him), he can have none to a place in the Church in heaven – unless we should suppose that those whom Christ by his word rejects here, he will nevertheless receive hereafter. And surely it is by the word that every Church pretends to judge; and it is by this rule, in the case before us, that the person in the judgment of the Church stands rejected.

Now is not this, to all intents and purposes, determining the merits of the cause? Do we not conclude that the person's error cuts him off from all ordinary possibility of salvation, by thus cutting him off from a place in the Church, out of which there is no ordinary possibility of salvation? Does he not henceforth become to us as a heathen man and a publican? Is he not reckoned among the number of those that are without, whom God judgeth? If not, what means such a solemn determination? Is it anything or is it nothing, for a person to stand rejected by the Church of God?

If such rejection confessedly leave the man still in the same safe and hopeful state as to his spiritual interests, then, indeed, it becomes a matter of mere indifference; for as to his civil and natural privileges, it interferes not with them. But the Scripture gives us a very different view of the matter; for there we see that those that stand justly rejected by the Church on earth, have no room to hope for a place in the Church of heaven. 'What ye bind on earth shall be bound in heaven' is the awful sanction of the Church's judgment, in justly rejecting any person. Take away this, and it has no sanction at all. But the Church rejecting, always pretends to have acted justly in so doing, and, if so, whereabouts does it confessedly leave the person rejected, if not in a state of damnation? that is to say, if it acknowledge itself to be a Church of Christ, and to have acted justly?

If, after all, any particular Church acting thus should refuse the foregoing conclusion, by saying: We meant no such thing concerning the person rejected; we only judged him unworthy of a place among *us*, and therefore put him away, but there are other churches that may receive him; we would be almost tempted to ask such a Church, if those other Churches be Churches of Christ, and if so, pray what does it account itself? Is it anything more or better than a Church of Christ? And whether, if those other Churches do their duty as faithful Churches, any of them would receive the person it had rejected? If it be answered that, in acting faithfully, none of those other Churches either could or would receive him, then, confessedly, in the judgment of this particular Church, the person ought to be universally rejected; but if otherwise, it condemns itself of having acted unfaithfully, nay cruelly, toward a Christian brother, a child of God, in thus rejecting him from the heritage of the Lord, in thus cutting him off from his Father's house, as the unnatural brethren did the beloved Joseph.

But even suppose some one or other of those unfaithful Churches should receive the outcast, would their unfaithfulness in so doing nullify, in the judgment of this more faithful Church, its just and faithful decision in rejecting him? If not, then confessedly, in its judgment, the person still remains under the influence of its righteous sentence, debarred from the kingdom of heaven; that is to say, if it believe the Scriptures, that what it has righteously done upon earth is ratified in heaven. We see no way that a Church acting thus can possibly get rid of this *awful conclusion*, except it acknowledges that the person it has rejected from its communion still has a right to the communion of the Church; but if it acknowledge this, whereabout does it leave itself, in thus shutting out a fellow-Christian, an acknowledged brother, a child of God? Do we find any parallel for such conduct in the inspired records, except in the case of Diotrephes, of whom the apostle says, 'Who loveth to have the pre-eminence among them, receiveth us not, prating against us with malicious words: and not content therewith, neither doth he himself receive the brethren, and forbiddeth them that would, and casteth them out of the Church.'

But, further, suppose another Church should receive this castaway, this person which this faithful Church supposed itself to have righteously rejected, would not the Church so doing incur the displeasure, nay even the *censure* of the Church that had rejected him?

158

and, we should think, justly too if he deserved to be rejected. And would not this naturally produce a schism between the Churches? Or, if it be supposed that a schism did already exist, would not this manifestly tend to perpetuate and increase it? If one Church, receiving those whom another puts away, will not be productive of schism, we must confess we cannot tell what would.

That Church, therefore, must surely act very schismatically, very unlike a Church of Christ, which necessarily presupposes or produces schism in order to shield an oppressed fellow-Christian from the dreadful consequences of its unrighteous proceedings. And is not this confessedly the case with every Church which rejects a person from its communion while it acknowledges him to be a fellow-Christian; and, in order to excuse this piece of cruelty, says he may find refuge some place else, some other Church may receive him? For, as we have already observed, if no schism did already exist, one Church receiving those whom another has rejected must certainly make one. The same evils also will as justly attach to the conduct of an individual who refuses or breaks communion with a Church because it will not receive or make room for his private opinions or self-devised practices in its public profession and managements; for does he not, in this case, actually take upon him to judge the Church which he thus rejects as unworthy of the communion of Christians? And is not this, to all intents and purposes, declaring it, in his judgment, excommunicate, or at least worthy of excommunication?

Thus have we briefly endeavoured to show our brethren what evidently appears to us to be the heinous nature and dreadful consequences of that truly latitudinarian principle and practice which is the bitter root of almost all our divisions, namely, the imposing of our private opinions upon each other as articles of faith or duty, introducing them into the public profession and practice of the Church, and acting upon them as if they were the express law of Christ, by judging and rejecting our brethren that differ from us in those things, or at least by *so* retaining them in our public profession and practice that our brethren cannot join with us, or we with them, without becoming actually partakers in those things which they or we cannot in conscience approve, and which the word of God nowhere expressly enjoins upon us.

To cease from all such things, by simply returning to the original standard of Christianity, the profession and practice of the primitive Church, as expressly exhibited upon the sacred page of New Testament Scripture, is the only possible way that we can perceive to get rid of those evils. And we humbly think that a uniform agreement in *that* for the preservation of charity would be infinitely preferable to our contentions and divisions; nay, that such a uniformity is the very thing that the Lord requires of the worship, discipline, and government of the Christian Church. Let *us* do as we are there expressly told *they* did, say as *they* said; that is, profess and practice as therein expressly enjoined by precept and precedent, in every possible instance, after *their* approved example; and in doing so we shall realize and exhibit all that unity and uniformity that the primitive Church possessed, or that the law of Christ requires. But if, after all, our brethren can point out a better way to regain and preserve that Christian unity and charity expressly enjoined upon the Church of God, we shall thank them for the discovery, and cheerfully embrace it.

Should it still be urged that this would open a wide door to latitudinarianism, seeing all that profess Christianity profess to receive the holy Scriptures, and yet differ so widely in their religious sentiments, we say, let them profess what they will, their difference in religious profession and practice originates in their departure from what is expressly revealed and enjoined, and not in their strict and faithful conformity to it, which is the thing we humbly advise for putting an end to those differences. But you may say, Do they not already all agree in the letter, though differing so far in sentiment? However, this may be, have they all agreed to make the letter their rule, or, rather to make it the subject-matter of their profession and practice? Surely not, or else they would all profess and practise the same thing.

Is it not as evident as the shining light that the Scriptures exhibit but one and the self-same subject-matter of profession and practice, at all times and in all places, and that, therefore, to say as it declares, and to do as it prescribes in all its holy precepts, its approved and imitable examples, would unite the Christian Church in a holy sameness of profession and practice throughout the whole world? By the Christian Church throughout the world, we mean the aggregate of such professors as we have described in Propositions 1 and 8, even all that mutually acknowledge each other as Christians, upon the manifest evidence of their faith, holiness, and charity. It is such only we intend when we urge the necessity of Christian unity. Had only such been all along recognised as the genuine subjects of our holy religion, there would not, in all probability, have been so much apparent need for human formulas to preserve an external formality of professional unity and soundness in the faith, but artificial and superficial characters need artificial means to train and unite them.

A manifest attachment to our Lord Jesus Christ in faith, holiness and charity, was the original criterion of Christian character, the distinguishing badge of our holy profession, the foundation and cement of Christian unity. But now, alas! and long since, an external name, a mere educational formality of sameness in the profession of a certain standard or formula of human fabric, with a very moderate degree of what is called morality, forms the bond and foundation, the root and reason of ecclesiastical unity.

Take away from such the technicalness of the profession, the shibboleth of party, and what have they more? What have they left to distinguish and hold them together? As for the Bible, they are but little beholden to it, they have learned little from it, they know little about it, and therefore depend as little upon it. Nay, they will even tell you it would be of no use to them without their formula; they could not know a Papist from a Protestant by *it*; that merely by *it* they could neither keep themselves nor the Church right for a single week. You might preach to them what you please, they could not distinguish truth from error. Poor people, it is no wonder they are so fond of their formula! Therefore, they that exercise authority upon them and tell them what they are to believe and what they are to do, are called benefactors.

These are the reverend and right authors, upon whom they *can* and *do* place a more entire and implicit confidence than upon the holy apostles and prophets; those plain, honest, unassuming men, who would never venture to say or do anything in the name of the Lord without an express revelation from Heaven, and there-fore were never distinguished by the venerable titles of Rabbi or Reverend, but just simple Paul, John, Thomas, etc. *These* were but servants. They did not assume to legislate, and, therefore, neither assumed nor received any honorary titles among men, but merely such as were descriptive of their office.

And how, we beseech you, shall this gross and prevalent corruption be purged out of the visible professing Church but by a radical reform, but by returning to the original simplicity, the primitive purity of the Christian institution, and, of course, taking up things just as we find them upon the sacred page. And who is there that knows anything of the present state of the Church who does not perceive that it is greatly overrun with the aforesaid evils? Or who that reads his Bible, and receives the impressions it must necessarily produce upon the receptive mind by the statements it exhibits, does not perceive that such a state of things is as distinct from the genuine Christianity as oil is from water?

On the other hand, is it not equally as evident that not one of all the erroneous tenets and corrupt practices which have so defamed and corrupted the public profession and practice of Christianity, could ever have appeared in the world had men kept close by the express letter of the Divine Law, had they thus held fast that form of sound words contained in the holy Scriptures, and considered in their duty so to do, unless they blame those errors and corruptions upon the very form and expression of the Scriptures, and say that, taken in their letter and connection, they immediately, and at first sight, as it were exhibit the picture they have drawn. Should any be so bold as to assert this, let them produce their performance, the original is at hand; and let them show us line for line, expression for expression, precept and precedent for practice, without the torture of criticism, inference, or conjecture, and then we shall honestly blame the whole upon the Bible, and thank those that will give us an expurged edition of it, call it constitution, or formula, or what you please, that will not be liable to lead the simple, unlettered world into those gross mistakes, those contentions, schisms, excommunications, and persecutions which have proved so detrimental and scandalous to our holy religion.

Should it be further objected, that even this strict literal uniformity would neither infer nor secure unity of sentiment; it is granted that, in a certain degree, it would not; nor, indeed, is there anything either in Scripture of the nature of things that should induce us to expect an entire unity of sentiment in the present imperfect state. The Church may, and we believe will, come to such a Scriptural unity of faith and practice, that there will be no schism in the body, no self-preferring sect of professed and acknowledged Christians rejecting and excluding their brethren. *This* cannot be, however, till the offensive and excluding causes be removed; and every one knows what *these* are. But that all the members should have the same identical views of all Divinely revealed truths, or that there should be no difference of opinion among them, appears to us morally impossible, all things considered. Nor can we conceive what desirable purpose such a unity of sentiment would serve, except to render useless some of those gracious self-denying and compassionate precepts of mutual sympathy and forbearance which the word of God enjoins upon his people.

Such, then is the imperfection of our present state. Would to God it might prove, as it ought, a just and humbling counterbalance to our pride! Then, indeed, we would judge one another no more about such matters. We would rather be conscientiously cautious to give no offence; to put no stumbling-block or occasion to fall in our brother's way. We would then no longer exalt our own opinions and inferences to an equality with express revelation, by condemning and rejecting our brother for differing with us in those things.

But although it be granted that the uniformity we plead for would not secure unity of sentiment, yet we should suppose that it would be as efficacious for that purpose as any human expedient or substitute whatsoever. And here we would ask: Have all or any of those compilations been able to prevent divisions, to heal breaches, or to produce and maintain unity of sentiment even among those who have most firmly and solemnly embraced them? We appeal for this to the history of all the Churches, and to the present divided state of the Church at large. What good, then, have those divisive expedients accomplished, either to the parties that have adopted them, or to the Church universal, which might not have been as well secured by holding fast in professions and practice that form of sound words contained in the Divine standard, without, at the same time, being liable to any of those dangerous and destructive consequences which have necessarily ensued upon the present mode?

Or, will any venture to say that the Scriptures, thus kept in their proper place, would not have been amply sufficient, under the promised influence of the Divine Spirit, to have produced all that unity of sentiment which is necessary to a life of faith and holiness; and also to have preserved the faith and worship of the Church as pure from mixture and error as the Lord intended, or as the present imperfect state of his people can possible admit? We should tremble to think that any Christian should say that they would not. And if to use them thus would be sufficient for those purposes, why resort to other expedients; to expedients which, from the beginning to this day, have proved utterly insufficient; nay, to expedients which have always produced the very contrary effects, as experience testifies.

Let none here imagine that we set any certain limits to the Divine intention, or to the greatness of his power when we thus speak, as if a certain degree of purity from mixture and error were not designed for the Church in this world, or attainable by his people upon earth except in so far as respects the attainment of an angelic or unerring perfection, much less that we mean to suggest that a very moderate degree of unity and purity should content us. We only take it for granted that such a state of perfection is neither intended nor attainable in this world, as will free the Church from all those weaknesses, mistakes and mismanagements from which she will be completely exempted in heaven, however sound and upright she may now be in her profession, intention, and practice.

Neither let any imagine that we here or elsewhere suppose or intend to assert that human standards are intentionally set up in competition with the Bible, much less in opposition to it. We fairly understand and consider them as human expedients, or as certain doctrinal declarations of the sense in which the compilers understood the Scriptures, designed and embraced for the purpose of promoting and securing that desirable unity and purity which the Bible alone, without those helps, would be insufficient to maintain and secure. If this be not the sense of those that receive and hold them, for the aforesaid purpose, we should be glad to know what it is. It is, however, in this very sense that we take them up when we complain of them, as not only unsuccessful, but also as unhappy expedients, producing the very contrary effects.

And even suppose it were doubtful whether or not those helps have produced divisions, one thing, at least, is certain, they have not been able to prevent them; and now, that divisions do exist, it is as certain that they have no fitness nor tendency to heal them, but the very contrary, as fact and experience clearly demonstrate. What shall we do, then, to heal our divisions? We must certainly take some other way than the present practice, if they ever be healed; for it expressly says, they must and shall be perpetuated forever.

Let all the enemies of Christianity say Amen; but let all Christians continually say: Forbid it, O Lord. May the good Lord subdue the corruptions and heal the divisions of his people. Amen and amen.

After all that has been said, some of our timid brethren may, possibly, still object, and say: we fear that without the intervention of some definite creed or formula, you will justly incur the censure of latitudinarianism: for how otherwise detect and exclude Arians, Socinians, etc? To such we would reply, that if to profess, inculcate, and practice neither more nor less, neither anything else nor otherwise than the Divine word expressly declares respecting the entire subject of faith and duty, and simply to rest in *that*, as the expression of our faith and rule of our practice, will not amount to the profession and practical exhibition of Arianism, Socinianism, etc., but merely to one and the self-same thing, whatever it may be called, then is the *ground* that we have taken, the *principle* that we advocate, in nowise chargeable with latitudinarianism.

Should it be still further objected that all these sects, and many more, profess to receive the Bible, to believe it to be the word of God, and, therefore, will readily profess to believe and practise whatever is revealed and enjoined therein, and yet each will understand in his own way, and of course practise accordingly; nevertheless, according to the plan proposed, you receive them all. We would ask, then, do all these profess and practise neither more nor less than what we read in the Bible – than what is expressly revealed and enjoined therein? If so, they all profess and practise the same thing, for the Bible exhibits but one and the self-same thing to all. Or is it their own inferences and opinions that they, in reality, profess and practise? If so, then upon the ground that we have taken they stand rejected, as condemned of themselves, for thus professing one thing when in fact and reality they manifestly practise another.

But perhaps you will say, that although a uniformity in profession, and it may be in practise too, might thus be produced, yet still it would amount to no more than a mere uniformity in words, and in the external formalities of practice, while the persons thus professing and practising might each entertain his own sentiments, how different soever these might be. Our reply is, if so, they could hurt nobody but themselves. Besides, if persons thus united professed and practised all the same things pray, who could tell that they entertained different sentiments, or even in justice suppose it, unless they gave some evident intimation of it? which, if they did, would justly expose them to censure or to rejection, if they repented not; seeing the offence, in this case, must amount to nothing less than an express violation of the expressly revealed will of God – to a manifest transgression of the express letter of the law; for we have declared, that except in such a case, no man, in our judgment, has a right to judge, that is, to condemn or reject his professing brother. Here, we presume, there is no greater latitude assumed or allowed on either side than the law expressly determines.

But we would humbly ask, if a professed agreement in the terms of any standard be not liable to the very same objection? If, for instance, Arians, Socinians, Arminians, Calvinists, Antinomians, etc., might not all subscribe the Westminster Confession, the Athanasian Creed, or the doctrinal articles of the Church of England. If this be denied, we appeal to historical facts; and, in the meantime, venture to assert, that such things are and have been done.

Or, will any say, that a person might not with equal ease, honesty, and consistency, be an Arian or a Socinian in his heart while subscribing the Westminster Confession or the Athanasian Creed, as while making his unqualified profession to believe everything that the Scriptures declare concerning Christ? to put all that confidence in him, and to ascribe all that glory, honour, thanksgiving, and praise to him, professed and ascribed to him in the Divine word? If you say not, it follows, of undeniable consequence, that the wisdom of men, in those compilations, has effected what the Divine Wisdom either could not, would not, or did not do, in that all-perfect and glorious revelation of his will, contained in the Holy Scriptures. Happy emendation! Blessed expedient! Happy, indeed, for the Church that Athanasius arose in the fourth century to perfect what the holy apostles and prophets had left in such a rude and unfinished state. But if, after all, the Divine Wisdom did not think proper to do anything more, or anything else than is already done in the sacred oracles, to settle and determine those important points, who can say that he determined such a thing should be done afterward? Or has he anywhere given us any intimation of such an intention?

Let it here be carefully observed that the question before us is about human standards designed to be subscribed, or otherwise solemnly acknowledged, for the preservation of ecclesiastical unity and purity, and therefore, of course, by no means applies to the many excellent performances, for the Scriptural elucidation and defence of Divinely revealed truths and other instructive purposes. These, we hope, according to their respective merit, we as highly esteem, and as thankfully receive, as our brethren. But further, with respect to unity of sentiment, even suppose it ever so desirable, it appears highly questionable whether such a thing can at all be secured, by any expedient whatsoever, especially if we consider that it necessarily presupposes in so far a unity or sameness of understanding. Or, will any say, that from the youth of seventeen to the man of fourscore – from the illiterate peasant, up to the learned prelate – all the legitimate members of the Church entertain the same sentiments under their respective formulas? If not, it is still but a mere verbal agreement, a mere show of unity. They say an amen to the same forms of speech, or of sound words, as they are called, without having, at the same time, the same views of the subject; or, it may be, without any determinate views of it at all. And, what is still worse, this profession is palmed upon the world, as well as upon the too credulous professors themselves, for unity of sentiment, for soundness in the faith; when in a thousand instances, they have, properly speaking, no faith at all; that is to say, if faith necessarily presupposes a true and satisfactory conviction of the Scriptural evidence and certainty of the truth of the propositions we profess to believe.

A cheap and easy orthodoxy this, to which we may attain by committing to memory a catechism, or professing our approbation of a formula, made ready to our hand, which we may or may not have once read over; or even if we have, yet may not have been able to read it so correctly and intelligently as to clearly understand one single paragraph from beginning to end, much less to compare it with, to search and try it by the holy Scriptures, to see if these things be so. A cheap and easy orthodoxy this, indeed, to which a person may thus attain, without so much as turning over a single leaf of this Bible, whereas Christ knew no other way of leading us to the knowledge of himself, at least has prescribed no other, but by searching the Scriptures, with reliance upon his Holy Spirit.

A person may, however, by this short and easy method, become as orthodox as the apostle Paul (if such superficial professions, such mere hearsay verbal repetitions can be called orthodoxy) without ever once consulting the Bible, or so much as putting up a single petition for the Holy Spirit to guide him into all truth, to open his understanding to know the Scriptures; for, his form of sound words truly believed, if it happen to be right, must, without more ado, infallibly secure his orthodoxy. Thrice happy expedient! But is there no latitudinarianism in all this? Is not this taking a latitude, in devising ways and means for accomplishing Divine and saving purposes, which the Divine law has nowhere prescribed, for which the Scriptures nowhere afford us either precept or precedent? Unless it can be shown that making human standards to determine the doctrine, worship, discipline, and government of the Church for the purpose of preserving her unity and purity, and requiring an approbation of them as a term of communion is a Scripture institution.

Far be it from us, in the meantime, to allege that the Church should not make every Scriptural exertion in her power to preserve her unity and purity; to teach and train up her members in the knowledge of all divinely revealed truth; or to say that the evils above complained of attach to all that are in the habit of using the aforesaid helps; or that this wretched state of things, however, general, necessarily proceeds from the legitimate use of such; but rather and entirely from the abuse of them, which is the very and thing that we are all along opposing when we allude to those subordinate standards. (An appellation this, by the by, which appears to us highly paradoxical, if not utterly inconsistent, and full of confusion.)

But, however this may be, we are by no means to be understood as at all wishing to deprive our fellow-Christians of any necessary and possible assistance to understand the Scriptures, or to come to a distinct and particular knowledge of every truth they contain, for which purpose the Westminster Confession and Catechism may, with many other excellent performances, prove eminently useful. But, having served ourselves of these, let our profiting appear to all, by our manifest acquaintance with the Bible; by making our profession of faith and obedience; by declaring its Divine dictates, in which we acquiesce, as the subject-matter and rule of both; in our ability to take the Scripture in its connection upon these subjects, so as to understand one part of it by the assistance of another; and in manifesting our self-knowledge, our knowledge of the way of salvation and of the mystery of the Christian life, in the express light of Divine revelation, by a direct and immediate reference to, and correct repetition of what it declares upon those subjects.

We take it for granted that no man either knows God, or himself, or the way of salvation, but in so far as he has heard and understood his voice upon those subjects, as addressed to him in the Scriptures, and that, therefore, whatever he has heard and learned of a saving nature, is contained in the express terms of the Bible. If so, in the express terms, in and by which 'he hath heard and learned of the Father'; let him declare it. This by no means forbids him to use helps, but, we humbly presume, will effectually prevent him from resting either in them or upon them, which is the evil so justly complained of; from taking up with the directory instead of the object to which it directs. Thus will the whole subject of his faith and duty, in so far as he has attained, be expressly declared in a 'Thus saith the Lord.' and is it not worthy of remark, that of whatever use other books may be, to direct and lead us to the Bible, or to prepare and assist us to understand it, yet the Bible never directs us to any book but itself.

When we come forward, we, as Christians, to be received by the Church, which, properly speaking, has but one book. 'For to it were committed the oracles of God,' let us hear of none else. Is it not upon the credible profession of our faith in, and obedience to its Divine contents, that the Church is bound to receive applicants for admission? And does not a profession of our faith and obedience necessarily presuppose a knowledge of the dictates we profess to believe and obey? Surely then we can declare them, and as surely, if our faith and obedience be Divine, as to the subject-matter, rule, and reason of them, it must be a 'Thus saith the Lord': if otherwise, they are merely human, being taught by the precepts of men.

In the case then before us, that is, examination for Church membership, let the question no longer be, What does any human system say of the primitive or present state of man? of the person, offices, and relations of Christ, etc., etc.? or of this, that, or the other duty? but, What says the Bible? Were this mode of procedure adopted, how much better acquainted with their Bibles would Christians be? What an important alteration would it also make in the education of youth? would it not lay all candidates for admission into the Church under the happy necessity of becoming particularly acquainted with the holy Scriptures? whereas, according to the present practice, thousands know little about them.

One thing still remains that may appear matter of difficulty or objection to some, namely, that such a close adherence to the express letter of the Divine word, as we seem to propose, for the restoration and maintenance of Christian unity, would not only interfere with the free communication of our sentiments one to another upon religious subjects, but must, of course, also necessarily interfere with the public preaching and expounding of the Scriptures for the edification of the Church. Such as feel disposed to make this objection, should justly consider that one of a similar nature, and quite as plausible, might be made to the adoption of human standards, especially when made as some of them confessedly are, 'the standard for all matters of doctrine, worship, discipline, and government.'

In such a case it might, with as much justice, at least, be objected to the adopters: You have now no more use for the Bible; you have got another book, which you have adopted as a standard for all religious purposes; you have no further use for explaining the Scriptures, either as to matter of faith or duty, for this you have confessedly done already in your standard, wherein you have determined all matters of this nature. You also profess to hold fast the form of sound words, which you have thus adopted, and therefore you must never open your mouth upon any subject in any other terms than those of your standard. In the meantime, would any of the parties which has thus adopted its respective standard, consider any of these charges just? If not, let them do as they would be done by. We must confess, however, that for our part, we cannot see how, with any shadow of consistency, some of them could clear themselves, especially of the first; that is to say, if words have any determinate meaning; for certainly it would appear almost, if not altogether incontrovertible, that a book adopted by any party as its standard for all matters of doctrine, worship, discipline, and government, must be considered as the Bible of that party.

And after all that can be said in favour of such a performance, be it called Bible, standard, or what it may, it is neither anything more nor better than the judgment or opinion of the party composing or adopting it, and, therefore, wants the sanction of a Divine authority, except in the opinion of the party which has thus adopted it. But can the opinion of any party, be it ever so respectable, give the stamp of a Divine authority to its judgments? If not, then every human standard is deficient in this leading, all-important, and indispensable property of a rule or standard for the doctrine, worship, discipline and government of the Church of God. But, without insisting further upon the intrinsic and irremediable deficiency of human standards for the above purpose (which is undeniably evident if it be granted that a Divine authority is indispensably necessary to constitute a standard or rule for Divine things, such as is the constitution and managements, the faith, and worship of the Christian Church), we would humbly ask, Would any of the parties consider as just the foregoing objections, however conclusive and well founded all or any of them may appear? We believe they would not.

And may we not with equal consistency hold fast the expressly revealed will of God, in the very terms in which it is expressed in his holy word, as the very expression of our faith and express rule of our duty, and yet take the same liberty that they do, notwithstanding their professed and steadfast adherence to their respective standards? We find they do not cease to expound, because they have already expounded, as before alleged, nor yet do they always confine themselves to the express terms of their respective standards, yet they acknowledge them to be their standards and profess to hold them fast. Yea, moreover, some of them profess, and, if we may conclude from facts, we believe each of them is disposed to defend by occasional vindications (or testimonies, as some call them) the sentiments they have adopted and engrossed in their standards, without at the same time requiring an approbation of those occasional performances as a term of communion. And what should hinder us, or any, adopting the Divine standard, as aforesaid, with equal consistency to do the same for the vindication of the Divine truths expressly revealed and enjoined therein?

To say that we cannot believe and profess the truth, understand one another, inculcate and vindicate the faith and law of Christ, or do the duties incumbent upon Christians or a Christian Church without a human standard, is not only saying that such a standard is quite essential to the very being of Christianity, and, of course, must have existed before a Church was or could be formed, but it is also saying, that without such a standard, the Bible would be quite inadequate as a rule of faith and duty, or, rather, of no use at all, except to furnish materials for such a work; whereas the Church of Ephesus, long before we have any account of the existence of such a standard, is not only mentioned, with many others, as in a state of existence, and of high attainments too, but is also commended for her vigilance and fidelity in detecting and rejecting false apostles. 'Thou hast tried them which say they are apostles, and are not, and hast found them liars.' But should any pretend to say that although such performances be not essential to the very being of the Church, yet are they highly conducive to its wellbeing and perfection. For the confutation of such assertion, we would again appeal to Church history and existing facts and leave the judicious and intelligent Christian to determine.

If after all that has been said, any should still pretend to affirm that the plan we profess to adopt and recommend is truly latitudinarian, in the worst and fullest sense of the term, inasmuch as it goes to make void all human efforts to maintain the unity and purity of the Church, by substituting a vague and indefinite approbation of the Scriptures as an alternative for creeds, confessions, and testimonies, and thereby opens a wide door for the reception of all sorts of characters and opinions into the Church. Were we not convinced by experience, that notwithstanding all that has been said, such objections would likely be made, or that some weak persons might possibly consider them as good as demonstration, especially when proceeding from highly influential characters (and there have not been wanting such in all ages to oppose, under various plausible pretences, the unity and peace of the Church), were it not for these considerations, we should content ourselves with what we have already advanced upon the whole of the subject, as being well assured *that* duly attended to, there would not be the least room for such an objection; but to prevent if possible such unfounded conclusions, or if this can not be done, to caution and assist the too credulous and unwary professor, that he may not be carried away all at once with the high-toned confidence of bold assertion, we would refer him to the overture for union in truth contained in the foregoing address.

Union in truth, among all the manifest subjects of grace and truth, is what we advocate. We carry our views of union no further than *this*, nor do we presume to recommend it upon any other principle than truth alone. Now, surely, truth is something certain and definite; if not, who will take upon him to define and determine

172

it? This we suppose God has sufficiently done already in his holy word. That men therefore truly receive and make the proper use of the Divine Word for walking together in truth and peace, in holiness and charity, is, no doubt, the ardent desire of all the genuine subjects of our holy religion. This, we see, however, they have not done, to the awful detriment and manifest subversion of what we might almost call the primary intention of Christianity.

We dare not, therefore, follow their example, nor adopt their ruinous expedients. But does it therefore follow that Christians may not, or cannot take proper steps to ascertain that desirable and preceptive unity which the Divine word requires and enjoins? Surely no; at least we have supposed no such thing; but, on the contrary, have overtured to our brethren what appears to us undeniably just and Scripturally evident, and which, we humbly think, if adopted and acted upon, would have the desired effect; adopted and acted upon, not indeed as a standard for the doctrine, worship, discipline and government of the Church, for it pretends not to determine these matters, but rather supposes the existence of a fixed and certain standard of Divine original, in which everything that the wisdom of God saw meet to reveal and determine, for *these* and all other purposes is expressly defined and determined; between the Christian and which, no medium of human determination ought to be interposed. In all this there is surely nothing like the denial of any lawful effort to promote and maintain the Church's unity, though there be a refusal of the unwarrantable interposition of an unauthorised and assuming power.

Let none imagine that we are here determining upon the merits of the overture to which, in the case before us, we find it necessary to appeal in our own defence against the injustice of the supposed charge above specified. To the judgment of our brethren have we referred that matter, and with them we leave it. All we intend, therefore, is to avail ourselves so far of what we have done, as to show that we have no intention whatsoever of substituting a vague indefinite approbation of the Scriptures as an alternative for creeds, confessions and testimonies, for the purpose of restoring the Church to her original constitutional unity and purity. In avoiding Scylla we would cautiously guard against being wrecked upon Charybdis. Extremes, we are told, are dangerous. We therefore suppose a middle way, a safe way, so plainly marked out by unerring wisdom, that if duly attended to under the Divine direction, the wayfaring men, though fools, need not err therein, and of such is the kingdom of God: 'For he hath chosen the foolish things of the world to confound the things that are wise.'

We therefore conclude it must be a plain way, a way most graciously and most judiciously adapted to the capacity of the subjects, and consequently not the way of subscribing or otherwise approving human standards as a term of admission into his Church, as a test and defence of orthodoxy, which even the compilers themselves are not always agreed about, and which nineteen out of twenty of the Lord's people cannot thoroughly understand. It must be a way very far remote from logical subtleties and metaphysical speculations, and as such we have taken it up, upon the plainest and most obvious principles of Divine revelations and common sense – the common sense, we mean, of Christians, exercised upon the plainest and most obvious truths and facts divinely recorded for their instruction.

Hence we have supposed, in the first place, the true discrimination of Christian character to consist in an intelligent profession of our faith in Christ and obedience to him in all things according to the Scriptures, the reality of which profession is manifested by the holy consistency of the tempers and conduct of the professors with the express dictates and approved examples of the Divine word. Hence we have humility, faith, piety, temperance, justice, charity, etc., professed and manifested, in the first instance, by the persons professing with self-application the convincing, humbling, encouraging, pious, temperate, just and charitable doctrines and precepts of the inspired volume, as exhibited and enforced in its holy and approved examples, and the sincerity of this profession evidently manifested by the consistency of the professor's temper and conduct with the entire subject of his profession, either by an irreprovable conformity, like good Zachariah and Elisabeth, which is of all things most desirable, or otherwise, in case of any visible failure, by an apparently sincere repentance and evident reformation.

Such professors, and such only, have we supposed to be, by common consent, truly worthy the Christian name. Ask from the one end of heaven to the other, the whole number of such intelligent and consistent professors as we intend and have described, and, we humbly presume, there will not be found one dissenting voice. They will all acknowledge, with one consent, that the true discrimination of

Christian character consists in these things, and that the radical or manifest want of any of the aforesaid properties completely destroys the character.

We have here only taken for granted what we suppose no rational professor will venture to deny; namely: that the Divine word contains an ample sufficiency upon every one of the foregoing topics to stamp the above character, if so be that the impressions which its express declarations are obviously calculated to produce be truly received; for instance, suppose a person profess to believe, with application to himself, that whole description of human depravity and wretchedness which the Scriptures exhibit of fallen man, in the express declaration and dismal examples of human wickedness therein recorded, contrasted with the holy nature, the righteous requirements, and inflexible justice of an infinitely holy, just, and jealous God, would not the subject-matter of such a profession be amply sufficient to impress the believing mind with the most profound humility, self-abhorrence, and dreadful apprehension of the tremendous effects of sin?

Again, should the person profess to believe, in connection with this, all that the Scriptures declare of the sovereign love, mercy and condescension of God toward guilty, depraved, rebellious man, as the same is manifested in Christ, and in all the gracious declarations, invitations and promises that are made in and through him for the relief and encouragement of the guilty, etc., would not all this, taken together, be sufficient to impress the believing mind with the most lively confidence, gratitude and love? Should this person, moreover, profess that delight and confidence in the Divine Redeemer – that voluntary submission to him – that worship and adoration of him which the Scriptures expressly declare to have been the habits and practice of his people, would not the subject-matter of this profession be amply sufficient to impress the believing mind with that dutiful disposition, with that gracious veneration and supreme reverence which the word of God requires? And should not all this taken together satisfy the Church, in so far, in point of profession? If not, there is no alternative but a new revelation; seeing that to deny this, is to assert that a distinct perception and sincere profession of whatever the word declares upon every point of faith and duty, is not only insufficient, as a doctrinal means, to produce a just and suitable impression in the mind of the believing subject, but is also insufficient to satisfy the Church as to a just and adequate profession; if otherwise, then it will necessarily follow, that not every sort of character, but that one sort only, is admissable upon the principle we have adopted; and that by the universal consent of all that we, at least, dare venture to call Christian, *this* is acknowledged to be, exclusively, the true Christian character.

Here, then, we have a fixed point, a certain description of character, which combines in every professing subject the Scriptural profession, the evident manifestation of humility, faith, piety, temperance, justice, and charity instructed by, and evidently answering to the entire declaration of the word upon each of those topics, which, as so many properties, serve to constitute the character. Here, we say, we have a fixed, and at the same time sweeping distinction, which, as of old, manifestly divides the whole world, however otherwise distinguished, into but two classes only. 'We know,' said the apostle, evidently speaking of such, 'that we are of God, and the whole world lieth in wickedness.'

Should it be inquired concerning the persons included in this description of character, whether they be Arminians or Calvinists, or both promiscuously huddled together? It may be justly replied, that according to what we have proposed, they can be nominally neither, and of course not both, for we call no man master on earth, for one is our Master, even Christ, and all we are brethren, the Christians by profession; and as such abstract speculation and argumentative theory make no part either of our profession or practice. Such professors, then, as we intend and have described, are just what their profession and practice make them to be; and this we hope has been Scripturally, and we might add, satisfactory defined, in so far, at least, as the limits of so brief a performance would admit. We also entertain the pleasing confidence that the plan of procedure which we have ventured to suggest, if duly attended to, if fully reduced to practice, would necessarily secure to the professing subject all the advantages of divinely revealed truth, without any liability to conceal, to diminish, or to misrepresent it, as it goes immediately to ascribe everything to God respecting his sovereignty, independence, power, wisdom, goodness, justice, truth, holiness, mercy, condescension, love, and grace, etc., which is ascribed to him in his word, as also to receive whatever it declares concerning the absolute dependence of the poor, guilty, depraved, polluted creature, upon the Divine will, power, and grace for every saving purpose; a just perception and correspondent profession of which, according to the Scriptures, is supposed to constitute that fundamental ingredient in Christian character; true evangelical humility. And so of the rest.

Having thus, we hope, Scripturally and evidently determined the character, with the proper mode of ascertaining it, to the satisfaction of all concerned, we next proceed to affirm, with the same Scriptural evidence, that among such, however situated, whether in the same or similar associations, there ought to be no schisms, no uncharitable divisions, but that they ought all mutually to receive and acknowledge each other as brethren. As to the truth of this assertion, they are all likewise agreed, without one dissenting voice. We next suggest that for this purpose they ought all to walk by the same rule, to mind and speak the same thing, etc., and that this rule is, and ought to be, the Divine standard. Here again, we presume there can be no objection; no, not a single dissenting voice.

As to the rule itself, we have ventured to allege that the New Testament is the proper and immediate rule, directory, and formula for the New Testament Church, and for the particular duties of Christians, as the Old Testament was for the Old Testament Church, and for the particular duties of the subject under that dispensation; at the same time by no means excluding the Old as fundamental to, illustrative of, and inseparably connected with the New, and as being every way of equal authority, as well as of an entire sameness with it in every point of moral natural duty, though not immediately our rule, without the intervention and coincidence of the New, in which our Lord has taught his people, by the ministry of his holy apostles, all things whatsoever they should observe and do, till the end of the world. Thus we come to the one rule, taking the Old Testament as explained and perfected by the New, and the New as illustrated and enforced by the Old; assuming the latter as the proper and immediate directory for the Christian Church, as also for the positive and particular duties of Christians as to all things whatsoever they should observe and do. Further, that in the observance of his Divine rule, this authentic and infallible directory, all such may come to the desirable coincidence of holy unity and uniformity of profession and practice, we have overtured that they all speak, profess, and practise the very same things that are exhibited upon the sacred page of New Testament Scripture, as spoken and done by the Divine appointment and approbation; and that this be extended to every possible instance of uniformity, without addition or diminution, without introducing anything of private opinion or doubtful disputation into the public profession or practice of the Church.

Thus and thus have we overturned to all intents and purposes, as may be clearly seen by consulting the overture itself; in which, however, should anything appear not sufficiently explicit, we flatter ourselves it may be fully understood by taking into consideration what has been variously suggested upon this important subject throughout the whole of these premises; so that if any due degree of attention be paid, we should think it next to impossible that we could be so far misunderstood as to be charged with latitudinarianism in any usual sense of the word. Here we have proposed but one description of character as eligible, or, indeed, as at all admissible to the rights and privileges of Christianity. This description of character we have defined by certain and distinguishing properties, which not only serve to distinguish it from every other, but in which all the real subjects themselves are agreed, without one exception, all such being mutually and reciprocally acknowledged by each other as legitimate members of the Church of God. All these, moreover, agreeing in the indispensable obligation of their unity, and in the one rule by which it is instructed, and also in the preceptive necessity of an entire uniformity in their public profession and managements for promoting and preserving this unity, that there should be no schism in the body, but that all the members should have the same care one for another; yet in many instances, unhappily, and, we may truly say, involuntarily differing through mistake and mismanagement, which it is our humble desire and endeavour to detect and remove, by obviating everything that causeth difference, being persuaded that as truth is one and indivisible wherever it exists, so all the genuine subjects of it, if disentangled from artificial impediments, must and will necessarily fall in together, be all on one side, united in one profession, acknowledge each other as brethren, and love as children of the same family.

For this purpose, we have overturned a certain and determinate application of the rule, to which we presume there can be no reasonable objection, and which, if adopted and acted upon, must, we think, infallibly produce the desired effect; unless we should suppose that to say and do what is expressly said and done before our eyes upon the sacred page, would offend the believer, or that a strict uniformity, an entire Scriptural sameness in profession and practice would produce divisions and offences among those who are already united in one spirit, one Lord, one faith, one baptism, one hope of their calling, and in one God and Father of all who is above all, and through all and in them all, as is confessedly the case with all of this character throughout all the churches. To induce to this we have also attempted to call their attention to the heinous nature and awful consequences of schism, and to that evil antiscriptural principle from which it necessarily proceeds.

We have likewise endeavoured to show, we humbly think with demonstrable evidence, that there is no alternative but either to adopt that Scriptural uniformity we have recommended, or else continue as we are, bewildered in schisms and overwhelmed with the accursed evils inseparable from such a state. It remains now with our brethren to determine upon the whole of these premises, to adopt or to reject, as they see cause; but, in the meantime, let none impeach us with the latitudinarian expedient of substituting a vague indefinite approbation of the holy Scriptures as an alternative for the present practice of making the approbation of human standards a term of communion; as it is undeniably evident that nothing can be further from our intention.

Were we to judge of what we humbly propose and urge as indispensably necessary for the reformation and unity of the Church, we would rather apprehend that there was a reason to fear a change of a very different nature; namely: that we aimed at too much strictness, both as to the description of character which we say ought only to be admitted, and also as to the use and application of the rule. But should this be the case, we shall cheerfully bear with it, as being fully satisfied that not only the common sentiment of all apparently sincere, intelligent and practical Christians is on our side, but that also the plainest and most ample testimonies of the inspired volume sufficiently attest the truth and propriety of what we plead for, as essential to the Scriptural unity and purity of the Christian Church, and this, we humbly presume, is what we should incessantly aim at. It would be strange, indeed, if in contending earnestly for the faith once delivered to the saints, we should overlook those fruits of righteousness, that manifest humility, piety, temperance, justice, and charity, without which faith itself is dead, being alone. We trust we have not so learned Christ; if so be we have been taught by him as the truth is in Jesus, we must have learned a very different lesson indeed. While we would, therefore, insist upon an entire conformity to the Scriptures in profession, that we might all believe and speak the same things, and thus be perfectly joined together in the same mind and in the same judgment, we would, with equal scrupulosity, insist upon and look for an entire conformity to them in practice, in all those whom we acknowledge as our brethren in Christ. 'By their fruits ye shall know them.' 'Not every one that saith unto me, Lord, Lord, shall enter into the kingdom of heaven; but he that doeth the will of my Father which is in heaven. Therefore whosoever heareth those sayings of mind, and doeth them not, shall be likened unto a foolish man which built his house upon the sand. Woe unto you scribes and Pharisees, hypocrites, for ye say and do not.'

We therefore conclude that to advocate unity alone, however desirable in itself, without at the same time purging the Church of apparently unsanctified characters, even of all that cannot show their faith by their works, would be, at best, but a poor, superficial, skindeep reformation. It is from such characters, then, as the proposed reformation, if carried into effect, would entirely deprive of a name and place in the Church, that we have the greatest reason to apprehend a determined and obstinate opposition. And alas! there are very many of this description, and in many places, of considerable influence. But neither should this discourage us, when we consider the expressly revealed will of God upon this point, Ezek. 44:6, 9, with Matt. 13 15, 17; 1 Cor. 5:6, 13, with many other Scriptures. Nor, in the end, will the multitude of unsanctified professors which the proposed reformation would necessarily exclude, have any reason to rejoice in the unfaithfulness of those that either through ignorance, or for filthy lucre sake, indulged them with a name and place in the Church of God. These unfaithful stewards, these now mistaken friends, will one day be considered by such as their most cruel and treacherous enemies.

These, then are our sentiments upon the entire subject of Church-reformation; call it latitudinarianism, or Puritanism, or what you please; and *this* is the reformation for which we plead. Thus, upon the whole, have we briefly attempted to point out those evils, and to prevent those mistakes which we earnestly desire to see obviated for the general peace, welfare and prosperity of the Church of God. Our dear brethren, giving credit to our sincere and well-meant intention, will charitably excuse the imperfections of our humble performance, and by the assistance of their better judgment correct those mistakes, and supply those deficiencies which in a first attempt of this nature may have escaped our notice.

We are sorry, in the meantime, to have felt a necessity of approaching so near the borders of controversy, by briefly attempting to answer objectives which we plainly foresaw would, through mistake or prejudice, be made against our proceedings; controversy making no part of our intended plan. But such objections and surmises having already reached our ears from different quarters, we thought it necessary to attend to them, that, by so doing, we might not only prevent mistakes, but also save our friends the trouble of entering into verbal disputes in order to remove them, and thus prevent, as much as possible, that most unhappy of all practices sanctioned by the plausible pretence of zeal for the truth – religious controversy among professors.

We would, therefore, humbly advise our friends to concur with us in our professed and sincere intention to avoid this evil practice. Let it suffice to put into the hands of such as desire information what we hereby publish for that purpose. If this, however, should not satisfy, let them give in their objections in writing; we shall thankfully receive, and seriously consider, with all due attention, whatever comes before us in this way; but verbal controversy we absolutely refuse. Let none imagine that by so saying, we mean to dissuade Christians from affording all the assistance they can to each other as humble inquirers after truth. To decline this friendly office would be to refuse the performance of an important duty. But certainly there is a manifest difference between speaking the truth in love for the edification of our brethren, and attacking each other with a spirit of controversial hostility, to confute and prove each other wrong. We believe it is rare to find one instance of this kind of arguing that does not terminate in bitterness. Let us, therefore, cautiously avoid it. Our Lord says, Matt. 17:7. 'Woe unto the world because of offences.' Scott, in his incomparable work lately published in this country, called his Family Bible, observes in his notes upon this place that our Lord here intends all these evils within the Church which prejudice men's minds against his religion, or any doctrines of it. The scandalous lives, horrible oppressions, cruelties, and iniquities of men called Christians; their divisions and bloody contentions; their idolatries and superstitions, are at this day the *great offences and causes of stumbling* to Jews, Mohammedans, and pagans in all the four quarters of the globe, and they furnish infidels of every description with their most dangerous weapons against the truth. The acrimonious controversies agitated among those who agree in the principal doctrines of the Gospel, and their mutual contempt and revilings of each other, together with the extravagant notions and wicked practices found among them, form the grand prejudice in the minds of multitudes against evangelical religion, and harden the hearts of heretics, Pharisees, disguised infidels, and careless sinners against the truths of the Gospel. In these and numberless other ways, it may be said: 'Woe unto the world because of offences,' for the devil, the sower of these tares, makes use of them in deceiving the nations of the earth and in murdering the souls of men. In the present state of human nature, it must needs be that such offences should intervene, and God has wise and righteous reasons for permitting them; yet we should consider it as the greatest of evils to be accessory to the destruction of souls; and an awful woe is denounced against every one whose delusions or crimes thus stumble men and set them against the only method of salvation.

We conclude with an extract from the Boston Anthology, which, with too many of the same kind that might be adduced, furnish a mournful comment upon the text; we mean, upon the sorrowful subject of our woeful divisions and corruptions. the following reply to the Rev. Mr. Cram, missionary from Massachusetts to the Senecas, was made by the principal chiefs and warriors of the six nations in council assembled at Buffalo creek, State of New York, in the presence of the agent of the United States for Indian affairs, in the summer of 1805. 'I am come, brethren,' said the missionary, 'to enlighten your minds and to instruct you how to worship the Great Spirit agreeably to his will, and to preach to you the Gospel of his Son Jesus Christ. There is but one way to serve God, and if you do not embrace the right way, you can not be happy hereafter.' To which they reply, 'Brother, we understand that your religion is written in a book. You say that there is but one way to worship and serve the Great Spirit. If there be but one religion, why do you white people differ so much about it? Why not all agree as you can all read the book? Brother, we do not understand these things. We are told your religion was given to your forefathers;

182

We, also, have a religion which was given to our forefathers; it teaches us to be *thankful* for all the favours we receive; to *love* one another, and to be *united*. We never quarrel about religion. We are told you have been preaching to the white people in this place. Those people are our neighbours, we are acquainted with them. We will wait a little to see what effect your preaching has upon *them*. If we find it does them good, makes them *honest*, and *less* disposed to cheat Indians, we will then consider again of what you have said.' Thus closed the conference. Alas, poor people! how do our divisions and corruptions stand in your way! What a pity that you find us not upon original ground, such as the apostles left the primitive Churches! Had we but exhibited to you their unity and charity; their humble, honest, and affectionate deportment toward each other, and toward all men, you would not have had those evil and shameful things to object to our holy religion, and to prejudice your minds against it. But your conversion, it seems, awaits our reformation; awaits our return to primitive unity and love. To this may the God of mercy speedily restore us, both for your sakes and our own, that *his way* may be known upon earth, and his saving health among all nations. Let the people praise thee, O God; let all the people praise thee. Amen, and amen.

6. A Statement of the Christian Faith, 1956

When the United Reformed Church was formed in 1972, the paragraph in the Basis of Union on formulations and declarations of faith deliberately included a twentieth-century statement from each of the Congregational and Presbyterian traditions to place alongside the classic seventeenth-century statements. The one chosen from the Presbyterian tradition was the Statement approved by the General Assembly of the Presbyterian Church of England in 1956.

The Presbyterian Church of England was formed in 1876 by a union of the Presbyterian Church in England (which consisted of congregations linked to the Church of Scotland before the Disruption of 1843 and related to the Free Church of Scotland subsequently) and the English Presbyteries of the United Presbyterian Church (a union of the branches of the Secession Church, which also included those English Presbyterian congregations from the seventeenth century which had remained trinitarian in their theology). Both partners took as their principal subordinate standard the Westminster statements as received by the Church of Scotland in doctrine, discipline, government and worship.

But, as with most Presbyterian churches in the nineteenth century, the development of evangelical theology led to a concern over the sense in which the Church understood and adopted the Confession, and what was involved for a minister in assenting to it at ordination. The main anxieties concerned the Confession's treatment of the extent of redemption, the total depravity of human beings since the Fall, the fate of those who died in infancy or without hearing the Gospel proclaimed, and religious toleration. The Synod of the Presbyterian Church of England approved a Declaratory Statement on the Westminster Confession in 1886. Discussion continued, however, and in 1890 a statement of Twenty-Four Articles of the Faith was approved by the Synod 'as a statement of the fundamental doctrines held and taught by this Church'.

In 1942 the General Assembly set up a special Committee on the Church's Doctrine, Standards and Witness to the Faith. The Committee reported in 1945 that it felt the Westminster Confession had lost its effectiveness as an expression of the Gospel to the contemporary world. The Assembly therefore instructed the Committee ' to produce an authorised statement of the Christian Faith which shall make it clear in what sense this Church now interprets Scripture, and which shall take an effective place in its life and teaching today'. A draft Statement was submitted to the 1953 Assembly with a full explanation of the aims behind it, and presbyteries were invited to comment. A revised Statement went to the 1955 Assembly, and after a further reference to presbyteries this Statement was approved by the General Assembly of 1956, 'as a declaration for this present time of the scriptural and historic faith'. An additional resolution reaffirmed the Assembly's right to interpret, alter, add to or modify her Subordinate Standards and formulas.

For further reading, see page 265.

A Statement of the Christian Faith

1 The Source of Christian Truth

1 The supreme and final source of truth in all that concerns God's relation to men and His purpose for them is the Lord Jesus Christ. In Jesus Christ, His Son, God has once for all made Himself known to men for their salvation.

2 God makes this saving truth known to men through the Bible, through the living tradition of the Christian Church, and through His dealings with men in their contemporary situation. In this revelation of God to men, the Bible has a place of unique authority.

3 The Bible is uniquely authoritative because it is the inspired record and interpretation of God's supreme act of self-giving and self-disclosure in Jesus Christ. The history of ancient Israel, as interpreted by the prophets, the fulfilment of that history in Jesus Christ, and the creation of the Church of Jesus Christ by the Holy Spirit, disclose and exhibit God's character and purpose, His love and saving power, in a way that is found nowhere else. All this the Bible sets forth in written words, so that through it men are confronted afresh in every generation with Christ, the living Word, and find God speaking to them in Him. As men enter deeply and seriously into this record, the Holy Spirit enlightens their minds and brings the truth to light in them. The study of the Bible is, therefore, primary and fundamental; advances in historical and linguistic knowledge are to be accepted and used as a gift of God to His Church.

4 Christian tradition embodies the insight and experience of former generations of Christians, and the accumulated knowledge of God's dealings with His people in all ages. It is expressed in various ways: in creeds and confessions, in liturgies and hymns, in theological and devotional writings. It is transmitted through the life and worship of the Church. It is to be received humbly and thankfully yet with discrimination, and tested always by the mind of Christ disclosed in Scripture.

5 God's action is not confined to the past. He is the living God who is at work in history in every age, and He is the source of all truth. New tasks are constantly unfolding before men, and new truths are discovered; by wrestling with these tasks

and appropriating these truths, within the living tradition of the Church and in the light of the Biblical revelation of God's nature and purpose, men enter more deeply into the knowledge of God and of His ways. The Church must resist the temptations to shut its eyes to new knowledge, to succumb to passing fashions of thought, or to ignore contemporary events which challenge its complacency. It must seek at all times to be open to the leading of the Holy Spirit, testing all things by the revelation of God in Jesus Christ.

2 God

1 There is one living and true God, infinite and eternal, who has made known His essential nature as Father, Son and Holy Spirit. These are not three Gods; nor are the Son and the Holy Spirit merely partial and temporary manifestations of God. He is one eternal Being – personal yet beyond man's conception of personality, surpassing human understanding in the mystery and richness of His threefold personal being, yet known through His own revelation of Himself and in the new life which is given by the love of the Father, the grace of Jesus Christ the Son, and the fellowship of the Holy Spirit.

2 All things have been created by God to fulfil His purpose; they are not the products of blind energy, or of an impersonal life-force. All things have their being in God and are sustained by Him; yet He is not merely the indwelling mind or soul of the world, nor is He in any way dependent on the world: He is above all, on Him all things depend, and the order, sublimity and beauty in His creation are but a partial expression of the infinite glory and majesty of His eternal being.

3 In the world of nature, there are sufferings and calamities which baffle man's understanding. Their origin and significance in God's creation are known only to Him; but nothing is beyond His knowledge and control, and nothing can frustrate His purpose of good. In the life of mankind, evil and wickedness abound; but against these God's holy and righteous will is inflexibly set. He is the source only of that which is good. For the furtherance of the good He is ever

active in history and in the lives of men. Men are not the helpless victims of fate or chance nor of any superhuman power of evil. Their whole being and life are within the grasp of God's manifold wisdom and providence, justice and mercy.

4 Through His coming in Jesus Christ His Son, God has revealed to men that He, the Creator and Sustainer of all things, all-wise and all-powerful, is holy love. All His actions towards men spring from this holy love. In love He created man; in love He judges him; in love He redeems him: His sovereign rule throughout all ages is the rule of love. The love of God goes forth freely to all men. It is not bestowed on them as a reward, for none can deserve it; nor is it withheld for their sinfulness, else none could receive it. Yet in loving He is also just. He opposes every form of unrighteousness, restrains and punishes sin, and by fatherly discipline seeks to lead men to walk in His ways.

5 God in His Holy Spirit is ever at work to make known to men His righteousness and power and His presence in the world. He alone quickens in men the desire to seek after Him and opens men's hearts and minds to the light which is in Christ, convicting them of sin, moving them to repentance and faith, and assuring them of forgiveness. In those whom God thus brings to Himself in Christ, His Holy Spirit dwells with transforming power, uniting them in love and service to God and to one another, and bringing into existence the new redeemed community which is the Church.

3 Man

1 God made men that they might forever have fellowship with Him as sons and with one another as brethren.

2 God gave men reason, and moral and spiritual insight, that they might know Him and hear His call and see His glory. He gave them power of choice, that as responsible persons they might do His will, and have the dignity and joy of serving Him in willing obedience and trust. He gave them the capacity to love and the need to be loved, and bound them to one another in families and communities, so that in mutual dependence and

in loyalty to one another they might find personal life in its fulness.

3 God has also inseparably linked man's life with, and made it dependent on, the natural order, not only as a part of that order, but so that through his reason he may rejoice in its beauty, discover its processes and laws, and act creatively in the world. In God's purpose for man there is no antagonism between body and spirit, nor between man's appreciation, exploration and control of nature and his fellowship with God. Only as men are rightly related to God, and to one another in God, can they be rightly related to the natural world, searching out and using its resources humbly, joyfully and for the common good.

4 Such is God's purpose. But all men sin in that they withhold from God their love and obedience, putting their own self-centred desires and purposes in place of God's will for them. Lacking thus its true centre in God, their life falls into conflict, frustration and misery. Sin destroys the balance of man's physical and spiritual nature; it brings him into subjection to his appetites; it distorts his judgment, so that he forms false ideals, and finds excuses for his wrong-doing, deceiving himself; it poisons his social relationships and breeds suspicion, ill-will and hatred, till even good impulses and good actions seem to him weakness and folly.

5 The whole human race in its continuity and solidarity is involved in sin and its consequences. Nevertheless no man can rightly blame others for his sins, or ascribe them wholly to the working of forces outside himself; nor can God be held responsible for sin, though the possibility of it was inherent in His creation of free persons. Nor again can the existence or action of spiritual powers of good or evil remove man's own responsibility before God. Every man is born into a life which is corrupted by the sins of his forefathers, but the refusal to yield his life in trust and obedience to the God who made him is always in some measure his own, and he is answerable for it. Each repeats in his own person the rebellion by which sin became dominant in the world. The longer men remain in this condition the more they are alienated from God, and the less able they are to know and do His good and perfect will.

6 Thus men being sinners are guilty before God and unable to save themselves. They are saved only by the redeeming act of God in Christ.

4 Salvation in Christ and Life in the Spirit

1 The redeeming act of God according to His eternal purpose, is His own coming into human life and history in Jesus Christ. His coming was not an isolated event, but the climax of a long process. God prepared the way by calling the people of Israel and binding them to Himself in a covenant of worship and obedience. To them He revealed His nature and will through the events of their history interpreted by His servants the prophets. When Israel proved rebellious and unfaithful to their high vocation, God continued to discipline, guide and inspire them, and in the fulness of time He sent His Son Jesus Christ, to be born of Mary through the Holy Spirit in the mystery of the Incarnation. He was the eternal Son of God made flesh; yet He was a truly historical person, born in Palestine in the reign of Augustus Caesar; His human nature was rooted in the previous history of the covenant people. He took to Himself man's whole nature and lived a truly human life, with its joys and sorrows, its duties and disciplines, its trials and temptations, yet without falling into sin. He was God incarnate, a perfect personality at once human and divine.

2 In Jesus Christ God was at work reconciling the world to Himself. This holy, loving and saving purpose Christ came to reveal and fulfil in His own person. He did this by living in selfless obedience to His Father, and in perfect fellowship with Him. His teaching, His works of healing and succour, His sharing in the needs of men, His refusal to separate Himself from them because of their sin, all demonstrated the presence and the power of the Kingdom of God in the world. He proclaimed that in Himself that Kingdom had come and was now present among men, so that their eternal destiny was bound up with their relation to Him. He called them to repentance and to the great decision to follow Him. But as men had rejected God, so they rejected Christ and crucified Him; yet God made this shameful death, by which men thought to rid themselves of Him, the means of redemption. In His death on the Cross Christ in obedience to the Father's will freely identified Himself with sinful man and offered Himself for the sin of the world. By this act of perfect obedience and love, and at immeasurable cost, He made atonement for sin, won the victory over it and broke the power of evil in the world. God vindicated this sacrifice and confirmed this victory by

raising Christ from the dead, thus overcoming for man the tyranny of death and proclaiming in act the final triumph of His holy love. God has exalted Him to His right hand, where He reigns in glory, the Head of His redeemed people the Church. As He came from the Father, and took upon Himself our humanity, so He has returned to the Father, and mediates between our humanity and the eternal being and counsels of the Most High.

3 By this great redeeming act in Christ God inaugurated a new era for mankind. By it He opened His Kingdom to all who put their trust in Christ. By it God gave to men in a new way the gift of the Holy Spirit and enabled them to live in His power.

4 It is by the Holy Spirit that men are moved to acknowledge their sinfulness and commit themselves in penitence and faith solely to the love and mercy of God in Christ. So committing themselves, they are forgiven; God accepts them, without condemnation, and, uniting them with Christ, takes them into sonship to Himself. He lifts them out of estrangement and enmity, liberating and creating anew in them the powers which sin had enslaved and destroyed. Their salvation in Christ is therefore in no sense their own achievement and merit: it is the free gift of God. In the mystery of His eternal counsel and purpose, He calls and enables them to be the servants of His redeeming activity in the world, and to share in His everlasting Kingdom of love in the world to come.

5 Thus in his new life the believer is united in Christ with the outgoing love of God. It is not a life simply of duty or obedience to rules, nor one governed only by the impulses of his own heart, but a life in which he steadfastly seeks in all situations, whether of prosperity or adversity, to have the mind of Christ, and thus to know and to do God's will of holy love. He is called to love all men, responding to their need, regardless of their deserts and without expecting reward. He is called to forgive, even as he knows himself to be forgiven. He is called to be victorious in suffering, in the faith that God overrules all things for good and that nothing can separate from His love. And in everything he is called to seek and to receive, through prayer and worship within the fellowship of the Church, the promised illumination, guidance and strength of the Holy Spirit.

6 In this high calling, the believer is not immediately made perfect; he is in continual conflict with the evil of his own heart, and has a deepening sense of his own sinfulness and need. Yet as often as

191

he turns to God in penitence, he finds pardon and grace sufficient for his need, and receiving anew the assurance that God will complete the saving work He has begun, he is enabled to live daily in the joy and peace of the Gospel.

5 The Church

1 The Church is the community in heaven and earth of those who, being united with Christ by faith, are reconciled to God. On earth it is manifested among all nations in particular Churches, in what to a greater or less extent the true Church is realised and embodied. It constitutes the new Israel of God, a people chosen and called out of all races and nations to be the servant of his redeeming purpose in the midst of mankind. Christ is the living Head of the Church, which is His Body. In Him the Church is one, holy, catholic and apostolic.

2 The Church is one because Christ dwells in it through the Holy Spirit, and those who are united with Christ are in unity with one another. Outward divisions are evidence that the Church on earth falls far short of its high calling, even though they do not destroy its inner unity. The Church must continually seek with grave searchings of heart to overcome such divisions and to give visible expression to the invisible unity which it has in Christ, for the greater effectiveness of its witness to Him.

3 The Church is holy, because the holy God has called it into being, consecrates it to Himself through Christ, and maintains its life through the Holy Spirit.

4 The Church is catholic or universal because it represents the new humanity which Christ came to create and into which He calls all peoples, and because it is commissioned to preach His Gospel to, and pray for, all mankind. The Church on earth has not fully attained this universality, which springs out of the love of Christ for all men; it must continually test its life by that love and rise above all exclusiveness whether of race or class or ecclesiastical tradition.

5 The Church is apostolic, because it is founded upon the same saving truth as the Apostles received through Christ's teaching and presence with them on earth; and because its commission to preach this truth to all nations is continuous with that which they received from Him. It must constantly test its message and teaching by the

apostolic faith and witness as set forth in the New Testament, if it is to avoid distortion or impoverishment of the Gospel.

6 The life of the Church is maintained in the fellowship of the Spirit through corporate worship, observance of the Lord's Day, the private devotion and consecration of its members, and their care for one another and for all men.

7 In the Worship of the Church the holy and eternal God, Father, Son and Holy Spirit, draws near and gives Himself to His people, calling and enabling them to yield themselves to Him in adoration, trust and obedience. The public worship of God is centred in the proclamation through word and sacrament of His saving work in Christ, and in the response of the worshippers in consecration, prayer and praise.

8 The two sacraments, Baptism and the Lord's Supper, set forth in symbolic form the redemptive work of Christ, and the Holy Spirit makes them means of grace to all who receive them in faith; they are not to be separated from the proclamation of the Gospel.

9 In the sacrament of Baptism Christ receives believers and their children into His Church. Baptism is administered with water in the name of the Father and of the Son and of the Holy Spirit, and signifies the out-going grace of God to all who repent and put their whole trust in Him, the washing away of their sin through the death of Christ, and the gift to them of newness of life in the family of God. It signifies also God's promise and assurance to them that in their new life thus begun His grace will be sufficient for every need. In infant baptism the same grace is given and promised to the child of believing parents. The child is received into the Church in the confidence that, nurtured and trained in a Christian home and in the fellowship of Christ's people, he will be led by the Holy Spirit in due time to make his own profession of faith in Christ as his Saviour and Lord.

10 The Sacrament of the Lord's Supper is the fullest expression of the Church's worship. It has its origin in the action of Christ at His last supper with His disciples, and His command to them to commemorate His death in like manner. By His own appointment the bread broken and the wine poured out shew forth His sacrifice on the Cross. When in obedience to His command believers gather round the table and eat the bread and drink the wine, the risen and ascended Lord is Himself present, and gives Himself to them for their spiritual nourishment and growth in grace. He assures them

of His unchanging love, gives them the peace of sins forgiven, and draws them into closer union with Himself and with the whole Church in heaven and upon earth. In response, the Church on earth unites in thanksgiving and offers itself afresh to His service; it seeks to make its imperfect obedience one with His perfect obedience and self-offering; and it looks forward to fulness of fellowship with Him when He shall come in His eternal Kingdom.

11 As the Body of Christ, the Church is called to a coherent and disciplined life in which every member has his place and ministry. Since the preaching of the Gospel and the sacraments of Baptism and the Lord's Supper are central in the life of the Church and in its work and witness in the world, there is a special Ministry to which Christ calls some of its members in every generation. They are ordained on His behalf by the Church to preach the Gospel, administer the sacraments, and give pastoral care and oversight to the members. Others are called to ministries of rule or administration. Every member is called to some form of service, according to the measure of Christ's gift to him. Through all these varied ministries, Christ builds up the Church in unity and love as the instrument of His saving purpose towards mankind.

6 The Social Order

1 God wills that men should live and work in fellowship with Him and with one another within the natural world which He has made, and in which He is Himself creatively at work. Out of this threefold relationship of God, men and the natural order spring the social institutions of human life in which God binds men together in mutual dependence, so that they have at all times reciprocal rights and duties under His rule. In the Christian life, these rights and duties are transformed into willing and loving service to God and men.

2 Society, in the purpose of God, is based upon the family, which God has designed to be a creative fellowship wherein children are cared for and loved as a trust from Him, and differences of sex, age and endowment are harmonised. The bond of the family is marriage, in which God ordains that a man and a woman shall vow themselves to each other in an intimate, exclusive and life-long union in fellowship with Him. Such union is the full expression of the

sex-relationship, and provides a stable home-environment in which children may develop happily, and learn their duties and privileges as children of God and members of the wider family of mankind.

3 In the social order of mutual dependence ordained by God, economic relationships have a necessary place. They are not governed merely by impersonal law or natural process, but lie within the creative purpose of God for men and for the world. Even though these relationships are perverted by human sinfulness, God is working through them to unite all men in His family, so that the needs of all may be met, the fear of want dispelled, and the opportunity for a full and free life secured to each. Selfish or wasteful exploitation of natural resources, misuse of wealth or leisure and acquiescence in injustice in economic life, are therefore contrary to God's will and a denial of His love.

4 Man shares in the creative energies with which God has filled the natural world, but in the exercise of these energies he fulfils himself only as he seeks through them to serve God and his fellow-men. Men and women are therefore called by God in their daily work not merely to earn a livelihood for themselves, but also to serve the community, and by the quality of their workmanship to glorify Him. In the arts and sciences in their various forms, God opens to mankind the way to a deeper wisdom and to a clearer vision of abiding values. He inspires gifted men to awaken the world to a fuller understanding, appreciation and enjoyment of truth, beauty and creative power of which He is Himself the source. In all these spheres, men are responsible to God for the right us of His gifts.

5 Political life also is part of the creative purpose of God in the social order. It is in accordance with His will that men should be organised under governments, to the end that evil-doing may be restrained, order upheld, just laws made and administered, and the unity, welfare and freedom of all the citizens promoted. All citizens therefore owe it to God and to one another to take a due part in the political life of the community and to respect the authority of government in its proper sphere. Those who govern must, however, recognise that both they and the citizens are in all things under the supreme authority of God's will. They must respect the rights of conscience, the rights of religious belief, and the Lordship of Christ in His Church. Should a government pursue a course contrary to the ends for which in the purpose of God it exists, or set itself up as an absolute authority, it may become the duty of

citizens to withhold their obedience. Upon Christians there rests the obligation, not merely loyally to fulfil the common requirements of citizenship, but also to pray for those who bear the responsibilities of government, and to seek to bring the mind of Christ effectively to bear upon the problems of the state and of community life.

6 In the providence of God, varieties of language, colour, race and nationality exist within mankind. It is God's will that these should not be made the occasion of exclusion and dissension, but rather than each should contribute its distinctive excellences to enrich the whole human family. Each nation is under obligation to God to live not merely for its own ends, but as a member of the family of nations, seeking to serve the good of all mankind, and being ready to acknowledge its own sins and failures. The refusal of men to recognise these obligations, and the wars and bitter antagonisms which spring from it, lay upon Christians the urgent task of witness and of reconciliation, for in Christ God has proclaimed the absolute worth of every human being, irrespective of nation, race or colour, and has shown both the way and the cost of restoring the broken unity of mankind.

7 The Fulfilment of the Christian Hope

1 The Christian hope is founded in Christ. He who is Victor over sin and death, who is Judge, and in whom all things shall be consummated, is the ground of our hope both here and for the world to come.

2 God gives eternal life to all who have faith in Him through Jesus Christ. This is a life of fellowship with the eternal God, begun in this present world and continued after death. It is a sharing in the victory over sin and death which God has wrought through Christ the Saviour and His resurrection, so that for those who are in Christ death does not bring extinction or mere survival but is a transition from one stage of eternal life to another. God has not disclosed the mode of the life hereafter, but inasmuch as it is continuous with the life now lived with Him, it will be a fully personal life.

3 In Christ judgment comes to all men, both in this world and in the world to come. They are responsible before God, and their lives, confronted by Christ's justice and mercy, have abiding significance both before and beyond death. Those who believe in Christ will find

in the world to come the joy of being with Him; those who have never known Christ will be judged according to the light they have had. At the last, God will finally judge all men; through Christ the hidden things of men's hearts will be made manifest and their eternal destiny declared. Whether God will ultimately bring all men to eternal life, or whether there will be some who have finally rejected His mercy in Christ, bringing condemnation on themselves, is not given to us to know.

4 According to His eternal purpose, through the coming again of Christ in glory, God will bring all things to their final consummation. The present sinful and imperfect order will be brought to an end, the whole creation renewed, and the fulness of the Kingdom of God established. What now appears to be but partial and evanescent good, or wasted effort and sacrifice, will then come to fulfilment; evil and injustice will be done away, the mystery of suffering made clear, the yearnings of men's hearts for their true life satisfied, and God's good purpose in the long travail of history vindicated. In the restored creation and in redeemed and glorified bodies His people will have in heaven the full enjoyment of Christ. The triumph and glory of the divine Kingdom, in which God shall be all in all, surpasses thought and imagination; but in the midst of the Throne will be the Lord Jesus Christ, crucified, risen, ascended; the triumph will be the triumph of God's perfect love, the glory His glory for ever.

7. A Declaration of Faith, 1967

The twentieth-century statement cited to represent the Congregational tradition is the Declaration approved by the Assembly of the Congregational Church in England and Wales in 1967.

When the Congregational Union was formed in 1832 it was agreed to present a Declaration of the leading articles of faith and discipline of the Congregational Churches, not as a binding standard or as terms of communion, but for the information of the public who, it was said, were apt to confuse Independents with either Methodists or Socinians (i.e., Unitarians). Such a Declaration of Faith was approved in 1833 – the Savoy Declaration being regarded as wordy and almost obsolete. The new Declaration represented a moderate Calvinism, heavily influenced by the subjective emphases of the Evangelical Revival. It was not much used, though it was printed in the *Congregational Yearbook* from 1858 to 1918. That practice began a year after controversies over the doctrine of two ministers, T.T. Lynch, whose book of poems entitled *The Rivulet* was held to be weak on the doctrine of the atonement, and Samuel Davidson, whose critical attitude to the Old Testament provoked controversy. The Declaration explicitly rejected the view that human formularies could ever be terms of communion (although only those whose general views were in accord with it were entitled to benefit from grants to aged or afflicted ministers from Congregational Union funds). It was never used as a basis for catechetical instruction.

In November 1958 the Council of the Congregational Union set up eight Commissions 'to elucidate the nature of the obedience to which God is calling us at this time'. Commission II was established to prepare a Statement of Faith. It was particularly concerned to meet 'new causes for scepticism and unbelief' with 'new forms of Christian thought'. *A Short Affirmation of Faith* was produced first, and approved after revision by the Assembly of 1961. The Commission then turned to the longer *Declaration of Faith*. A draft was published and comments invited in 1964 from Congregational and other churches. The revised form was accepted by the Assembly of the Congregational Church in England and Wales in 1967, together with *A Short Affirmation of Faith*, 'as representative statements' and both were commended to the churches.

For further reading, see page 265.

A Declaration of Faith

Introduction

1 *The purpose of this Declaration*

Christian faith includes the beliefs and practices to be found in Christian churches and in the experience of individual Christians. It displays variety and development; its content is as far-reaching as life itself; it cannot be compressed into one precise formulation whose adequacy and purity of statement will command assent from all Christians. But, if it cannot be defined, it can be declared. Christian faith is publicly declared in many things that Christians say and do, corporately and individually. For the most part, these are partial declarations which make clear some facet of Christian belief or some aspect of faithful Christian living. But from time to time churches are moved to offer a considered, balanced and detailed statement of the convictions which shape Christian life and thought. At the meetings of its Council on November 17th and 18th, 1958, the Congregational Union of England and Wales called for the preparation of such a statement.

As a first step, *A Short Affirmation of Faith* was prepared; it was submitted, revised after criticism from the churches, and re-submitted in May 1961, as 'a summons to faith within our own churches.' This present Declaration is meant to serve wider purposes. It attempts, in radically different circumstances, to do what was envisaged in the Declaration agreed upon at the Savoy, London, on October 12th, 1658, when Congregationalists offered an account of the faith held in their churches and of the order observed in them 'that others, especially the Churches of Christ, may judge of us accordingly.' A first draft, submitted in May 1964, was revised after criticism from the churches; and the final version was submitted to the renamed and reconstituted Congregational Church in England and Wales in 1967 to be accepted, together with the *Short Affirmation* as a representative statement.

Declarations of this character have often been associated with particular crises in the history of the Church and designed to refute particular errors or misrepresentations. The context of the present Declaration is a climate of uncertainty about Christian faith, within the Church as well as outside it. New causes for scepticism and unbelief have appeared with advances in knowledge and experience during the past three centuries. In this period, too, God has guided his Church towards new forms of Christian thought, and these, though fruitful, have been unsettling.

The Declaration seeks to make clear how, in the texture of contemporary life and with full acknowledgement of difficulties both new and old, those who make it are constrained to be, and choose to be, Christian. Their faith is presented through positive affirmations, arranged in an order which they believe to be appropriate though it is not traditional. The Declaration as a whole tries to state, honestly and clearly, what is generally held by those who speak through it. The detail of its formulation is not imposed upon any as a definition of what must be held; but it has been received by the Congregational Church in England and Wales as an acceptable statement of truths which each church member is summoned to make his own in his own way. It is published with sufficient authority for those within our churches or outside them who wish to consult it as a representative statement to do so reliably.

What is said in the Declaration must be taken up by churches and individuals and made real through their vitality and variety of testimony. It is open for criticism by theologians in our own and in other churches and requires to be supported by fuller explanations which they can offer. There is work to be done also by skilled apologists in defending it and in commending it to particular persons or groups in the modern world. But there are immediate uses for the Declaration as it stands. It will be read by some who are not Christian. They may begin with no direct or urgent interest in these matters, if they have hitherto relied upon impressions, and possibly upon misunderstandings, of ways in which Christians are supposed to have thought, the Declaration may help them judge more fairly. Christian readers who belong to churches differently ordered from ours may, we hope, be convinced by reading the Declaration that Congregationalists also belong to Christ and are fellow-members with them in the one Church of Christ. To Christian readers in our own churches the Declaration is offered as a help to clarity and certainty. Above all it is hoped that the Declaration may help many, outside our churches as well as within them, to find and sustain a living faith in God.

2   The Congregational Church in England and Wales

How should the people whose Declaration this is be identified? First, we are Christians. We trust in the Lord Jesus Christ and live under his direction. Our hope for ourselves, for the whole Church of Jesus Christ, and for the universe, is in God who has revealed himself in Jesus Christ. Our faith in God through Jesus Christ sets us firmly in Christ's Church and we are united with all who through the centuries have shared the Church's life and sought for true renewal of it in every age. In belief we are for the most part at one with other Christians from whom we are separated by church order.

What are now known as Congregational churches were first formed in this country in the sixteenth century. They attempted to display in their organization and life what was thought to have been the truly New Testament character of the Church's life, worship, ministry and forms of government. They had affinities both with the Calvinist and with the Anabaptist traditions in the Reformation of the Western Christian Church. We maintain our Church life in dissent from the Church of England, and we have the specific name, Congregationalist, in addition to that of Christian; but this is of secondary importance and we would be glad if we could be Christian without further label.

Congregationalists played their part, as did all other Christians, in creating and perpetuating the division which has appeared within the one Church of Jesus Christ. In our separated state we look with longing for the full yet flexible unity of the Church as a gift which will help it to be more obedient and more effective in its witness to its Lord. Yet, we must still affirm that, for the Church, unity of organization must remain secondary to obedience to the Gospel. We believe that to insist upon an unbroken identity of organization, or upon an office determined by traditional links, or upon identity of theological statement with any particular period of the past, as essential to the valid existence and continuity of the Church, narrows the Church and hardens it in a way contrary to the will of the

Lord Jesus Christ. Any features of our obedience which distinguish us from other groups of Christians are there, not to separate us from the whole company of Christ's people, but to keep open the way to the full freedom and fellowship of the whole Church of Christ.

3   Christians and non-Christians

Christians have been deemed by some to be complacent and imperceptive about the conditions in which human life and human culture are sustained, and these charges have frequently been justified. Yet Christian faith and membership of the Christian Church need not restrict either human vision, or human sensitivity, or human concern. Bound up with their fellow-men in the common concerns and opportunities of human life, Christians must open their minds to great human problems, old and new, to which men should be fully sensitive in any serious declaration of faith. We do not seek to hide but rather to express genuine uncertainties and difficulties which are felt alike by the Christian and non-Christian in modern circumstances. The power of Christian faith is made clearer and the nature of Christian certainty more evident through honest declaration of the struggle with doubt which is part of the believer's experience.

We are Christians, and it is from our place within the Church of Jesus Christ that we declare the faith by which we live. Christians are separated from many of their fellow-men by their convictions. They are often separated too, and unnecessarily, by avoidable misunderstanding. Important Christian convictions, even if not generally shared, can at any rate be noted and understood. Christian belief in God includes an affirmation of God's active hostility to wrongdoing in the public and private life of mankind. Christians ask all men at least to note and understand their conviction about this. They make the same plea about their affirmation that Jesus Christ has supreme and saving authority over the public life of mankind and over human history, and not only, as some suppose them to say, over the private lives of individuals in this world and over life in a world beyond death.

With these convictions Christians diverge from many of their fellow-men; but at the same time they share with them insights and concerns which arise on the common ground of experience, and plain statement about some convergent attitudes will obviate common misconceptions. Christians are aware that men have new things to learn in their struggle to find a moral way of living, and that new solutions have to be sought for problems of public order and government. At present they face, as a common human concern, the problems and dangers posed by the development of technical power. They welcome the scientific exploration of the universe, for which Christian faith is no substitute. They are deeply thankful for the enlargement of man's understanding of the physical universe and for the improvement of man's physical condition and environment. Their belief in God is not hostile in principle to scientific enterprise, and they are confident that no development in man's power over the resources of the universe can remove man or the universe from the sovereign power of God.

It is from the fullest possible engagement with mankind's ordinary and current life and thought that Christians must declare their faith. Christians respond to the Gospel of Jesus Christ and are constrained to worship God. There are pressures upon them to abandon this worship and the faith which it expresses, but they do not prevail against the constraint of the Christian Gospel. There are intellectual conflicts and practical frustrations which tell heavily against Christian belief and hold others back from sharing it. Christians know that their faith would be worthless if it gave them immunity from difficulties in some world of make-believe. Its truth and power appear when, by responding with God's help to the pressures and difficulties, Christians reach a more perceptive understanding of their faith and act with greater maturity in Christian ways.

4   The language of Christian conviction

The words we have to use in describing where we stand are widely regarded as meaningless or untrustworthy. It is not the words themselves that are the stumbling-block, but rather the claim that they refer to great and trustworthy realities. Scepticism attacks any confidence in God, and particularly in God revealed through the Bible and present among us in Christ. If this is uncertain there can be no confidence in the sovereignty of God, in the claims of the Church or its importance; there can be no confidence in God's final purpose for the universe and no serious respect for his claim on the life and conduct of mankind.

These considerations explain the shape given to the Declaration. It tries to show clearly that a faith expressed in Christian affirmations can be strong and certain. Assurance does not come to us, however, by virtue of our own resourcefulness in thought or in speech. Assurance comes to men from God who claims us, judges us, transforms and holds us. It becomes real for any man when the content of Christian affirmation brings into his life its own inherent truth and power.

The language of Christian conviction must always be difficult to those who do not share it (and even to those who do) because of its double-sided character. On the one hand it is a stammering, groping language, seeking to express in symbolic terms a knowledge of him who in his majesty remains to a great extent unknown and in many respects unknowable, even in the light of his revelation. On the other hand it is firm confident language, testifying that God puts himself within our range of speech and must not be thought of in less than Christian terms. The humility and the confidence of Christian language belong together. They have been menaced both by a false arrogance and by a false uncertainty. Faith requires of us boldness, guarded by critical awareness, in speech.

Words, however, merely focus past experience, unless they can create new experience. The great words upon which any expression of Christian faith must be built come to life only as they become personal possessions through personal commitment to God revealed in Jesus Christ. Our way towards the truth is this way of personal commitment in response to God's gracious dealings with us in Christ as he is disclosed through the Bible in the Church. This does not mean a belittling of man's mind, but rather a calling forth of man's rational, critical and creative powers in response to the certainty which is in God.

Declaration

We make this Declaration of Faith as members of the Christian churches bound together by covenant to form the Congregational Church in England and Wales. Our faith is in God, through Jesus Christ, in the Holy Spirit.

In the Church we live under the constraint of the Holy Spirit; we know the grace of God in Jesus Christ and trust it as sufficient for the redemption of men and women in all their need; our lives are exposed to the claim of God and we learn about his will for human beings both before and after death. Our task is to make clear the truth we have found. We declare it is a testimony to the churches of our own order, and to the churches of other orders within the one Church of Christ, and also to groups and to individuals who are outside the Christian allegiance.

We affirm first the reality, the grace, and the triune being of God; we declare our trust in him as sovereign over the universe; we declare our belief that he has brought the Church into being to serve his liberating purpose for all mankind; we declare our belief that he will accomplish his purposes with grace and glory; we acknowledge what he requires of us and of all mankind and affirm that he himself is enabling men to fulfil this requirement.

We offer our Declaration to the God whom we worship in Christian faith, as a tribute to his glory. We pray that he will prevent whatever is wrong in it from doing harm. We pray that he will use whatever is right in it to nourish faith. The kingdom and the power and the glory are his for ever.

1 God Is

1 We declare first that God exists. He is himself the only cause and ground of his own being; self-existent, self-determining, eternal. He needs nothing other than himself to be what he is. His complete perfection is a harmony of infinite richness. Whatever else exists depends, by contrast, on factors other than itself for being and character and worth. At best its perfection is always partial and limited. It is a creature, and, ultimately, the creation of God. God is the Lord of all being and his authority extends everywhere. He is the source of all that is, and everything exists through his generosity. He gives himself to men out of his freedom and love so that in faith they can know him, trust him and obey him.

2 Men can neither know God nor speak faithfully about him without his help. The universe is not able to contain or fully to disclose his eternal greatness; he is not to be sought or found as

one of its items or aspects, nor as the totality of items and aspects. Although his presence reaches intimately into the inward recesses of human experience, men nevertheless do not recognize him. His being transcends all human powers of perceiving. But God, mighty and mysterious, gives himself to be our God and calls forth from us faith and worship.

Faith in God is more than the affirmation of beliefs. It is confident trust in God; it is the response of a man's whole life to God's claims; it finds its necessary expression in worship. In worship men surrender their human interests, in adoration, to a Lord whose influence upon their being and well-being they wholly trust. When worship is directed to finite powers, human life is intensified but is also distorted. If worship is to be given at all, it must be given to the Lord of all being who alone is worthy of it. Christian worship of God is given in response to news, heard and believed; to the Gospel which Jesus Christ has given to his Church.

We know God, as a man may know his friend, because through this Gospel God gives himself to be known and trusted by human beings. Though the splendour of his being remains veiled from us, we acknowledge him to be the rightful authority over every human heart. Men must obey him, and through obeying love him; men must love him, and through loving obey him. God seeks from all human beings a self-giving in love and freedom which answers to his own. From this central conviction all other Christian convictions derive their power and certainty.

3 Among our fellow-men there are many who have no such confidence in God. They are aware of powerful influences other than God which mould and dominate men's environment and men themselves, and which suggest ways of life making for greater well-being and fulfilment of destiny; but they are aware of nothing which transcends such influences. They deal with these influences, either as ultimate forces to which men must abandon themselves, or as powers to be manipulated with irreligious self-confidence for man's advantage. Such powerful influences are not God, and we believe that it is damaging and wrong for any man to entrust his life to idols or to be himself the idol in whom he trusts.

There is one who has supreme claim upon human life; he is God. His claim is rightfully made and is for men's good. It is a holy claim, requiring the disavowal of all rival claims. Men who practise idolatry in their ignorance of God bring their lives under his adverse judgement. Their resistance to his judgement interposes a further barrier between themselves and God. God gives himself to men, from beyond the frontiers of human finitude and through the barriers of human rebellion, as the Lord of all being whose judgement upon them is conceived and carried out in forgiving love. He gives himself to be known, trusted and obeyed as their God. Knowing him in this relationship, Christians are able to take account also of evils other than human rebellion which distort his creation and offend against the supremacy we ascribe to God. Because of these evils many withhold from God the faith and worship which are his by right. In the light of his self-giving we have confidence that he will overcome all evil, free his creation from distortion, and bring it to share in his own glory, a glory that will exceed all our powers of praise.

4 Since he is the Lord of all, we expect the thoughts of men everywhere to turn towards God. With many who are not Christian, we cannot believe that this universe is an uncreated self-sustaining system, having no purpose other than its own functioning. With many, too, we cannot limit the meaning of a human being's life to those dealings with things and with other people which occupy him from birth to death. From these starting-points many have been moved to inquire about God. Many also have been moved by the inexplicable claims of truth, beauty and goodness. In their questioning about life's source and meaning, many do not use the word 'God' at all, but may nevertheless learn much about the ways of him whom they cannot acknowledge. Others are able, as we are, to reach a conviction that human life is in the care of God, and that he seeks association with all who live it, and admits them to some knowledge of purposes which give lasting meaning and value to all that men do and suffer. The Lord of all being so conceals his presence that man's aspiring quest is always precarious and often unrewarded. We do not say that it is bound to end in the falsehood of identity. But we are obliged to make plain that our own assurance of God has its particular ground of confidence, distinct from grounds shared by all religious men. We welcome every sign of commonly shared awareness, but where similar affirmations rest on different foundations divergent meanings often lie below the surface of words used in common. It is from our own ground of confidence alone that we are entitled to appraise the testimony of others from other grounds.

5 The revelation of God takes place where, confronted with realities in which he is at work, human conscience is awakened and instructed by his love and his judgement. The ground of Christian confidence is that God has disclosed himself to us through Jesus Christ; supremely in the human life Jesus lived, his death and his resurrection; but also in ancient Israel where there was preparation for his coming; and in the Church which since his coming has drawn its life from him. In Jesus Christ we affirm the presence and action of God as well as the effort and achievement of a man. In transparent goodness Jesus achieved the full stature of manhood; he defeated the pressure of sin at its strongest; raised from the dead and with the power to give himself by the Holy Spirit to his fellow-men, he brings the deliverance of God to all who trust in him. God himself, out of his great love, acted in Jesus Christ with judgement and mercy to meet and overcome the evils infecting his creatures because of alienation from their Lord. Faith in God becomes fully certain and definite and fruitful when it is the response given by men and women to the authority of God expressed in Jesus Christ. Through him we have the pardon of God and peace with God. Our struggle for life and for faith does not cease, but nevertheless we rest secure in God.

6 From this ground of confidence, we draw out the truth that God reveals himself with infinite generosity even though there be no true discernment nor any true obedience. No limits can be set to his generosity; none therefore may claim to measure in advance how much knowledge of God may be reached from other than Christian grounds. From our own Christian starting-point we make wider affirmations which others again may be willing to endorse on other grounds.

God may reveal himself to men and women in their reflections upon human life. In God's purpose for the universe man has a distinctive place. Men and women are created to live in relationship with God, both individually and corporately. They have special responsibilities and duties towards him, and God offers himself to them through the simplicities and the intricacies of human life.

God is at work in the events of human history and, if his work be discerned, there is revelation of himself to men in this sphere. We do not affirm this solely or chiefly about history which involves Christian institutions or wider religious interests. It is to be found in every part of mankind's story.

There is revelation of God to be seen in the structures of the universe and in its various components, more especially where these display orderliness and harmony and beauty. In so far as the physical universe can be seen as God's creation it serves to enlarge men's knowledge of him.

God is self-revealing and he is present everywhere. This we affirm; but there is much that is enigmatic and uncertain about this widely offered revelation. With Christian knowledge of God we benefit from it, and seek to benefit more fully. Yet no man can know with true certainty what it means to turn to God and believe in him, or what it means to disobey his will and ignore his purpose, until he has recognized God where God identifies himself with the human race, in the person of Jesus Christ. Response to God's wider revelation which is not rooted at this central point of disclosure is at best insecure and at worst perverse.

7 We acknowledge an obligation to attend to everything God may have to say to us through human religious aspirations and religious experience, not only in Christianity, but also in the other religions practised in the world.

Christians cannot afford to boast of their own spirituality. Religion may be the channel of the human spirit's response to its Creator and Redeemer; it may also be the channel of idolatrous distortions of human life. From such idolatrous distortions the practice of the Christian religion has been by no means free. As human beings, moreover, Christians may be inferior to representatives of other religions, and must be humble before them and ready to learn from their human qualities. We are ready also to say that something of what is given to mankind in non-Christian religion may, as Jesus Christ makes it part of his own truth, be part of the Christian inheritance. In holding the Christian faith, therefore, we are ready and willing to look over the frontiers of the Christian Church to see what God in Christ is doing among those who ignore or resist his Gospel. Beyond these frontiers we see many who have reached and have declared truth which we believe to be of God; but we do not see any revelation of God to which, apart from Christ, we could respond as his sure and certain self-disclosure. The revelation of God in Christ is no mere supplement to such a wider revelation; nor is it one form among many of a general revelation. Faith in God through Jesus Christ provides for us definite understanding of the word 'God' and of the word 'faith'.

8 We believe that God has revealed himself through a course of history which had as its central event the life of God made man in Jesus of Nazareth. The revelation is clear and it is decisive. The irreplaceable records of that revelation, and our only access to it, are the documents bound together in the Old and New Testaments of the Bible. Through the Bible God continues to draw men and women into fellowship with himself and keeps them faithful. Faith born and nourished from this source by his Spirit grows clearer and more certain for those who offer themselves to God by worship, love and obedience, through Jesus Christ.

In this faith men are delivered from denial of God's claim on them, and from distrust of his purpose for them, into a life of fellowship with him. They come to know that the whole universe depends upon God; that he is more intimately present to men, even if they repudiate him, than is the experienced world, or other people, or even their own selves; and that he is active in the corporate life of mankind, calling men through all life's detail to fellowship with him in truth and righteousness.

The Christian believer shares with his fellow-men much perplexity and frustration, but remains sure that God exists and that his love is real and reliable. In the believer's experience there is nothing which avails to overthrow God's rightful claim upon men or to weaken God's power to save men and keep them for his own.

We affirm the reality of God. We do so because we share the conviction that he has revealed himself in Jesus Christ. From this ground of confidence we go on to speak about his character which is expressed in all that he does.

2   God is Gracious

1 God, known and worshipped through Jesus Christ, is before all else a God who gives himself with unlimited and overflowing generosity. The name of this free self-giving is grace. The grace of God calls forth our utmost gratitude and trust.

2 Christians know God and his grace because he has created through the faithfulness of Jesus Christ a new relationship between man and God. Disqualified as sinners for life with God, Christians nevertheless know themselves to be living at peace with him. They live as sinners forgiven and recreated by God who, in giving himself

to them, empowers them to become what he made them to be. We acknowledge the grace of God in a new life of gratitude and find then that there is grace in all God's dealings with his creatures.

3 His authority expressed in the conditions of our existence, no less than his mercy revealed in Christ, exhibits his grace. Time, space, all natural human powers and human relationships, are his gifts to men; in conferring them he shares with us his own capacity to be. With these gifts, and within the framework they provide for life on earth, he gives the opportunity to know him and to love him as faithful Creator. He gives himself to men, more intimately, as God the Father whose will they know and should gladly obey and upon whose care they may rely. The opportunity to know God as Creator and Father is so offered that men may accept it in freedom, or may by their own choice neglect or refuse it. In various ways men have neglected the offer or refused it; they still do so. In consequence they make the world wretched. God seeks to rescue men from this wretchedness and to repair and improve the state of his creation. This active compassion most clearly exhibits his grace.

4 God's grace is expressed in mercy. This we know by fellowship with Jesus Christ. In this fellowship we are able to recognize that there is treason to God within his universe, the treason called 'sin' which his mercy meets and overcomes. In our flesh and in our world Jesus gave to God the obedience man should be giving. Alone among men he was guiltless of surrendering to temptation or of promoting evil. In death he endured the evil produced by sin at work in his fellow-men and their society. From the way in which men turned against Jesus or away from him as he went to his death Christians learn to recognize sin and the treason of it. It is human behaviour, done in deliberate self-will, which at the same time expresses bondage to corrupting conditions; behaviour in which men turn destructively against God, against fellow-men, and against their own integrity. Having kept his own manhood clear of sin, Jesus was able to present before God and men the consequences of its presence in others, with perfect loyalty both to God who hates it and to men who have made it part of themselves. Men who know that wrongdoing invites God's hostility learn at the Cross that God deals with the offence of sin in his world by grace, forgiving the wrongdoer but utterly condemning his wrongdoing. The grace of God suffices to meet and overcome the whole indignity of sin.

5 Christians are themselves deeply involved in the treason of sin and know this the more clearly because they live in the light of God's mercy. They recognise sin and must speak about it, though they cannot wholly explain it or account for it. They are able in penitence to repudiate it; but such repudiation does not in itself suffice to emancipate them from it.

In its wider sense the word 'sin' designates a condition of blindness and of bondage and of rebellion against God. The word is also used more narrowly to designate a particular act of wrongdoing. Sin appears in human life wherever men capitulate in their selfishness to the lure of wrong choices and are involved in the wrongdoing of particular sins.

Behaviour which does not accord with God's wisdom displays the blindness of sin: sometimes men are able to see the way of wisdom but disregard it, and sometimes they do not see it at all; in either case their folly is a sinful offence. Behaviour marked by feeble resistance, or none at all, to what is wrong in prevailing circumstances displays the bondage of sin: sometimes the power to overcome circumstances is within reach and sometimes not; in either case to capitulate to evil is a sinful offence. Men whose minds are closed against the truth of God and whose wills are closed against his love act with the rebelliousness of sin: sometimes their infidelity is deliberate, sometimes it is the product of neglect or indifference, and sometimes it has never been challenged by any call to belief; in all cases their relation with God is a sinful one and what they do through self-determination is a sinful offence. The more men persist in self-centred rebellion, the more blind they become and the more impotent in the grip of sin as bondage. A sinner damages himself in every act of wrongdoing; sinning narrows life's possibilities and warps its actuality; it exposes men to tragedy and infests their world with the rottenness of decay.

Sinners, though in many ways helpless victims in the grip of sin, are nevertheless held responsible for their sinful offences. God's way with sinners includes the gift of conscience, whereby sinners carry in some measure the burden of their sin and wrongdoing. The burden is felt as 'guilt'. Not all guilt makes for healing and renewal. Misconceived guilt, arising from inadequacy, is a damaging burden on human life and should be lifted by remedial skill. Guilt arising from wrongdoing can pave the road to release by forgiveness, and men may bear its burden without damage until that end is reached.

Sin is at its most damaging and most dreadful when the sinner feels no trace of guilt. It belongs to the grace of God that he should bring the burden of sinfulness and the weight of responsibility to a focus in the sinner's conscience and open the way for the sinner to seek forgiveness and release. In all their sin men are able to turn to the grace of God and find healing for themselves, and, within this healing process, opportunity to make some reparation for damage done by their sin to others.

6 Because we can reckon with sin in the light of God's forgiving grace we are able to affirm the worth of all that is created and preserved by the grace of God the Father. Human life in particular, though corrupted by sin, remains immeasurably valuable. The freedom men have and their inventive powers make possible the personal life which men develop as bodily creatures in this material world. By discovery and experiment men have learnt, and are still learning, new patterns of life for themselves and new ways of influencing and using their environment. We owe thanksgiving and praise to God for the goodness preserved and enhanced because of his patient and providential grace. Yet at all points this goodness is open to be corrupted by sin. And we have no confidence that any scientific discovery, any political or economic or psychological adjustment, can overcome man's sin and enable him to live in peace. The greater an achievement, moreover, the more deadly may be the influence of sin upon it; and the more urgent therefore becomes the need of transforming grace.

7 God has met man's great need by his own initiative, constrained by nothing except his love; in Jesus of Nazareth, in whom his grace was incarnate, God came himself to emancipate the world. Holy·in his utter hostility to sin, God has reconciled to himself man who is sinful. He has released mankind from slavery to evil and has given to us a foretaste of life under his own everlasting sovereignty. This redeeming grace of God is triumphantly present in the life, the death, the resurrection and the reign of Jesus Christ.

8 The life of Jesus Christ is presented for us in records of his words and deeds and of his attitudes and reactions throughout a short public ministry. The records bring before us with sufficient clarity a man wonderfully perfect in the ways of human love and human self-giving towards God and towards fellow-men. He calls men to discipleship through gentle yet penetrating teaching, through encouragements and warnings, through stern challenges

214

and searching rebukes. All his words mediate to men, freshly and graciously, a newly authoritative encounter with truth. His acts of creative passion bring healing and joyful hope where there was ground only for despair. Both deeds and words spring from an inner experience of which those closest to him saw something: his faith, his prayer, his effort and steadfastness in obeying the Father and his fidelity through sustained anguish. From Jesus as he lived on earth God received perfect human obedience. His life was a perfect expression of human love to God and to his fellow-men. We believe that it was also a deed of grace done by God, yet done in manhood common with our own.

9 Jesus died by crucifixion. He anticipated and accepted this death, and the path which led towards it, with perfect human grace. At that moment of history three things met in decisive encounter: the grace of God concentrated in holy love for men needing to be emancipated; the true love and obedience of one man towards God; sinfulness in the human race, taken to the point of hardened and active hatred. Here, in a mystery of holy love and anguish which men do not and cannot fathom, sin failed, and failed decisively, to divide the acts of man from the life of God. On the Cross hatred was absorbed, in suffering endured to the depths of spiritual dereliction and the giving up of life itself; but the love at work at this meeting point of God's life and man's was not deflected and not frustrated. Sin and all creatures corrupted by sin were nakedly exposed to God's judgement; but his judgement was grounded in the love which prevailed, and it secured to his creatures a future. In this future they exist by the emancipating grace of God as living testimonies to his judgement and love. Under these conditions men can take up life for the future as from a new birth. They can live as new creatures whose sole and sufficient security comes, in forgiveness, from God's grace in the death of Jesus.

10 By the resurrection of Jesus God vindicated him and delivered him completely from the death into which he had fully entered. We acknowledge that no exact description can be given either of the resurrection event or of the way in which death's effects were overcome. We share with the original witnesses to his resurrection their faith in God who wrought it and in Jesus whom it vindicated. Jesus, given back to them as their living friend, was given to them anew as their Lord; so too he is given to us. His ministry and teaching now awaken belief that a new way of hope and trust and fulfilment is

being opened for mankind. His complete fidelity to love and his complete opposition to sin were taken to a victorious climax in the darkness of death. In his resurrection sinfulness and death were robbed of their seemingly inevitable and lasting hold upon human life. From his risen life the triumph of grace strikes home to the lives of his fellow-men and undermines both sin and the fear of sin, death and the fear of death. We echo and prolong the confident praise of God which rings throughout the New Testament and could not conceivably be sustained had Jesus not been raised from the dead.

11 We believe not only that Jesus lives but also that he has been exalted to reign. The authority to which the whole universe is subject is Jesus; he is the judge who decides what is right and he is himself the standard by which right is judged. As man he was both crucified and raised from the dead; and in his exalted manhood he reigns. From this comes our confidence and our concern for the true development of humanity in all human things. We believe, too, that he has under his control all the things in men themselves and in their environment which threaten to frustrate the purpose of God. The manner and effectiveness of his control are still veiled from us, as they were veiled when he established his authority upon the Cross. But we see evidence of his reign wherever men are released from the terror of things which threaten God's purpose and from bondage to them. And we look confidently for the full splendour of his reign which is yet to come.

12 God's emancipating grace in Jesus Christ is made effective in men's lives through the Holy Spirit. Men are not able of themselves to step out of the blindness and bondage and rebellion of sin; but God meets their need to do so by his grace. He grants to sinful men a new way of living, one which expresses the freedom of sonship in a world belonging to God the Father. This life is grounded upon reconciliation between God and forgiven sinners. It is both the gift of God and man's achievement of true selfhood. God awakens sinners to their need; he exposes the hatefulness of sin by overcoming it; he raises up the sinner to live in fellowship with Jesus Christ, with faith in God and true kindness towards his fellow-men; he brings sinners within the People of God, newly created as the Church of Jesus Christ. Christians know God's direct action upon their own lives, and upon the Church into which they are incorporated; and they speak of God as the Holy Spirit.

God the Holy Spirit has created the Church as a new society in this world where believers are incorporated with Christ for the life of grace. The Church depends upon God for necessary reform and constant renewal. God by his Spirit brings its members ever and anew into his obedience and into peace with him through faith and love and hope. He intensifies their awareness of his demands as he leads men further into the obedience which his demand requires. In all the work of his Spirit God provides a foretaste of the resources with which men will live in everlasting fellowship with him.

God the Holy Spirit comes into individual human lives and enables men to acknowledge Jesus as Saviour and Lord. He interprets to them God's grace in Jesus Christ; he strengthens them so that they can respond in gratitude; he turns them away from self-preoccupation towards the goodness of God; he lifts the burden of guilt so that they are able to grow in the ways of love and fresh obedience.

Men respond imperfectly to this work of God and are not at once lifted completely out of sin's grip. Christians at present have to struggle towards the future; but the Holy Spirit is with us in this struggle and his is Lord of the future. Neither the damage already done by sin, nor the unremitting pressure of sin persisting until our death, will undo the new and gracious relationship into which God accepts forgiven sinners who have seen and loved the goodness which is in Jesus Christ. God's grace in the work of the Holy Spirit is the climax of his self-giving. It is the ground of final assurance that his grace will prevail.

3 God is One

1 There is no God other than he whose grace we have declared. Both Old and New Testaments affirm, in opposition to all human idolatries, that he alone is God and he is one God. We echo their testimony from our own convictions about what he has done for the world in Jesus Christ and from the experience of living by Christian faith in him.

2 Through Jesus Christ we have been shown who God is and what he is. He is the Father, loved and obeyed by Jesus Christ. He is the son, distinct from the Father yet united with him in one being

and life, incarnate in Jesus Christ. He is the Holy Spirit, distinct from Father and Son yet the same God, bestowed through Jesus Christ. From this threefold acknowledgement we go on to declare that God is three-in-one and one-in-three. We have the duty to show, if we can, that our threefold knowledge is knowledge of one God; but we do not claim that the mystery of God's being is thereby explained.

3 We believe in God the Father. All things are subject to his rightful authority and gracious purpose, and in his will is our peace. These convictions are expressed in both Testaments of the Bible and they are ours too. God the Father is the Lord known, loved and obeyed by Jesus of Nazareth through life and through death. He is the God whose wisdom, love and power availed to vindicate Jesus by raising him from the dead. Jesus responded with perfect love to the Father's love for him; and, through this perfect love which binds Jesus to the Father and to mankind, the Father's love seeks all mankind. It has reached into our lives and set us free to follow Jesus in the knowledge and love and obedience of Christian discipleship.

Knowing God to be the eternal Father, we live with sober confidence that the universe is his good creation and is a world where every human life is within his gracious purpose and under his intimate care. Such faith is continually being tested by much that we do not understand. At the same time it keeps strong in us the resolution always to seek the truth and to live by it however disturbing it may be; for wherever truth is before us it expresses to us the trustworthy authority of God the Father. The truth of God, eternally Father Almighty, has been clarified and made certain for us through Jesus of Nazareth, whose communion as Son with the Father through the Holy Spirit is eternal within the being of God.

4 We believe in God the Son. We see Jesus first as a man who knows the will of God and does it with freedom and love exceeding what is expected in a servant and found only in a son. His role in the world is unique: the Spirit-anointed Servant-Lord depicted in the Old and New Testaments as Messiah or Christ. Manhood was uniquely perfected in the response of Jesus to God the Father. In him there is a sonship without defect or strain. This sonship, we believe, has a foundation in God other than the sonship by creation and adoption to which the rest of mankind may aspire. We affirm that it was the eternal Son of God who came to the world in Jesus of Nazareth.

His words come home to us as the words of God himself. His deeds come home to us as the deeds of God himself. His redeeming compassion comes home to us as the redeeming compassion of God himself. All three, taken to their climax in the dying and resurrection of Jesus, convince us that we have found God not only through Jesus but in him. Exalted now to the majesty of divine power and love, he is our living Lord and Saviour Jesus Christ. We acknowledge him, so exalted, to be at all times God the Son eternally united with the Father in the one life of God.

From him our sonship is derived. God unites us to him by faith, and works within us through love to make our lives like his. This hope is for all mankind. All men are called to give themselves in worship to God through his Son; and he himself is to be worshipped with the Father and the Spirit in the unity of God's eternal being.

5 We believe in God the Holy Spirit. God himself conveys to men the gift of sonship granted to them in fellowship with Jesus Christ. By interpretation and persuasion he builds them into his new creation. This work is done by God personally present and active in the depths of human life. Men have used the name 'spirit' to speak of God as he penetrates with disembodied power and loving care into every part of his creation and brings his will to effect. They have used the same name for other influences acknowledged though not perceived; and to distinguish God from other so-called spirits they speak of him as the one and only holy spirit. The Holy Spirit is a personal name, together with Father and Son, for God himself. It is by fellowship with Jesus Christ that Christians have come to know him in this mode of subsistence.

God the Holy Spirit is at work when men learn through the events and words of the Bible how God gives himself in Jesus Christ. He is at work when men take their place in the community of the Church, and when by his help they find and fulfil in that community new possibilites of love and reconciliation with their fellow-men. The Holy Spirit is present whenever men seek to be led by God through contemporary events; with his support they may truly find a way forward and walk in it with the integrity of faith. His gracious presence is not confined to the Church; for even where the Spirit is not understood in relation to Jesus Christ, where his presence is undiscerned, where his very existence is denied, there too God works perpetually in the Holy Spirit to enlarge the possibilities of human life and to open the way for faith and sonship.

God the Holy Spirit penetrates into every part of human experience as Lord and life-giver. His work is not directly to disclose himself, but rather to make known through the Son the mind and will of the Father and to fulfil them. Yet when, through his action, men give themselves in worship to the Son, and through the Son to the Father, they give themselves also to the Spirit as Lord eternal, one with the Father and the Son.

6 We believe in one God. He has disclosed himself to men through his Son, physically present in human history as the man Jesus Christ. Through Jesus Christ we know God to be the Father whose grace and glory are reflected to us in the Son's obedience. We know too that the Son is united with the Father in the Spirit and in this communion is rightly to be worshipped. The knowledge, faith and worship which we declare are ours through one emancipating work, arising from one mind, one love, one God. It is this one God whom, with all Christians, we serve and adore.

God, the only God, reveals himself in the fatherly creation and government of the world; in the life, death, resurrection and reign of Jesus Christ our Lord; in the awakening of faith and love and hope, and their nourishment, in the hearts of men and in the life of the Church. We cannot comprehend God in the profundity of his eternal being, but we affirm with confidence that what he has revealed himself to be, this he eternally is: Father, Son and Holy Spirit, one God. To him be praise and glory for ever.

4   God is Sovereign over the Universe

1 We believe that God reigns over the universe. Plain evidence of his rule is not there for all to see; and Christians, no less than other men, are troubled by perplexity and doubt when they reckon with the facts of sin, wrongdoing and cruelty, of natural disaster, disease and death. Yet God calls men, in fellowship with Jesus Christ, to respond with complete trust to his wise and constant sovereignty. The universe, we believe, is his workmanship, and it is good. We are confident that he governs it, everywhere, all the time, with steadfast loyalty to his creatures; and that men may wholly trust his universal rule. We make no claim to full or clear understanding of how God's sovereignty works within the processes of the

physical universe or even in the course of human history, and we do not see a complete and satisfying goodness either in nature as it now is or in the patterns of human history. But, in Christian faith, we believe in God's rule: we look for hints and traces of it, guided by what we know of God through Jesus Christ, and we find them, both in the order and beauty of physical reality and in the histories of individuals and of societies. In detail we may misread the signs of God's government, but this does not shake our confidence that he does rule and that he is active everywhere in the universe. We are ready to affirm that all men's practical living in this universe depends for its worth on the sovereignty of God; and we repudiate any notion that the universe is under the sway of fate or chance, or that it is abandoned to anarchy.

2 We declare the character of Christian confidence in God's sovereignty and the ground on which it rests when first we affirm wisdom, love, power and serenity in God, from our knowledge of him through Jesus Christ, and then speak about the providence with which he reigns.

3 It is with wisdom, love, power and serenity that God knows and cares and rules throughout his universal domain. We speak about each attribute in turn, but each time with the rest in view. For it is in the expression of his love, made effective by his power and arising from his serentiy, that God is seen to be wise. It is because he is wise and powerful and serene in his loving that we entrust ourselves to him with a love responding to his own. We look to his power with confidence and hope because the power of God is the practice of wisdom and love grounded in serenity. We acknowledge his serenity with thankfulness, for if his wisdom, love and power were not conceived in peace and joy they would not bring to the realm of God the full joy and peace which he promises.

4 We affirm the wisdom of God. We cannot prove it. Some things that we experience are apparently at variance with it. But we believe in Christ and know that God is trustworthy. As we read his purpose to emancipate mankind through Jesus Christ and taste the fruits of its accomplishment, we are persuaded that all God's purposes are conceived and fulfilled in perfect wisdom. In all his purposes, and in the mastery required for their accomplishment, God acts with knowledge that is all-embracing and wholly true, and does so with unshakeable constancy and goodness. In God knowledge combines with goodness in ways beyond our highest experience. This is his

221

wisdom. In faith we rely upon its infinite resource with unlimited confidence.

5 We affirm in God the strong and loyal impulse to be for others all that in their interest he can be. This is his love. We cannot prove it. Some events in human history apparently contradict it; and we are not wholly able to interpret what it means for creatures other than human beings. But we believe in Christ and respond through all times of sorrow and bewilderment to the love declared in him. In love God has brought his human creatures into being; in love he has saved them in Christ; in love he prepares them for his final kingdom. Their freedom to rebel against their maker, to ignore their saviour, to resist the love which seeks their final glory, is itself a signal expression of the love God has for them and will never renounce. His love is wonderful beyond human praise; for in loving them God brings unwavering support to ungrateful and unworthy creatures. His limitless concern, self-initiated and expressed in his own self-giving, is the ground in God of all human hope.

6 We affirm the power of God. We are not able to trace out in detail the workings of the power he exerts; and there are manifestations of power in the universe which appear to suggest that all is not under his control. But we know something of God's power at its source; for we know Christ, the Son of the Father who sustains the physical world and makes it serve his purposes, the Son whose life was strong enough to overcome human death, from whom we receive the Holy Spirit with his transforming power. Power in God is the exercise of his authority, which is sovereign over all creatures. By his power he can create and sustain, he can save and could damn. In every use of his power God remains true to himself and to what he has revealed that he is. To separate his power from his wisdom, his love and his serenity would be to undo the meaning of the name God. His power is neither magical nor capricious. It expresses God's freedom to make his wisdom and love effective. Within the limits of his own consistency the freedom is absolute, for there is no power outside himself by which God could be coerced. From lives already being transformed by the power of God in Christ we affirm that the Lord whom we worship is God, almighty in his wisdom and love and serenity.

7 We affirm the serenity of God. He lives in the blessedness of everlasting joy and peace. Of this we are assured through Jesus Christ. But through him we also know that serenity, so far from

separating God from the struggles of his creatures, reinforces his compassion for them and is the ground of its stability and strength. God is seeking to give his own serenity to human beings, to be in them a source of strength and stability, not only in times of rest and calm but also in the experience of work and struggle. By sharing God's blessedness so far as they are able, men come to live with surer and deeper consideration for one another. To know God's delivering grace and to wonder at his sacrifice for us is also joyfully to adore in God the blessedness which cannot be shaken and the joy which cannot be taken away.

8 Under the rule of God men build up their lives in this universe over a course of time. What they have already become in past time is brought into the present; it is modified by what happens in the present moment; it is taken into the future for good or ill. We believe that this happens always under the providential care of God. In his dealings with Israel this has been made plain; and the truth of it was confirmed not only in the teaching of Jesus but also by the course of his life.

We affirm the providential care of God. By his grace he preserves what would otherwise perish; by grace he concurs with what happens in the present moment; by grace he governs its passage into the future in order to fulfil his good purposes. His providential care is exerted throughout with loving respect for the freedom and integrity of his creatures, hiding his action unless men freely turn to him in the response of faith. It is possible therefore to maintain, as many men do, that creatures merely follow a course of development intrinsic to them in their situation. But when, in the new freedom of integrity of Christian faith, men turn to God with knowledge and trust, they taste the benefits of his providential care and must speak of it out of their own experience.

We turn to God for guidance, and he shares with us the wisdom in his own purposes. We turn to him for support, knowing that we are inadequate to the demands of every present moment, and we have the support of his loyal love. We turn to him with prayers that his power may be perfected even in our weakness. We turn to him in the hope of sharing his serenity, so that we may do our part with good humour and truly human compassion. The prayers do not go unanswered and the hope is fulfilled. We do not know how God's sovereign care is exercised over creatures other than ourselves; but we believe that what he is to us he must also be in some comparable mode to them. We affirm the universal providence of God's rule.

9 In every event, and in all aspects of every event, God is active; in disaster and in success, in situations which menace human hopes and in situations which raise them high there is nothing which evades his knowledge, will and care. Human beings know this as they respond to his personal care and derive from it the guidance and support which God is waiting to give. They respond by learning from the facts which make up the event. God's activity is in these facts; it does not stand out as an additional factor, open to inspection or debate. Christians must learn, and learn by experience as all men do, how to live in God's world as it is. They must learn by examining life as others live it, not only as individuals but also in families, nations and other social groups. But they will interpret the evidence always in the light of the knowledge they have of God through Christ.

The Christian is called in every situation to express thanks and obedience to God in mind and deed, as Jesus did. Divine care, human experience, and Christian obedience belong together. God's personal care and help are found in this process of response to it. They cannot be affirmed as factors which, when present, excuse men either from learning by experience or from living as God requires. God's help is given to men in ways which evoke from them the maximum initiative and responsibility. If, then, the Christian is frequently perplexed and uncertain, he is not therefore dismayed. Perplexity and uncertainty turn him towards God for help and direction and also call out his own best effort. His life is doubly enriched as a result.

10 Of one thing the believer is certain; in every situation he can turn to God who is active in it. He can turn to God in situations of hardship and heartbreak, in his individual experience or in that of groups which engage his loyalty or in the history of nations; the presence of God in sovereign power will make it possible for the pain in such situations to help rather than harden those who must endure it. He can turn to God in situations of achievement and joy, whether the experience is his own or that of his family, of his social group or of mankind as a whole; the presence of God in sovereign power will save the believer from a false pride and from a false security. No situation in life, no discovery about the physical universe, no insight into the making of man or of history, should turn anyone away from God's love for him in Jesus Christ.

With each fresh occasion for personal knowledge of God's personal love and care, our confidence in his sovereignty over the universe is strengthened and renewed.

5   *God is Sovereign over the Church*

1 We worship God through Jesus Christ within the Christian Church. This Church is the whole company of believers, drawn from all humanity irrespective of nation, colour, race or language. God has called it into being to worship him and to make known and effective his purpose for all mankind. The Church is founded upon Jesus Christ. It can have for its own life his risen life which he is able and willing to share with all who, like members joined in one body, are joined to him through faith and by the Holy Spirit. Loyalty to Jesus Christ includes loyalty to his people.

2 The Church, we believe, is God's own creation, graciously given and graciously used by him to carry out his purpose in this world. God seeks to draw all mankind into fellowship with himself. God was in Christ reconciling the world to himself and nothing must ever obscure the fact that Jesus Christ has identified himself with all humanity and not only with the Church. God's concern, God's love and God's action in Christ are for all men and women and for every aspect of their being. It is for the sake of his liberating purpose towards all mankind that the Church exists, and its corporate life serves to build up Christians in faith and love and hope so that they may serve this purpose. The loyalty which Christians give to the Church includes both grateful acceptance of the form and task which God gives to it and watchful concern that in all respects it should follow its Lord as the servant of all mankind.

3 God creates the Church to be one, holy, catholic and apostolic; this we know by faith in Christ. In so far as God already enables the Church to be one and to be holy, those within it become living Church members; in so far as he already enables the Church to be catholic and apostolic, its members live by love enriched with depth and vision and are confident in mission; this we know also from experience. But the Church as Christians know it is not yet as God would have it be. In varying degrees and aspects it is disunited,

unholy, narrowed by false rigidities and untrue to its apostolic origin and mission; any defect in any one of these respects carries with it defects in all. Yet, in faith and from experience, we declare that God does enable his Church to be what he requires. He uses special features of his people's life together as means which bring them to live by grace under the Lordship of Christ in the present world. These means of grace are God's gifts to his Church, gifts entrusted to human hands and therefore vulnerable to human misconception, ingratitude and lack of faith. His enabling power is freely offered: in so far as it is accepted, the Church is what he would have it be; in so far as it is rejected, it is not. In the sovereignty of grace God is present to his Church, in living authority through Christ its Lord and with the power of the Holy Spirit; and in his hands the means of grace are sufficient to bring the Church to unity, holiness, catholicity, and apostolicity as he intends.

4 From our particular experience within the whole Church of Christ we seek now to express the understanding and confidence we have about these means of grace and about the structure of Church life which God creates through them. The fundamental principle, which we share with other Christians, is that Church life must be so ordered as most fully to express the Lordship of Christ and to enable the Church to fulfil its mission in the world at each and every place and time. In part we know already what this means. But we know, too, that the Church must constantly look to the judgement of God upon its own life. Where its thought and practice are reformed and renewed in love and obedience answering to God's grace, true life for the Church will be re-born.

5 God creates the Church through the Bible. The Bible is the record of God's revelation of himself in the life of ancient Israel where there was true knowledge of him; of his revelation in the life, death and resurrection of Jesus Christ where in our fellow-man he was personally and uniquely present among us; of his revelation in the testimony of Christ's apostles and in the life of those who first heard and believed. In this revelation the living and eternal God discloses the truth about himself which is to be found in all his dealings with mankind. By knowing this record and steeping itself in the details the Church is able to hold fast to the revelation of God and accord to it the authority which it rightfully has over all the Church's life and thought.

The Bible must be read with fully critical attention if the Church is to discern the truth which is binding and not be in bondage to what is not binding; for the Bible is not free from human error and confusion and contradictions. It is a trustworthy means of grace, not in the sense that it is impervious to criticism but in the sense that through its records we are able to know God reliably and trust him confidently. Through the words of the Bible God in Christ speaks directly to believers and brings home to their lives and to the life of the Church the reality of his claims and his promises. There are in the Church other means and agencies which serve to bring its life and thought under the Lordship of Christ; but all of them are rooted in God's revelation of himself in the Bible, and by it they are also to be judged.

6 God requires the Church to remember its own history. He calls it to study expressions by the Church of its faith and thinking, the institutions of the Church and its standards of action, decisions by Councils, and the practice of piety; and events which display the Church's course in this world. No one period has an overriding claim on the attention of the contemporary Church; there is much to learn not only from periods of vitality and expansion but also from dull and dead periods. But we acknowledge with particular thankfulness the great affirmations of Christian faith which we have from the past: the Apostles' Creed, the Nicene Creed, the *Te Deum*, together with notable Confessions and Catechisms produced at the Reformation. They direct us to the Bible's whole message and we follow them in so far as they lead us to God in Christ.

God calls his Church to scrutinize its life hitherto with open historical attentiveness; to consider the experience of any who have claimed the Christian name whether or not they satisfy particular theological standards for being the Church; and to discern where in past times Christian communities were obedient and where they were disobedient. We have fellowship with earlier generations by appreciating the questions which they met and answered in their own way. Through this fellowship God gives to us his own help and guidance when, for the sake of present obedience, we give our minds to questions which earlier generations did not always answer with lasting satisfaction and some cases did not have to face.

7 God dwells in his Church by his Spirit and the obedient Church will learn with his aid what God wants it to think and to do now. The Church must often do this in times of uncertainty and

227

confusion. It should not look for results which are spectacular in human eyes, its own or those of unbelievers. It is sufficient if in restrospect it is plain, even to hostile observers, that the Church has sought the will and purpose of God and not its own selfish ends. The Church should pray for grace so to decide and so to act that, because of what is done and the way it is done, men find it easier and not harder to worship God and to persist in faithful and confident Christian living. God calls on the Church to open channels for the free action of his grace within each congregation and within all wider associations for Church life, and to preserve liberty of conscience so that the fullest response of obedience to God may be offered in love and freedom.

8 God calls the Church into renewed love and obedience to himself through its worship. The worship of the Church is expressed in many ways; through prayer and praise, through the reading of the Bible and the proclamation of Christ in preaching, through the sacraments of Baptism and the Lord's Supper, through many and varied acts of devotion and Christian ordinances, and through teaching and fellowship which prepare members for discipleship and deepen it. God gives himself to his people when they truly worship him.

God's gift of himself comes through his Word. It comes in Jesus Christ who is the Word of God made man. Preaching, which takes up the Bible's testimony to him and makes it contemporary with the hearers, has an essential place at the centre of Christian worship. To preach Christ is to proclaim him and to apply his truth to the mind and conscience of believers and unbelievers. It is done under obedience to God and with faith that God will speak his own Word to those who hear. The Word of God declared in preaching is the Word enacted and confirmed in the ordinances of Baptism and the Lord's Supper.

When, in Christ's name, the Church observes the ordinance of Baptism, it makes explicit at a particular time and place and for a particular person what God has done in Christ for all his creation. With that person and for him the Church claims the benefit of God's promise to bless believers and their children. It undertakes to receive and to nourish within its fellowship the one who is baptized. Through this ordinance children are brought with their believing parents into the life of grace. The response of those baptized in infancy must be fulfilled in considered acknowledgement of Jesus as Lord when they are of an age to give it and to undertake willing service and responsibility in the Church's life through membership of a particular church.   When in accord with Christ's own action at supper on the night of his betrayal and arrest, the Church observes the ordinance of the Lord's Supper, Christ is present in his risen power to renew his covenant fellowship with his people and theirs with him. He brings the particular church assembled at his table into renewed fellowship with the whole Church on earth and in heaven. Through the symbolic meal, with its traditional elements of bread and wine, he restores the Church in its pilgrimage through this world by giving himself afresh to its members and by taking up their lives into his own self-offering. At this Supper the Church looks back with special thanksgiving to the death of Christ, which the Supper proclaims and interprets as the accomplishment of God's eternal purpose; it also looks forward to the final establishment of God's sovereignty.

The worship of the Church, obediently and faithfully designed, brings those who participate in it to the point where they are open to Christ's message, receptive to his judgement, exultant in his promise, and empowered to be his disciples. It is offered to God in pure response to his glory and grace; he uses it as a means of grace to the worshippers, to renew them in love for their service and witness in the world.

9 God keeps the Church faithful to its calling through its members. He lays upon them the duties of membership in a particular church, duties which are also opportunities for them to express their faith. It is their duty to share in public worship and to practise private devotion; the quality of membership is closely linked with worship and each influences the other for better or worse. It is their duty also to uphold Christian standards in their daily living. They must use, too, the freedom which is theirs to join in building up the fellowship of the Church and to share in the decisions which shape its life and service.

God surrounds and supports each individual Christian with the faithfulness, the devotion, the initiative and the service of fellow-Christians. In true Church membership the Christian responds, not only with personal faith in Christ but also with active good will towards his fellow-Christians especially those with whom he is in constant association. By this life together in the Church's fellowship of the Holy Spirit, all the members of the Church

229

help to bring others to Christ. They help one another to turn from self-concern towards Christ; they keep one another steadfast to him; they support one another in patient and honest dealings with all men; they awaken and maintain a lively awareness of God's mission to all mankind. Through the power of this life together, a congregation expects to be used by God for bringing others into the life of the Church.

Through constant caring for the well-being of a particular church and of those fellowships of churches and those Church enterprises to which it is committed, Christians learn together how to make a common Christian judgement expressing practical love and obedience to God. They grow in discipleship when together they seek the Holy Spirit's guidance and each tests his own attitude in the light of attitudes adopted by others. Members meet, in the domestic life of the Church, bringing experience gained in the daily life of the world which helps to suggest where the paths of wisdom and of service should run. From their meeting they go out again to daily life with fresh experience of reaching Christian decisions in the fellowship of the Church, strengthened to share again with men of all faiths and of none in making decisions which will best uphold the dignity and well-being of all who are affected. In this process God is able to make Church membership fruitful beyond the Church's domestic life. He teaches his Church again and again that it does not live for itself but for its ministry of love and service and witness, and in the local neighbourhood of each particular church and to the ends of the earth.

10 There is a ministry to be fulfilled by the whole Church, through all its individual members and through its corporate life. God keeps his Church loving and obedient by requiring from it wise care and deep compassion for the lives of individual persons and for the social life of mankind.

For the better practice of its own corporate life and worship and for the better exercise of membership by individuals, God has given to the Church from the beginning a special office of ministry within its own structure. The appointment of men and women to this office by the gift and calling of God is acknowledged by the Church. It sets these servants apart to lead in its worship and teaching and in the ordering of its life, and to lead and strengthen their fellow-members in Christian faith and compassion and in claiming the world for Christ.

There is division in the Church through disagreements about the forms and authorization of internal ministries. We are firmly persuaded that unity must always be threatened by a belief that one and only one mode of authorization is tolerable for the Church's ministries. The refusal of fellowship, grounded upon such a belief however sincerely held, is an offence against Christ and his Gospel. No particular form of ministry and no mode of authorization, however venerable and precious, ensure that the Church is actually obedient to its Lord. A desire for security, strong in all human affairs, prompts the search for a ministry which can do this; but that search contradicts the character of mature Christian faith.

Nevertheless, the ministry of the Church found within its own structure is God's instrument and not man's. Those set apart for its tasks are to be trained with great care and appointed with due solemnity. Their office should have recognition from the whole Church; and with other Christians we look for paths of reformation to take us to this goal in truth and obedience. But we rejoice that even in the divided Church God uses ministries undertaken in faith and love to bless his Church and to build it up in Christ. As he has used them in the past, so he will continue to use them, in the sovereignty of his grace.

11 By these principal means of grace God creates his Church under the Lordship of Jesus Christ and helps it to fulfil its mission. In the practice of Church life his gifts are open to misconstruction and misuse; and when the Church allows its own self-regard to obstruct the purpose God has for it, his means of grace are perverted. In seeking, as it must, to cleanse its life from such abuse, the Church must attend to God's direction that in life and thought his Church points beyond itself.

God calls his Church to point beyond itself to Christ. He is its Lord; it is his community and only under him is it the instrument through which God's will is done. Christians rightly feel affection and loyalty for the Church and have confidence in it, but these are kept in place and surpassed by their fidelity to Christ. Whenever the Church claims for itself the obedience owed to its Lord, it falls away from its true character.

God calls his Church to point away from itself not only to Christ but also to men and women with their personal opportunities and needs. The Church exists to share with Christ his care for men and women. To treat their actual needs as less important than the

Church's own habits or convenience is to turn from the service of God to the service of self.

God calls his Church to point away from itself not only to Christ and mankind but also to the final Kingdom of God. In this world the Church is given by God as an essential part of life in Christ Jesus; and to share with all its members in worship, fellowship and service is a source of joy. But the Church exists to serve the coming of God's full sovereignty and in the splendour which is to come he will draw all the life of the Church into his Kingdom.

Under this self-denying discipline of witness made in faith and love and hope the Church is enabled by God to become what he creates it to be; one, holy, catholic and apostolic.

12 The unity of the Church of Christ is a fact because Christ is really present with his people. It is established by his presence, but it must also be expressed in the fellowship of all Christian people with their Lord, and with the Church of past centuries, and with Christians in their own immediate neighbourhood, and with Christians throughout the world. So far-reaching a requirement is not easily fulfilled. By good things as well as by bad the expression of unity has been broken and the gift has been forfeited, though never, by the grace of God, withdrawn. God calls his Church to find fresh visible expressions of the unity it already has and to move towards the complete unity which in Christ he seeks to give. In striving to answer his call the Church must move towards more complete expression of its character as holy and catholic and apostolic.

13 The Church is holy because it belongs to God; he has called it into being and it is owned and used by him. He keeps it as his own through the Lord Jesus Christ and obedience to him is the condition by which its holiness is sustained. The Church expresses holiness by the purity of true response to God, unadulterated with evil; and the New Testament emphasizes that the obedience of holiness, arising from clean hearts, becomes visible in deeds of constant and consistent love. So exacting a requirement of God's grace calls for disciplines within the Church's life that members may be strengthened when they must offer resistance or make renunciations in face of evil, and the half-hearted may be encouraged to commit themselves more deeply to the standards God expects from his Church.

The Church's sensitivity to the touch of the Holy Spirit has at no time been sufficient for full obedience. The Church is still in process of being redeemed and therefore in process of reaching obedience.

Members feel sorrow because they fail to produce the harvest of the Holy Spirit. They feel disquiet because the communities whose life they share fail to lead a sufficiently disciplined life. A proof that God keeps the Church holy is that individuals and communities within it are moved to care about shortcomings as they grow towards maturity in the mind of Christ. Knowing their own need as sinners for the forgiveness of Christ and for patient forbearance from their fellow-members, they learn how in God's Church the strong must bear with the weak and must guard against their own possibilities of failure. The joy of being nourished and sustained as a member of Christ's community overrides for believers the pain of belonging to a Church not yet perfect. Misconceived anxieties about holiness bring much trouble and division into the Church's life; but in this joy there is power to heal.

14 The Church is catholic because Jesus Christ is universal both in his Lordship and in his care for his people. Through Jesus Christ God endows his Church with truth and love and power that it may live for him throughout the world and through the ages and serve his purpose for all human beings in all aspects of their life. This universal character is the catholicity given to the Church in Christ. In practice the Church often refuses to be catholic. Yet, narrowed and divided though it is, the Church is aware in all parts of being called by the Gospel to catholicity; and Jesus Christ remains the ever-present source of the catholicity to which it is called.

The Christian Church exists historically in the form of particular churches, locally present with varying scope and organization at times and places throughout the world. Through his means of grace, God makes it possible for particular churches, everywhere and at all times, to display fellowship in the Gospel and fellowship with all Christians, and so through Christ to express in that place the catholicity of the whole Church within which each particular Church has its life. Particular churches must obey the universal call of their Lord. We reaffirm our Congregational conviction that the wholeness of Christ's universal Church may be present in local congregations, as well as in wider associations, where God gathers people together in constant relationship for worship, for fellowship, for service and for witness to the world, under the care of Christ their Lord.

Failures in catholicity have arisen from breaches of fellowship; and breaches of fellowship from failures in catholicity. Fellowship in the Church is strained by hostility arising from differing conceptions of the community life through which the Church expresses itself whether locally or universally, from differences in judging how submissive the Church should be to national or social pressures, from differing ways of expressing the Gospel theologically. Fellowship is strained by false rigidities which narrow the boundaries of Christ's Church; it is strained equally by vagueness, shallowness and superstition which diminish the truth and power and love of Christ in his Church. Separations have occurred through lack of patience in dealing with differences and defects; selfish indifference to the well-being of the whole Christian Church causes separations and perpetuates them. Christians, loyal to principle and concerned for truth, have been obliged to separate from others and this has occasioned hostility, sometimes on one side only and sometimes on both. Breaches within the Church do not of necessity diminish the catholicity with which separate churches live in response to their universal Lord; but in varying degrees this consequence is everywhere apparent in practice.

Christ renews his gift of catholicity to the Church whenever his people seek the truth together in love. God is calling Christians from all traditions to reach out with sympathy to each other that his purpose for all human beings in all aspects of their life may be fully served. Christians should respond by learning from other traditions and by making known their own. They must pray for humility, patience and understanding, that they may see truth to which they have been blind and come to value riches they have failed to appreciate. Knowing that rigidity and shallowness are to be found in us as well as in others, we pray that God will deliver us and all Christian communions into true catholicity.

15 The risen and exalted Lord sends his Church with a witness to make in all the world and with a mission to the world arising within its witness. This is its apostolic calling. Authorized by the Holy Spirit, it is in the world to declare from generation to generation the Gospel of Jesus Christ. Its integrity as Christ's apostolic Church appears most plainly in its fidelity, as witness, to the testimony of Christ's first apostles; in its continuity of concern for true worship; and in the care it expresses for the world whose Lord and Saviour is Jesus Christ. The mission of the Church is discharged through these functions: to publish the

234

truth about Jesus Christ and to lead the world in worship to God through him; in the power of the Spirit to build up its members in faith and goodness; to produce in and through their corporate life the practice of human living grounded on reconciliation; to win from all who have not heard of God's grace in Jesus Christ a glad acknowledgement in faith and life; to warn men of God's perpetual hostility to evil and to urge that they abandon wrong-doing; to give loving service to mankind for Christ's sake; to seek and pray for the coming of God's reign on earth and to prepare for the fullness of his kingdom when God shall be all in all. In discharging its mission the Church is hampered by clumsiness, timidity, indifference and worldliness; and blemish in any aspect of mission impairs the witness it is commissioned to give. The grace of God renews apostolicity beyond each fault by sending the Church to work afresh, in the strength of his forgiveness.

16 The Church of Jesus Christ is visible wherever it responds to the gracious presence and sovereign claims of God. It is seen in men and women who hold faithfully to the news of God's love in Jesus Christ declared in the Bible; in those who cherish such continuity with the Church of past centuries as will enable them to be obedient to God's will in the present; in those who seek fellowship with all Christian people; in those who practise patience, tolerance, understanding and forgiveness, both within the fellowship of the Church and in their dealings with all human beings; in those who constantly seek, with eagerness and humility, for fresh light on the ways of active Christian discipleship; and in those who seek, without wearying, to bring the world, near and far, to an acknowledgement of the Lordship of Christ. In them the Church and God's sovereignty over it are made plain together. Many people regard the Church with sentimental and even supersti-tious veneration. To many others its very name has a harsh and ugly sound. Many others, again, ignore it, despise it, or regard it without hope. We acknowledge that the sinfulness of Christian people has contributed to this state of affairs. But no sinfulness in the Church can obliterate the wonderful and glorious fact that God draws Chris-tian believers into this community and imparts to it the risen life of Jesus Christ. We know from our own experience that the reality of true Church life as the New Testament speaks of it is not always to be seen; but it is sufficiently present to be known and enjoyed.

In affirming it we affirm through it the gracious sovereignty of God.

6 *God will Triumph*

1 God's purpose for the physical universe is for the most part hidden from us in mystery; we do not suppose that its only function is to provide support and discipline for men's bodies and minds during their lifetime on earth. We are certain that God's purpose will be worthy of his own majesty, and that it will be consistent with the dignity and splendour apparent in the universe to minds instructed through scientific inquiry. Yet we do not know, either in Christian faith or through scientific inquiry, what God will do with his creation when he completes the open expression of his sovereignty.

2 God's purpose for mankind has been disclosed, we believe, in Jesus Christ. By raising him from the dead, God made us certain that this purpose will not be frustrated by anything which sin and death can do. His dealings with individuals will be in the setting of his whole dealing with mankind. How his purpose for mankind will work out remains enigmatic to us in very many respects. Yet through his deed of grace in Jesus Christ we have intimations sufficient to make us look forward with confident hope to all that he intends: a new and wonderful fellowship between God and mankind and within it a new fellowship of man with man. This expectation helps to determine the way we live now. Through Jesus Christ we know that already we have our being in the world God brings to light in him and are members of his one human family in heaven and earth.

3 In faith we expect God to complete his purpose of all mankind and for each individual person by endowing men beyond their death with new resources for being alive unto God in fellowship with Jesus Christ. In the powers already granted through the gift of the Holy Spirit, Christians have a foretaste of the new being. It has, for its indispensable grounds, the judgement of God through which men will know at last the whole truth about themselves, and the saving love of God which removes all condemnation from

those joined in manhood with his obedient Son their Saviour Jesus Christ. For those who trust the grace of the Lord Jesus Christ the judgement of God's holy love is the gateway to his everlasting mercy.

4 Whether every human being will be able to endure so searching a judgement and thankfully to take back his life from the judge's hands, we do not know. Those who do, will live henceforth transfigured in the glory of God's perfected creation. That God should discard from this creation any creature precious to him is inconceivable. Yet we are sure that God will for ever respect human freedom and will not impose salvation upon any who may be everlastingly recalcitrant. Human beings are warned not to harden themselves in opposition to God or seek to defeat his gracious purpose. To be banished from the presence of the Lord and from the glory of his power is a prospect to be envisaged by the rebellious with appropriate fear. Yet, in affirming this, we know Christ as the Good Shepherd who seeks until he finds, and we disclaim any right to speak of limits beyond which the patience and compassion of God are exhausted.

5 God's wisdom, love and power will be fully vindicated in the triumph of his purposes for the universe and for the corporate life of mankind within it. This triumph is presented in the Bible as the outcome of a final conquest by God of all evil powers which at present bring human life into the blindness and bondage and rebellion of sin. Our minds cannot bring into focus this aspect of God's dominion; but we are encouraged to believe that the long struggle for right in which mankind shares will have its satisfying outcome when God brings his sovereignty to triumphant completion.

6 We look forward to acts of God which bring final transformation to human life and admit human beings to share in his own eternal joy and felicity. Creatures have been called into being to reflect the unimaginable glory of the everlasting God. Cleansed from sin we shall see God in Christ Jesus in open splendour, and he will make us like himself. We do not know in what universal framework human lives so transfigured will be set; nor how in that framework God's other purposes for his created universe will be fulfilled. We do know that God is the source, the guide and the goal of all that is, and that in his serenity he sees the end from the beginning. He lives in the blessedness of everlasting joy and

peace, and his creatures will share in that blessedness and rejoice in it.

7 God Requires Obedience from Human Life and Blesses it

1 God's will for all human beings is that they should come to live in love and obedience to him and in mutual responsibility and love to one another. This is the life which he requires from all men and seeks to give to all men. By faith in Jesus Christ man find new freedom to meet God's requirement and to receive his gift in their course of life through this world. From this basis Christians seek, with men of other faiths and of none, for standards of human action which will maintain and enhance the fullness and dignity of human living among all men everywhere. The Christian has specific insights and duties because of his allegiance to Christ and his Church; and these enable him to look in a Christian way at the opportunities and duties he shares with all his fellow-men. But he will see what these opportunities and duties are, and will derive strength to fulfil them in faith, only as he enters into the general experience of human life. And he must be ready to acknowledge signs of true human obedience and of God's blessing wherever Christ may lead him to see them.

2 It is within God's purpose that human beings should seek fullness in developing their gifts of mind and of body and enjoying the satisfactions open to them. Yet, as we know from the example of Jesus Christ, this is not an overriding aim. Human life is lived in a world where God's rule does not yet openly prevail; and all men, in all respects, are far from being perfect in the ways of obedience to God. Developments and satisfactions which, to human judgement, promise greater fullness of life may in practice corrupt that fullness rather than enhance it; they may be beyond possible attainment because the world is as it is; they may be incompatible with deeper obligations of obedience to God and with love to men. Frustration of particular hopes and purposes is therefore something men must be ready to accept, and to accept without bitterness. The way to fuller life, moreover, may lie through a demand that men willingly give up something of their own natural development if love to God or men should require this.

3 Looking to Jesus Christ, we are persuaded that dignity in human life is attained through obedience to God and love for fellow-men. In Jesus Christ himself human dignity is complete. From him the same dignity is imparted to other lives, sometimes directly through Christian faith and obedience, and sometimes indirectly through the influence of Christian tradition upon human imagination and behaviour.

Every expression of this dignity may serve to guide and invigorate those who see it. It is expressed wherever men go beyond the limits set by prudence and calculation in fulfilling the common duties which God lays upon us all; and wherever men show a Christ-like generosity of faithfulness and love. To these possibilities all men are explicitly summoned by Christ's word and example.

In their response as disciples, Christians have an inexhaustible obligation to show how faith works through love in fulfilling all life's ordinary duties. They have no superior standing in God's sight. But those who accept Jesus Christ as Saviour and Lord and live in his way gain insights which reveal life's dimensions and values; and they are set free to share in life with willing and joyful self-forgetfulness.

The obligation to conduct human life in a Christian way cannot be reduced to a code of rules, though rules may have a place in helping to express it. Certainly it is not presented as a law to be imposed on all regardless of belief. There are many, not Christians, who through the attractive power of Christ's gift live with something of the same insight and freedom which Christians receive, and Christians are thankful for every expression of the true human dignity which his gift makes possible.

4 Men live by using the provisions of the physical universe. Christ's word and example require us to turn the resources of nature to men's material and spiritual advantage. This is God's universe, and his will is that men should improve their understanding of it by scientific investigation and should reshape the conditions of human life by technological wisdom and technical power in ways which maintain and enhance human dignity. Christians are confident that every enlargement of true understanding will show a universe which may still be apprehended as God's creation, and their confidence does not carry with it any restriction on scientific freedom. Equally, the belief that the world is God's creation and therefore good does not imply passive and cautious acquiescence

in what is or what has been. Yet here, as everywhere in human life, human enterprise can bring peril as well as reward. When men take ways which are not in fact ways of obedience to God, they not only do wrong, but in so doing expose human life to distortion, narrowing and disaster. In disobedience men have used technical power in the past and may use it in the future to their own hurt, by exploiting the universe greedily or indifferently and ignoring their responsibility for the well-being of all living creatures and of future generations. But misplaced reverence for the physical world is equally disobedient; so too is the failure of nerve which makes men shrink from extending their control within it. All mean in dealing with the world are dealing with God to whom it belongs. Those who deal with it wisely and responsibly are doing his will.

5 Men live in relations with one another. Their life shows marks of obedience to God and evidence of his blessing when they deal with one another in responsible fellowship, respecting, caring for and serving one another. God's sovereignty in Jesus Christ is not confined to the private lives of individuals. He claims supreme authority over the public life of mankind.

This does not confer upon his Church any right to the control of public affairs, but it does impose upon Christians a responsibility to share actively in common human concern about the institutions through which mankind's corporate life is expressed and about their interacting claims: those institutions through which men seek political well-being, cultural and educational ends, the doing of professional and economic business, and the domestic institutions of home and family. These are within God's realm, where his will is that men should respond to his sovereignty through Jesus Christ. Fullness and dignity of life as revealed in him call for both individual liberty and corporate unity. When the individual's self-expression enriches the community and when a community's corporate discipline protects and exalts the individual spirit, then God is obeyed.

Men who are obedient, though they set appropriate value on permanence and stability, will be alert to the call for change and development. God's purposes are fulfilled when men create social institutions which restrain injustice and oppression and leave an open way for people to live together in freedom and fellowship. They are God's servants (whether they know it or not) who construct social frameworks which acknowledge each man's dignity and set him free to choose his own way and be responsible for his choice, no matter what his nation, race, religion or politics may be. They are God's servants, too, who resist measures that degrade human life, restrict its necessary freedom, or minimize community effort and responsibility. Christians must be ready to share in the effort required to preserve and improve good government, and, as occasion may demand, must be awkward in thought and in practice, in resistance to public authorities whose acts increase the difficulty of living human life in a Christian way.

6 In the wider associations of mankind, economic, cultural and political, we believe that fidelity to God's intention for human life is reflected in these principles:

> that there should be respect for the impartial rule of law and for duly constituted authority – only so is man delivered from self-destructive anarchy;

> that law should win men's respect when it sets limits to the advantages of selfishness at the expense of the whole community;

> that, together with law, there should be freedom to obey God rather than men, and freedom for fair and humane dealings beyond legal requirements;

> that all men, whatever power they exercise, must be answerable to others for the just use of power, be it in the form of wealth or intellect or birth or education or office or status or political influence;

> that human effort should have as its ultimate justification the well-being of persons as persons;

> that there should be constant concern for those in need, not only for neighbours in a particular society but anywhere in the world;

> that need should be met in such a way that the personal lives of the needy are respected.

7 The family, based on the lifelong marital commitment of husband and wife, though it takes many forms, is indispensable to the health of any social order. Marriage is the condition which allows most fully for personal love and respect between man and woman. Here God's intention may be plainly seen. It is in the marital commitment that sexual intercourse has its rightful place; and it is wrong to deprive children of the early support and training they should be given in a family home. Because the interplay of personal lives can produce havoc as well as happiness, the family may be a sphere of

bitterness, tyranny and frustration. When God's intention is fulfilled it is a sphere in which husband and wife, parents and children, can learn respect and trust, love and forgiveness, patience and humour, understanding and faithfulness, the ways of sacrifice and the ways of rejoicing.

8 God has brought mankind into existence as a human population within the physical universe. As part of the animal creation, mankind shares with other living creatures a common environment and appetites and basic resources for living. Men have exceptional powers for cultivating their environment and are able by their work to have dominion over other creatures. Human obedience to God includes respect for the life of fellow-creatures and where men wantonly exploit their dominion over animals, plants or inorganic resources, God's purpose is violated. It is honoured where animals are treated with humane wisdom and where vegetable and mineral resources are used with skill and forethought.

9 A mark of true humanity is to be sensitive to beauty. The glory of God is reflected in the order of the universe, in the majesty and terror of great immensities, in variety of light and colour and sound, in the charm which the bodies of living things can display. Mankind's response to its physical environment in the form of work can be graced with elegance and distinction where, in the form of play, there is added response which creates and reveals beauty. The enjoyment of beauty, especially if unrelated to all that makes for human well-being, can blind men to God even in their appreciation of the beauty he makes possible; the inordinate pursuit of beauty may close their lives to other aspects of his call upon them. But where beauty is wantonly neglected or destroyed, the world is impoverished and God's purpose is dishonoured.

10 Human living is invested with dignity and worth when men find the ways of obedience to God. God is calling all human beings in all circumstances to live as he requires; he gives his blessing to those who follow his ways, some acknowledging and others not acknowledging him whose requirement they are. His call is obeyed when men strive to protect their fellows from impoverishment and sickness and physical calamity. It is obeyed in all efforts to seek true interdependent fellowship and freedom for mankind. He calls men to fight for what is right and humane when there is tyranny and oppression. He calls them to maintain their human protest against what is wrong even if it should be plainly to their own hurt to do so.

In face of selfishness, stupidity, short-sightedness, inertia and malice, in themselves, as well as in others, he calls men to act with kindness, intelligence, imagination, courage and devotion.

Where practices hitherto accepted present an intolerable threat to humane living, God calls men to abandon such practices and to find new ways of dealing with the matters at stake. As with slavery in the past, so now men must search their conscience about the resort to war, which brings shameful exploitation and corruption and waste of life, human and non-human, and of the earth's resources. In all his requirements God calls men to act with faith in face of risk. He calls them to live in this world as his pilgrim people, with no security except that which is theirs through abiding in him as they actively obey his will.

11 Individually and in their social groups men must struggle to find and follow the ways of obedience. This is plain to us not least from the history of the Church itself where obedience and disobedience are intermingled. The problems which confront men are posed for them by the physical setting in which they have to act, by past history, by their own convictions and intentions and by the intentions and convictions of those who must share in finding and accepting some solution. Solutions less satisfactory than are possible will be reached when men act without ideals. This is liable to happen also when men, determined to accept nothing less than the ideal, show no critical awareness that an ideal may serve to mask less noble motives. Men should act with convictions, firmly held though always open to revision and held with tolerance and respect for those whose convictions differ. Solutions arrived at on this basis, though imperfect in themselves, may serve to fulfil God's requirement, if they are accepted with patience and goodwill.

God calls each individual person to act with a right attitude to his own life as well as to other people and to God himself. Each must listen to what God teaches him both through what happens to him and in what he does. God looks to him for generosity and compassion towards other people; and he expects a man to be ready to suffer even when he is in the right. God seeks to draw each man to himself and to win his acknowledgement of God as the Lord who lays rightful claim to human obedience.

12 Believing as we do that men may give practical obedience to God without acknowledging him whom they obey, we affirm also that wherever this requirement is fulfilled it is by his help. Though

failure to worship God in Jesus Christ is always a hurt to human life, it does not destroy the real obedience rendered to God by the practice of intellectual integrity, patience, compassion, striving for what is right, sacrifice for friends, courage, faithfulness. Human beings, who in these ways co-operate with God through some aspects of their life, display the influence of his grace. For this we give thanks to him, humbly and joyfully, whether or not they themselves acknowledge God.

13 Yet God's purpose for human life will be fulfilled only in men and women who respond to his leading. Some men who do not worship God are in some respects a shining example to their fellows, Christian as well as non-Christian. But, for all men, failure to worship God reduces the standards they can attain in actual living. It leaves men alienated from the source of human integrity. God calls all human beings to worship him with gratitude and trust, and blesses them wherever self preoccupation is lost in praise and adoration of his goodness.

14 The worship of God in Jesus Christ does not absolve anyone from, nor is it a substitute for, the proper qualities of human living. Nor do Christians enjoy any kind of privileged position in which they are emancipated from the discipline, drudgery and difficulty associated with human living. Church attendance and Church loyalty, where not made impossible by circumstances, are primary conditions for the practice of Christian living; but their strict observance in no way compensates for defects in daily practice – lack of integrity, absence of self-sacrifice, failure in loving-kindness, or refusal of responsible service. Nor does Christian faith give answers to technical problems which can be solved only in the light of relevant knowledge. Christians must learn from truth and goodness wherever they are to be found. The special task entrusted to them is to show in practice what help Christian faith provides for the living of ordinary human life.

8   God Shares his Joy with Men in their Christian Discipleship

1 To all who live in obedience to him and have fellowship with him, God gives a share in his eternal joy. Christians enter upon that life, when, confronted through Christ's presence with the grace and

glory of God, they commit themselves in faith as disciples. In the life Christ offers to his disciples there is freedom from sin and power to overcome sin's distorting effects. With freedom and power to transcend sin's miseries, there is joy for men.

No Christian is holy as Christ is holy; freedom from sin is not yet complete in Christian experience. In themselves human beings are not worthy of life in full fellowship with God, nor capable of it. They need continual forgiveness and renewal as their means to freedom. They need power from God, sufficient to transform what they are, to sustain what they become, and to strengthen them for new deeds of faith and obedience. Through God's grace these needs are met, not once only but again and again in the lives of those actively committed to Christian discipleship. Christians therefore share that joy in living which the eternal God has in himself.

2 The freedom which comes with forgiveness is freedom from whatever hinders fellowship with God. It is known in experience as a growing liberation from fears and obsessions. Recalcitrant Christians, all too slowly, find themselves able and willing to turn from a life selfishly centred in their own well-being and haunted by fear for their own interests to a life of outgoing care for the well-being of others.

The new freedom is a disciplined freedom. It is nurtured through continual acknowledgement of unworthiness before God and a willingness to be changed in every relationship. Christians, further-more, often have to learn through suffering. Christian faith leads men to act against many selfish instincts and often against the grain of society. Its discipline may be painful and burdensome, not only because of resistances which take their toll, but also because at times faith may find no better expression than in necessary but uneasy compromise. But it is discipline which liberates men from the prison-house of self for life with God and with fellow-men. Its pains, accepted in faith, can enlarge the power to love.

3 Apart from the grace of God in Jesus Christ the Christian life would be too high and exacting for any to reach and sustain. But with his grace, God brings into human lives his own wise and loving power. Men and women, called in Christian discipleship to share the corporate life of God's faithful people, receive power, each according to his need and opportunity; power to love God in response to his own loving, power to obey him, power to learn from him and hold fast to his ways despite external and internal

dissuasives. There is power for each as all participate in the worship of the Church and in its local and world-wide life and mission; as all learn from the Church of the centuries and discover God's call in a new day; as each in daily living remembers the present reality of those who with open vision enjoy the glory of God in his triumphant sovereignty. Men and women are transformed and sustained and invigorated by the power God gives them. They learn more of the mind of Christ and learn to display it as their own mind by letting his sacrificial love have free course in themselves. Their fellowship with Jesus Christ is able to grow and to become more evident.

To many who do not share it, the Christian life appears to consist largely of strenuous endeavour to maintain moral standards and to fulfil duties and responsibilities which others evade without apparent loss. That Christian discipleship has its burdens and costliness is not to be denied. But, as experienced from within, the cost is accepted willingly and the burdens are lightened. Some things which, without faith or with flagging faith, seem to be intolerably burdensome are not seen as burdens at all. Constant attendance at public worship and responsibility for church affairs, prayer in private and reading of the Bible, and loyalty to Christian allegiance in everyday life: these are duties, but duties accepted as God's gracious gifts. They provide faith with strong and joyful confirmation and make it living and powerful.

4 With freedom from fears and with power to overcome evils there is also promised to the Christian a share in God's own eternal joy. This joy, which seeks men through pain as well as through peace and pleasure, is ours through faith. It is not ours unconditionally. It springs from the continuing activity of God's Holy Spirit. We lose it if we set ourselves in opposition to God. Alike in public worship and private devotion and in the situations of every day, it is necessary repeatedly to turn to him that we may discern the true needs of others and respond anew to the leadings of his Spirit in meeting them. Only so can our faith, our will to obey and our joy increase and be kept fresh.

The joy in Christian discipleship answers to and fulfils what God affirmed to man once and for all in the life, death and resurrection of the Lord Jesus Christ. It also points forward in promise. In gratitude for all that God has done and continues to do for man in Christ, we give joyful loyalty to him now and trust him for the future.

In fellowship with God through Christ we are able to bear with patience the unsolved enigmas of our earthly life. We seek to interpret its mystery in the light of God himself and by his power. We live in joyful hope of coming, through Christ, to share in the final glory when the victory over evil already gained will be entire.

5 In God alone is our faith, our hope, our love. In him they are begun, continued and perfected. To him be praise and glory throughout his creation for ever.

8. The Basis of Union of the United Reformed Church, 1981

It may be helpful to conclude this selection of documents by printing the full text of the Basis of Union of the United Reformed Church, as revised in 1981.

In 1965 the Joint Committee for Conversations between the Congregational Union of England and Wales and the Presbyterian Church of England published *A statement of convictions on which a united Church, both catholic and reformed, might be built*. This Statement contains the nucleus of the material which subsequently appeared in the Basis of Union as presented for discussion in 1968 and 1969. It reached its final form as paragraph 7 of the Scheme of Union published in 1970. The Basis of Union is concerned with the nature and purpose of the Church and the United Reformed Church, and with the faith and ministry of the United Reformed Church. At a number of points the Basis draws on phraseology from the Presbyterian Statement of 1956 and the Congregational Declaration of 1967.

The Basis of Union adopted in 1972 was further revised as a result of the conversations which took place between the United Reformed Church and Churches of Christ in Great Britain and Ireland between 1972 and 1976. Some of the amendments removed references to the Congregational and Presbyterian partners of 1972 and replaced them with references to the United Reformed Church; others included specific references to Churches of Christ. The most substantial changes came in the paragraphs on Baptism and Ministry. Paragraph 7(14) was amended to take account of the recognition of dual convictions about baptism, and paragraph 7(21) was amended to allow for the introduction of auxiliary (or non-stipendiary) ministry. These amendments were finally approved in 1981 when the Re-formed Association of Churches of Christ joined the United Reformed Church.

The Basis of Union of The United Reformed Church

Basis of Union

7. This clause sets out the Basis of Union.

The Church and the United Reformed Church

(1) There is but one Church of the one God. He called Israel to be his people, and in fulfilment of the purpose then begun he called the Church into being through Jesus Christ, by the power of the Holy Spirit.

(2) The one Church of the one God is holy, because he has redeemed and consecrated it through the death and resurrection of Jesus Christ and because there Christ dwells with his people.

(3) The Church is catholic or universal because Christ calls into it all peoples and because it proclaims the fullness of Christ's gospel to all men.

(4) The Church is apostolic because Christ continues to entrust it with the gospel and the commission first given to the apostles to proclaim that gospel to all peoples.

(5) The unity, holiness, catholicity and apostolicity of the Church have been obscured by the failure and weakness which mar the life of the Church.

(6) Christ's mercy in continuing his call to the Church in all its failure and weakness has taught the Church that its life must ever be renewed and reformed according to the Scriptures, under the guidance of the Holy Spirit.

(7) The United Reformed Church humbly recognises that the failure and weakness of the Church have in particular been manifested in division which has made it impossible for Christians fully to know, experience and communicate the life of the one, holy, catholic, apostolic Church.

(8) The United Reformed Church has been formed in obedience to the call to repent of what has been amiss in the past and to be reconciled. It sees its formation and growth as a part of what God is doing to make his people one, and as a united Church will take, wherever possible and with all speed, further steps towards the unity of all God's people.

(9) The United Reformed Church testifies to its faith, and orders its life, according to this Basis of Union, believing it to embody the essential notes of the Church Catholic and Reformed. The United Reformed Church nevertheless reserves its right and declares its readiness at any time to alter, add to, modify or supersede this Basis so that its life may accord more nearly with the mind of Christ.

(10) The United Reformed Church, believing that it is through the freedom of the Spirit that Jesus Christ holds his people in the fellowship of the One Body, shall uphold the rights of personal conviction. It shall be for the Church, in safeguarding the substance of the faith and maintaining the unity of the fellowship, to determine when these rights are asserted to the injury of its unity and peace.

The United Reformed Church and the Purpose of the Church

(11) Within the one, holy, catholic, apostolic Church of the United Reformed Church acknowledges its responsibility under God:

> to make its life a continual offering of itself and the world to God in adoration and worship through Jesus Christ;
> to receive and express the renewing life of the Holy Spirit in each place and in its total fellowship, and there to declare the reconciling and saving power of the life, death and resurrection of Jesus Christ;
> to live out, in joyful sacrificial service to all men in all the variety of their physical and spiritual needs, that ministry of caring, forgiving and healing love which Jesus Christ brought to all whom he met;
> to bear witness to the lordship of Christ over the nations in all the variety of their organised life.

The Faith of the United Reformed Church

(12) The United Reformed Church confesses the faith of the

Church Catholic in one God, Father, Son and Holy Spirit. It acknowledges that the life of faith to which it is called is a gift of the Holy Spirit continually received in Word and Sacrament and in the common life of God's people. It acknowledges the Word of God in the Old and New Testaments, discerned under the guidance of the Holy Spirit, as the supreme authority for the faith and conduct of all God's people.

(13) The United Reformed Church believes that, in the ministry of the Word, through preaching and the study of the Scriptures, God makes known in each age his saving love, his will for his people and his purpose for the world.

(14) The United Reformed Church observes the gospel sacrament of baptism into Christ as a gift of God to his Church, and as an appointed means of grace. Baptism is administered with water in the name of the Father and of the Son and of the Holy Spirit. It is the sacrament of entry into the Church and is therefore administered once only to any person.

When the Church observes this sacrament it makes explicit at a particular time and place and for a particular person what God has accomplished in Christ for the whole creation and for all mankind – the forgiveness of sins, the sanctifying power of the Holy Spirit and newness of life in the family of God. In this sacrament the Church affirms its faith in the action of God in Jesus Christ; and takes corporate responsibility for those receiving baptism, promising to support and nourish them as it receives them into its fellowship. Baptism may be administered in infancy or at an age of responsibility. Both forms of baptism shall be made available in the life of every worshipping congregation. In either case the sacrament of baptism is a unique part of the total process of Christian initiation. When baptism is administered at an age of responsibility, upon profession of faith, the baptized person at once enters upon the full privileges and responsibilities of membership. When baptism is administered to an infant, upon profession of faith by his parent(s), he is placed under the nurture of the Church that he may be led by the Holy Spirit in due time to make his own profession of faith in Christ as his Saviour and Lord, and enter upon the full privileges and responsibilities of membership. These two patterns of Christian initiation are recognised by the United Reformed Church.

The profession of faith to be made prior to baptism by a believer or at an age of responsibility by one baptized in infancy is indicated in Schedule A.[1] This profession, and its acceptance by the Church which shares in it, is a necessary part of the process of initiation and whenever possible it should be made at a celebration of the Lord's Supper.

The United Reformed Church includes within its membership both persons whose conviction it is that baptism can only be appropriately administered to a believer and those whose conviction it is that the infant baptism also is in harmony with the mind of Christ. Both convictions are honoured by the Church and both forms of baptism are understood to be used by God in the upbuilding of faith. Should these differences of conviction within the one Church result in personal conflict of conscience it will require to be pastorally reconciled in mutual understanding and charity, and in accordance with the Basis of Union, in the first instance by the Elders' Meeting of the local congregation, and if necessary by the wider councils of the Church. No one shall be required to administer a form or mode of baptism to which he has a conscientious objection, nor shall the form or mode of baptism used in any instance be one to which conscientious objection is taken by the person seeking baptism or by the parent(s) requesting baptism for an infant.

(15) The United Reformed Church celebrates the gospel sacrament of the Lord's Supper. When in obedience to the Lord's command his people show forth his sacrifice on the cross by the bread broken and the wine outpoured for them to eat and drink, he himself, risen and ascended, is present and gives himself to them for their spiritual nourishment and growth in grace. United with him and with the whole Church on earth and in heaven, his people gathered at his table present their sacrifice of thanksgiving and renew the offering of themselves, and rejoice in the promise of his coming in glory.

(16) The United Reformed Church gives thanks for the common life of the Church, wherein the people of God, being made members one of another, are called to love and serve one another and all men

---

[1]   Admission to the full privileges and responsibilities of membership of the Church shall be in accordance with paragraph 9(1) and (2)(vi) of the Structure [not reprinted here] and with Schedule A.

and to grow together in grace and in the knowledge of the Lord Jesus Christ. Participating in the common life of the Church within the local church, they enter into the life of the Church throughout the world. With that whole Church, they also share in the life of the Church in all ages and in the Communion of Saints have fellowship with the Church Triumphant.

(17) The United Reformed Church at the date of formation confesses its faith, in the words of this statement:–

We believe in the one living and true God, creator, preserver and ruler of all things in heaven and earth, Father, Son and Holy Spirit. Him alone we worship and in him we put our trust.

We believe that God, in his infinite love for men, gave his eternal Son, Jesus Christ our Lord, who became man, lived on earth in perfect love and obedience, died upon the cross for our sins, rose again from the dead and lives for evermore, saviour, judge and king.

We believe that, by the Holy Spirit, this glorious gospel is made effective so that through faith we receive the forgiveness of sins, newness of life as children of God and strength in this present world to do his will.

We believe in the one, holy, catholic, apostolic Church, in heaven and on earth, wherein by the same Spirit, the whole company of believers is made one Body of Christ, to worship God and serve him and all men in his kingdom of righteousness and love.

We rejoice in the gift of eternal life, and believe that, in the fullness of time, God will renew and gather in one all things in Christ, to whom, with the Father and the Holy Spirit, be glory and majesty, dominion and power, both now and ever.

(18) The United Reformed Church, under the authority of Holy Scripture and in corporate responsibility to Jesus Christ its everliving head, acknowledges its duty to be open at all times to the leading of the Holy Spirit and therefore affirms its right to make such new declarations of its faith and for such purposes as may from time to time be required by obedience to the same Spirit.

At the same time the United Reformed Church accepts with thanksgiving the witness borne to the Catholic faith by the Apostles' and Nicene Creeds. It recognises as its own particular heritage the formulations and declarations of faith which have been valued by Congregationalists, Presbyterians and members of Churches of Christ as stating the gospel and seeking to make its implications clear.[2]

Ministry in the United Reformed Church

(19) The Lord Jesus Christ continues his ministry in and through the Church, the whole people of God called and committed to his service and equipped by him for it. This service is given by worship, prayer, proclamation of the gospel and Christian witness; by mutual and outgoing care and responsibility; and by obedient discipleship in the whole of daily life, according to the gifts and opportunities given to each one. The preparation and strengthening of its members for such ministry and discipleship shall always be a major concern of the United Reformed Church.

(20) For the equipment of his people for this total ministry the Lord Jesus Christ gives particular gifts for particular ministries and calls some of his servants to exercise them in offices duly recognised within his Church. The United Reformed Church recognises that Christ gives himself to his Church through Word and Sacrament and through the total caring oversight by which his people grow in faith and love, the exercise of which oversight is the special concern of elders and ministers. Those who enter on such ministries commit themselves to them for so long as God wills: the United Reformed Church having solemnly acknowledged their vocation and accepted their commitment shall appoint them to their particular ministry and give them authority to exercise it within the Church, setting them apart with prayer that they shall be given all needful gifts and graces for its fulfilment, which solemn setting apart shall in the case of ministers and elders be termed ordination.

(21) Some are called to the ministry of the Word and Sacraments. After approved preparation and training, on receiving a call they

[2] E.g. among Presbyterians: the Westminster Confession, 1647; A Statement of the Christian Faith, 1956; among Congregationalists: the Savoy Declaration, 1658; A Declaration of Faith, 1967; among Churches of Christ: Thomas Campbell's Declaration and Address, 1809.

are ordained and inducted to their office. They are commissioned to conduct public worship, to preach the Word and to administer the Sacraments, to exercise pastoral care and oversight, and to give leadership to the Church in its mission to the world.

Within this ministerial calling some offer themselves for ministry at such places and under such conditions of service as are decided under the oversight of the councils of the United Reformed Church; they may be called to be ministers of local churches, or missionaries overseas, or to some special and approved ministry.

Others serve as auxiliary ministers, under the same oversight but continuing in other occupations, earning their livelihood within them, and sharing in all the circumstances of a 'secular' calling.[3] Auxiliary ministers shall normally serve under the leadership of a full-time minister.

The preparation and training for the full-time ministry shall be of a more extended and developed nature than that for the auxiliary ministry. If auxiliary ministers offer themselves for the full-time ministry, and are recognised as candidates for it, they shall undertake such further preparation and training as is required under rules decided by the General Assembly.

Full-time ministers whose place and form of service become dependent upon an agency not under the discipline of the General Assembly become, for such time as this is the case, auxiliary ministers, except where the General Assembly agrees, either for specific categories or individuals, to their continued recognition as full-time ministers.

(22) Some are called to be elders. They share with ministers of the Word and Sacraments in the pastoral oversight and leadership of the local churches, taking counsel together in the Elders' Meeting for the whole Church and having each a group of members particularly entrusted to his pastoral care. They shall be associated with ministers in all the Councils of the Church. Elders elected by the Church Meeting, are ordained to their office and are inducted to

---

[3] Ordained elders of Churches of Christ in Great Britain and Ireland at the date of unification with the United Reformed Church may choose either to be inducted as auxiliary ministers or to serve as elders as described in paragraph (22). Those choosing to serve as auxiliary ministers shall be offered opportunity of suitable further training as outlined above.

serve for such limited period as the Church which elects them shall determine.[4]

(23) In the Presbyterian Church of England some have been ordained to the office of deaconess and appointed to a local church to give instruction in the Christian faith, to exercise pastoral oversight together with the minister and elders, and when invited to do so to conduct public worship and to preach the Word. The United Reformed Church shall receive and recognise both their ministry and the candidature of those in training for the office of deaconess at the time of union.

(24) Other full and part-time ministries recognised by the uniting Churches at the time of union shall continue to be exercised in the United Reformed Church without further commissioning, subject always to the decisions of the General Assembly. The United Reformed Church shall determine from time to time what other ministries may be required and which of them should be recognised as ministries in the whole Church. It shall decide how those who are to exercise them shall be set apart.

(25) The worship of the local church is an expression of the worship of the whole people of God. In order that this may be clearly seen, the United Reformed Church shall (a) take steps to ensure that so far as possible ordained ministers of the Word and

---

[4] Elders elected for the first time after the formation of the United Reformed Church shall be ordained and inducted to that office. Serving deacons of the Congregational Church in England and Wales and serving elders of the Presbyterian Church of England shall continue to serve on the Elders' Meeting of the local church for such period as shall be determined by the Church Meeting. Serving elders of Churches of Christ in Great Britain and Ireland who choose to serve as elders at the date of unification with the United Reformed Church and serving deacons of Churches of Christ at the date of unification shall continue to serve on the Elders' Meeting of the local church for such period as shall be determined by the Church Meeting. Subsequently, all elders shall be eligible for re-election, and those elected shall enter on their office by induction. On re-election, those not previously ordained may, if they so desire, be ordained before induction.

Elders of the United Reformed Church, or serving deacons of the Congregational Church in England and Wales at the time of union, or serving deacons of Churches of Christ in Great Britain and Ireland at the date of unification, on removing to another local church are eligible for election by that church to the Elders' Meeting, and if elected are then inducted.

The ordination and/or induction of elders shall be carried out in the course of public worship by the minister, or one of the ministers, of the local church (or during a pastoral vacancy, the interim moderator) acting with the serving elders (see Schedule B).

Sacraments are readily available to every local church; (b) provide for the training of suitable men and women, members of the United Reformed Church, to be accredited by District Councils as lay preachers; (c) make provision through District Councils, in full consultation with the local churches concerned, for the recognition of certain members of the United Reformed Church, normally deaconesses, elders or accredited lay preachers, who may be invited by local churches to preside at baptismal and communion services where pastoral necessity so requires. The pastoral needs of each situation shall be reviewed periodically by the District Council in consultation with the local church. Apart from ordained ministers of the United Reformed Church and of other Churches, only such recognised persons may be invited.[5]

(26) The ordination and induction of ministers (including auxiliary ministers) shall be in accord with Schedules C and D. Appropriate affirmations of faith shall also be made by those entering upon other ministries within the life of the Church. In the United Reformed Church all ministries shall be open to both men and women.

---

[5] Those in Churches of Christ in Great Britain and Ireland authorised to preside at baptismal and communion services at the date of unification with the United Reformed Church may continue to do so for such period as shall be determined by the District Council. Subsequently, only ordained ministers (including auxiliary ministers) or those authorised under the provisions of this clause shall preside.

SCHEDULE A *(See paragraph 7(14) in the Basis of Union)*

Affirmation of Faith to be made at admission to the full
privileges and responsibilities of membership of the Church.

It is the responsibility of the minister and Elders' Meeting, before
bringing the names of candidates to the Church Meeting, to be
assured of the sincerity of their intention. After adequate preparation, and acceptance by the Church Meeting, candidates shall
be publicly admitted to the full privileges and responsibilities of
membership of the Church of Jesus Christ and in particular to the
membership of the local church.

This act may include the laying on of hands as a sign of the
commissioning of those called by God to the service of Jesus
Christ. Acceptance of candidates, as also their acceptance of their
commission, shall be signified by the giving and receiving of the
right hand of fellowship.

Thereafter they shall be commended to the love and care of their
fellow-members.

During the act of admission public profession of faith and of
commitment to the Church shall be made –
Either: (a) By question and answer thus:–

1   Do you confess your faith in one God, Father, Son and Holy
Spirit,
taking the Father to be your Father,
the Son to be your saviour and Lord,
the Spirit to be your helper and guide?
I do.

2   Do you promise, in dependence on God's grace,
to be faithful in private and public worship;
to live in the fellowship of the Church and to share in its
work;
and to give and serve, as God enables you, for the advancement of his kingdom throughout the world?
I do.

3   Do you promise, by that same grace, to follow Christ and to
seek to do and to bear his will all the days of your life?

I do.

4   And do you trust in his mercy alone to bring you into the fullness of the life of the world to come?
I do.

Or: (b) in the form of a declaration such as the following:
I confess my faith in one God, Father, Son and Holy Spirit,
taking the Father to be my Father,
the Son to be my saviour and Lord,
the Spirit to be my helper and guide.
I promise, in dependence on God's grace,
to be faithful in private and public worship;
to live in the fellowship of the Church and to share in its work;
and to give and serve, as God enables me, for the advancement of his kingdom throughout the world.
I promise, by that same grace, to follow Christ and to seek to do and to bear his will all the days of my life; and
I trust in his mercy alone to bring me into the fullness of the life of the world to come.

Or: (c) in the forms customarily used in the uniting Churches before union.

SCHEDULE B

Affirmations to be made by Elders at Ordination and Induction.

NOTE
The service, which takes place at public worship, shall include a statement regarding the functions of the elders taken from Schedule D and from paragraphs 7(19), (20) and (22) in the Basis of Union.

Afterwards the presiding minister shall say to the elders-elect:
In the light of this statement of the nature, faith and order of the United Reformed Church and concerning the functions of the

eldership, the elders-elect are now asked to answer the following questions:

1   Do you confess again your faith in one God, Father, Son and Holy Spirit?
    I do.

2   In dependence on God's grace do you reaffirm your trust in Jesus Christ as saviour and Lord and your promise to follow him and to seek to do and to bear his will all the days of your life?
    I do.

3   Do you believe that the Word of God in the Old and New Testaments, discerned under the guidance of the Holy Spirit, is the supreme authority for the faith and conduct of all God's people?
    I do.

4   Do you accept the office of elder of the United Reformed Church in this congregation and do you promise to perform its duties faithfully?
    I do.

SCHEDULE C *(See paragraph 7(26) in the Basis of Union)*

Affirmations to be made by Ministers at Ordination and Induction.

NOTE
The service will also include the reading of the Statement contained in Schedule D, and provision will be made for a statement to be made concerning the circumstances of the call. The minister may also make a personal statement of his own call to that office.

The presiding minister shall say immediately after the reading of the Statement:
A.B., do you undertake to exercise your ministry in conformity with this statement?
    I do.
    He shall then ask:

1   Do you confess anew your faith in one God, Father, Son and Holy Spirit?
    I do.

2   Do you believe that the Word of God in the Old and New Testaments, discerned under the guidance of the Holy Spirit, is the supreme authority for the faith and conduct of all God's people?
I do.

3   Do you believe that Jesus Christ, born into this world, living as a man among men, dying upon the cross, raised from the dead and reigning for evermore, is God's gift of himself to the world whereby his love and mercy are revealed, offering to all men forgiveness, reconciliation and eternal life? And will you faithfully proclaim this gospel?
This I believe and this I will proclaim.

4   Do you believe that the Church is God's people, gathered by his love to serve him in reconciling the world to himself?
I do.

5   Are zeal for the glory of God, love for the Lord Jesus Christ and a desire for the salvation of men, so far as you know your own heart, the chief motives which lead you to enter this ministry?
(At induction to a new charge, the question shall end 'to enter on the duties of the ministry in this place'.)
They are.

6   Do you promise to fulfil the duties of your charge with all fidelity, to lead your people in worship, to preach the Word and administer the Sacraments, to exercise pastoral care and oversight, and to give leadership to the Church in its mission to the world?
I do.

7   Do you promise to live a holy life and always to maintain the truth of the gospel, whatever trouble or persecution may arise?
I do.

8   Do you promise as a minister of this Church to seek its purity, peace and true prosperity, to cherish brotherly love towards all other Churches and to endeavour always to build up the one, holy, catholic and apostolic Church?
I do.

9   And all these things do you profess and promise as the Lord Jesus Christ shall give you grace and strength to fulfil the same?
I do.

SCHEDULE D

A statement concerning the Nature, Faith and Order of the United Reformed Church.

(To be read aloud at Ordination and Induction Services).

1   The United Reformed Church confesses the faith of the Church Catholic in one God, Father, Son and Holy Spirit.

2   The United Reformed Church acknowledges that the life of faith to which it is called is a gift of the Holy Spirit continually received in Word and Sacrament and in the common life of God's people.

3   The United Reformed Church acknowledges the Word of God in the Old and New Testaments, discerned under the guidance of the Holy Spirit, as the supreme authority for the faith and conduct of all God's people.

4   The United Reformed Church accepts with thanksgiving the witness borne to the Catholic faith by the Apostles' and Nicene Creeds, and recognises as its own particular heritage the formulations and declarations of faith which have been valued by Congregationalists, Presbyterians and members of Churches of Christ as stating the gospel and seeking to make its implications clear.

5   The United Reformed Church testifies to its faith, and orders its life, according to the Basis of Union, believing it to embody the essential notes of the Church Catholic and Reformed. The United Reformed Church nevertheless reserves its right and declares its readiness at any time to alter, add to, modify or supersede this Basis so that its life may accord more nearly with the mind of Christ.

6   The United Reformed Church, under the authority of Holy Scripture and in corporate responsibility to Jesus Christ its everliving head, acknowledges its duty to be open at all times to the leading of the Holy Spirit and therefore affirms its right to make such new declarations of its faith and for such purposes as may from time to time be required by obedience to the same Spirit.

7   The United Reformed Church, believing that it is through the freedom of the Spirit that Jesus Christ holds his people in the fellowship of the One Body, upholds the rights of personal conviction. It

shall be for the Church, in safeguarding the substance of the faith and maintaining the unity of the fellowship, to determine when these rights are asserted to the injury of its unity and peace.

8 The United Reformed Church declares that the Lord Jesus Christ, the only king and head of the Church, has therein appointed a government distinct from civil government and in things spiritual not subordinate thereto, and that civil authorities, being always subject to the rule of God, ought to respect the rights of conscience and of religious belief and to serve God's will of justice and peace for all men.

9 The United Reformed Church declares its intention, in fellowship with all the Churches, to pray and work for such visible unity of the whole Church as Christ wills and in the way he wills, in order that men and nations may be led more and more to glorify the Father in heaven.

The following alternative form of the Statement is authorised for use.

With the whole Christian Church
the United Reformed Church believes in one God,
Father, Son and Holy Spirit.

The life of faith to which we are called
is the Spirit's gift
continually received
through the Word, the Sacraments
and our Christian life together.

The highest authority
for what we believe and do
is God's Word in the Bible
alive for his people today
through the help of the Spirit.

We accept with thanksgiving to God
the witness to the catholic faith
in the Apostles' and Nicene creeds.

We acknowledge the declarations
made in our own tradition
by Congregationalists, Presbyterians and the Churches of Christ
in which they stated the faith
and sought to make its implications clear.

We conduct our life together
according to the Basis of Union
in which we give expression to our faith
in forms which we believe contain
the essential elements of the Church's life,
both catholic and reformed;
but we affirm our right and readiness,
if the need arises,
to change the Basis of Union
and to make new statements of faith
in ever new obedience to the Living Christ.

Held together in the Body of Christ
through the freedom of the Spirit,
we rejoice in the diversity of the Spirit's gifts
and uphold the rights of personal conviction.
For the sake of faith and fellowship
it shall be for the Church to decide
when differences of conviction
hurt our unity and peace.

We believe that
Christ gives his Church a government
distinct from the government of the state.
In things that affect obedience to God
the Church is not subordinate to the state,
but must serve the Lord Jesus Christ,
its only King and Head.
Civil authorities are called
to serve God's will of justice and peace for all humanity,
and to respect the rights of conscience and belief.

We affirm our intention
to go on praying and working,
with all our fellow Christians,
for the visible unity of the Church
in the way Christ chooses,
so that people and nations
may be led to love and serve God
and praise him more and more for ever.

Further Reading

The Apostles' and Nicene Creeds
Praying Together: A Revision of Prayers We Have in Common (Norwich: The Canterbury Press, 1989).

J.N.D. Kelly, *Early Christian Creeds*, third edition, London 1972.

Confessing One Faith: Towards an Ecumenical Explication of the Apostolic Faith as expressed in the Nicene-Constantinopolitan Creed (381), World Council of Churches Commission on Faith and Order, Geneva, 1987.

The Westminster Confession
Text: S.W. Carruthers, *The Westminster Confession of Faith*, Manchester 1937.

A.F. Mitchell & J. Struthers (eds), *Minutes of the Sessions of the Westminster Assembly of Divines*, Edinburgh 1874.

A.F. Mitchell, *The Westminster Assembly: Its History and Standards*, London 1883.

R.S. Paul, *The Assembly of the Lord: Religion and Politics in the Westminster Assembly and the 'Grand Debate'*, Edinburgh 1985.

The Savoy Declaration
Text: A.G. Matthews (ed), *The Savoy Declaration of Faith and Order 1658*, London 1959.

W. Walker, *Creeds and Platforms of Congregationalism*, New York 1893.

R.W. Dale, *History of English Congregationalism*, London 1907.

A. Peel, *The Savoy Declaration of Faith and Order 1658*, London 1939.

G.F. Nuttall, *Visible Saints*, Oxford 1957.

A.P.F. Sell, *Saints: Visible, Orderly and Catholic*, Geneva 1986.

Thomas Campbell's *Declaration and Address*
Text: W. Robinson (ed), *Declaration and Address*, Birmingham 1951.

F.D. Kershner, *The Christian Union Overture*, St Louis, Mo 1923.

L.G. McAllister, *Thomas Campbell: Man of the Book*, St Louis, Mo 1954.

D.M. Thompson, 'The Irish Background to Thomas Campbell's *Declaration and Address*', *Journal of the United Reformed Church History Society*, iii, May 1985.

D.M. Thompson, *Let Sects and Parties Fall*, Birmingham 1980.

A Statement of the Christian Faith
Text and Commentary: M. McAra, *Commentary on A Statement of the Christian Faith* (in seven parts), London n.d.

S.W. Carruthers, *Digest of the Proceedings of the Synods of the Presbyterian Church of England, 1876-1905*, London 1907.

Declaration of Faith
Text and a collection of essays: R. Tomes (ed), *Christian Confidence*, London 1970.